TEN
MODERN
SCOTTISH
NOVELS

Other AUP Titles of Interest

A BLASPHEMER AND REFORMER
A Study of James Leslie Mitchell—Lewis Grassic Gibbon
William K Malcolm

LITERATURE OF THE NORTH
Edited by David Hewitt and Michael Spiller

GRAMPIAN HAIRST
An Anthology of Northeast Prose
Edited by William Donaldson and Douglas Young

THE LUM HAT AND OTHER STORIES
Last Tales of Violet Jacob
Edited by Ronald Garden

THE GREEN MAN OF KNOWLEDGE
and other Scots Traditional Tales
Selected and Edited by Alan Bruford

TEN
MODERN
SCOTTISH
NOVELS

Isobel Murray and Bob Tait

ABERDEEN UNIVERSITY PRESS

First published 1984
Aberdeen University Press
A member of the Pergamon Group
© Isobel Murray and Bob Tait 1984

The publisher acknowledges subsidy from the
Scottish Arts Council towards the publication
of this volume.

British Library Cataloguing in Publication Data
Murray, Isobel
    Ten modern Scottish novels
    1. English fiction—Scottish authors—
    History and criticism   2. Scottish
    fiction—20th century—History and
    criticism
    I. Title   II. Tait, Bob
    823′.912′09   PR8603
ISBN 0 08 028494 9
ISBN 0 08 028493 0 (flexi)

Printed in Great Britain
The University Press
Aberdeen

In memory of Joseph Tait
1911–1983

Contents

CHAPTER ONE

Introduction

Scottish fiction is still a very poor relation of English fiction in the scale of critical attention it receives. Even the very best critical accounts, such as that of Francis Russell Hart in *The Scottish Novel: A Critical Survey* (1978), tend to be just that: surveys, with little or no room for the considered attention to individual novels that is taken for granted in the criticism of English fiction. It is a primary intention of this book to begin to redress that balance.

So we have selected ten novels from the last fifty years and subjected them to careful reading and investigation. We make no claim that these are the best ten novels of that period, but we would suggest that they are ten of the best. Some of these novels virtually choose themselves and would figure in any critic's choice of ten: *A Scots Quair* and *The Silver Darlings* are two examples. The arbitrary factor of whether books are currently in print or not has inevitably prevented us from choosing from the whole field: sparing us some dilemmas, no doubt, but restricting choice more than we would have wished. For instance, this meant that we could not include Naomi Mitchison's *The Bull Calves*. Eric Linklater's *Juan in America* illustrates another kind of problem of choice. It made a welcome re-appearance in hardback while we were writing this book. Had we known of this earlier we might, of course, have included it. On the other hand, something else of interest would have had to go. These are the familiar practical and judgemental problems of a project such as this.

We looked for a selection of novels reasonably spaced over the fifty years, in the hope that the sum of the investigation would produce not only ten individual analyses but at least some pointers to cultural preoccupations in literary Scotland during the past half century. We found in the first place extraordinary variety. There is considerable variety in technique, from the innovative and experimental modes of Grassic Gibbon, through highly individual adaptations of all kinds of traditional and new novel forms, to the recent strikingly unusual juxtaposition of realistic and fantastic modes by Alasdair Gray. The writers themselves have a widely diverse range of backgrounds, both in terms of social class or occupations and in terms of the geographical settings they choose and the historical

periods in which they set their novels. It would be too much to say that
these novelists have quite different readerships in mind, but there are
substantial differences in intention and emphasis. Some, like Kennaway
and Spark, seem to address the international audience for fiction in
English, while many of the others are concerned primarily to find and move
a Scottish audience.

Close reading of almost any ten modern Scottish novels can only, we
believe, heighten the impression of a degree of cultural diversity and
fragmentation astonishing in so small a country. At times it seems as if
there is not one Scotland but many. McIlvanney and Williams, for
example, assert the importance of looking scrupulously at working-class
experience: and that is a kind of experience so different from much of what
we are likely to encounter in earlier fiction or the real settings of the rural
north, or the northern isles, the officers' mess or an Edinburgh girls' school,
that we seem to be transported to a different place. Individual novelists,
finding themselves writing from within such different cultural frameworks,
have to resort to ingenious distinctive stratagems in order to convey
precisely the spirit and quality of the ways of life they are concerned with.
The more those ways of life (e.g. urban industrial working-class life) have
been ignored, undervalued or sentimentalised in the past, the more
complex the writer's task. Precedents are scarce or dangerous; and often a
readership has had to be won over or established afresh.

Most of our writers face challenges of that kind in one way or another.
Gibbon's varied use of literary modes is evidence of one such struggle.
Gunn not only asserts the claim of neglected aspects of history: he also
wants to put forward a vision of a basis for social values very different from
those prevailing in a modern industrial society. MacColla challenges
preconceptions and prejudices of a traditional readership. McIlvanney
must draw on that readership while trying to confront a wider population
with a far from comforting picture of their history. And so on.

Such a variety of subject matter and approach can certainly be seen as a
source of great difficulties for the Scottish novelist. But on the whole we
would argue that vigour and variety here make for strength. In poetry the
figure of Hugh MacDiarmid bestrides the Scottish Renaissance like a
colossus: and a figure so dominant is clearly a mixed blessing. In fiction,
although we have incontestably great novelists such as Gibbon and Gunn,
there has been no such overweening presence. Once Gibbon had reinforced
the anti-Kailyard salvoes of George Douglas Brown and John
MacDougall Hay, there was considerable freedom for novelists to develop
in their own chosen directions, although all our authors seem aware that
kailyards have not simply vanished forever from the Scottish scene.
Vigilance is necessary. There is much to re-consider and new ground to

explore. So we would suggest that even these ten novels, chosen from so many others, indicate a real renaissance of fiction in the last fifty years, after Scotland's long slumber in the Kailyard. In 1929 Neil Gunn defined the way forward which our novelists have followed in very different ways:

> The Renascent Scot is—must be—intolerant of the Kailyairder, that is, of the parochial, sentimental, local-associative way of treating Scotland and the Scots. He wants to treat of Scotland as rock and sea and land—a unique and wonderful rock and sea and land—and he wants to treat of Scotsmen as real projections of *homo sapiens* (rather than as kirk-elderish grannies), and he wants to complete his picture in a way that will not only make self-satisfied Scotsmen sit up but will make the cultured of the world take notice. That may sound rather a big claim. But considered in its creative aspect, it is merely the modest claim to serve the ends of Literature.

The ten individual analyses point up the variety we indicate. All the more striking, then, that we found similar preoccupations recurring in different forms. In a society whose culture is so markedly fragmented it is not surprising that often these preoccupations are concerned with social bonds or their impossibility. The analyses also add up to something else, grounds sometimes for endorsing but more often for qualifying some of the glib generalisations we all commonly make about Scottish fiction: grounds too for offering new but invariably tentative generalisations.

We were surprised, for example, on surveying the field to see how importantly comic elements feature in most of the novels. In an often grim world, Scottish novelists have frequently had recourse to different techniques and modes of comedy. *A Scots Quair* depends markedly on the humour of the different folk voices and on the wry humour of Chris herself. *The Prime of Miss Jean Brodie* is a comic masterpiece of wit, balance and juxtaposition, effortlessly exposing the weakness of humankind in a girls' school story. And in very different ways the comic impulse contributes significantly to the success of *From Scenes Like These, Greenvoe, Docherty, Fergus Lamont* and *Lanark*.

For all their rejection of Kailyard cosiness, comfort and complacency, our novelists are not blind to the positives of the small cohesive community. It is possible to discern in many of them a yearning for a pre-industrial, pastoral Scotland—and in the case of *Greenvoe* or *Fergus Lamont*, it is impossible to miss it. *And the Cock Crew, The Silver Darlings* and *Sunset Song* all look back to pre-industrial times with some mixture of elegy, celebration and regret. In these novels as well as in *Docherty* and in *Lanark* we are struck by a yearning for solidarity, for the very possibility of a sense of common purposes and values which would be life-giving rather than life-destroying. To create such a community in contemporary Scotland is, of course, not a task which novelists can be expected to undertake alone; but all our authors implicitly demonstrate the human longing for such benign social bonds, or in the case of *From Scenes Like These* savagely expose their absence. There are other variants too on this theme. They may contemplate artificial communities which both share and betray common purposes and values, like the battalion in *Tunes of Glory* or the girls' school in *The Prime of Miss Jean Brodie*.

If our fractured national culture and communal divisions preoccupy and move all our novelists to some extent, this may help to explain the selective emphasis with which aspects of Scottish history importantly recur in their fiction. While popular historical novels still hark back to the dramatic and romantic figures of Wallace, Bruce, Mary Queen of Scots and Bonnie Prince Charlie, these do not feature here. The Disruption in the Scottish church which so concerned Barrie and Maclaren and provided much of their subject matter does not feature here either. And no serious novelist has as yet exploited the fictional possibilities of the 'Red Clyde' and its attendant myths. This last is a particularly curious omission, perhaps, in view of the now frequently acknowledged importance of working-class life and politics to any understanding of the making of modern Scottish culture. In fact, the class struggle in political terms is more underplayed than one might expect.

However, one historical phenomenon has been rediscovered and has become an important part of literary consciousness during the past fifty years—the Highland Clearances. The myths and realities of the Clearances effectively sum up, dramatise and express the nostalgia for a pastoral Scotland in which community and shared values are paramount. They have come to epitomise pain and protest at deracination and division. Neil Gunn did most to remind Scottish readers of the Clearances and he had to do considerable primary research for this purpose himself in the 'thirties. In *Butcher's Broom* (1934) he dwelt not only on the cruelty and suddenness of the evictions, but more on the continuity with previous generations and the co-operative, healthy social units which were to be uprooted. *The Silver Darlings* stresses the triumphant way in which the evicted people make a new life and retain their solidarity, but the Clearances are never forgiven or forgotten. We never forget that: 'The landlord had driven them from these valleys and pastures, and burned their houses, and set them here against the sea-shore to live if they could and, if not, to die' (12).

And the Cock Crew tackles the actual phenomenon of the Clearances head on, yet MacColla need give us very little account of the process of eviction: the subject is inherently powerful and poignant, inspiring pity or anger in the reader as the novelist desires. So, later novels can afford to be much more indirect still. A literary memory informs and reinforces our reading of *Greenvoe*, for example, so that we need no hint of authorial anger at the eviction of the people and the clearing of the island to make way, not for sheep, but for something baleful and colossally threatening. Fergus Lamont, deracinated by his own monumental folly, becomes preoccupied with the Clearances, not just with the story of Donald of Sutherland and his sad return to desolate Strathnaver, but with his perceptions of other 'clearances': from the evicted family that troubles his childish mind to the fates of the contemporary Donalds of Sutherland, returning home after the Great War to the broken promises that await them. Deracination, then, and the need to restore meaningful social bonds, are recurrent concerns.

Perhaps one of the commonest generalisations about the Scottish novel is that it is very taken up with Calvinism and with attitudes and behaviour springing from the Calvinist tradition. Our study of these ten novels certainly bears that out. We found even more attention to Calvinism and its inheritance than we had expected, and we were interested to note how many different aspects of the creed and its psychology have been anatomised.

In *Sunset Song*, the ironically named Reverend Gibbon is a gross hypocrite, preaching one kind of sexual behaviour and practising quite another. And more importantly, the authoritarian John Guthrie is a harsh and judgemental man, victim and promoter of a harsh and judgemental tradition. Fergus Lamont's unforgiving grandfather is out of the same stable. But in *And the Cock Crew* MacColla's target is twofold. He hates a creed that he sees as naysaying, banishing fun and sport and art, and in extremity condemning every feature of this world as sinful and unimport-ant. He also, through Fearchar, attacks the doctrine of Election, and the way in which confidence in his Election can make a man over-confident in his judgement, and over-judgemental.

The dangers of Election, and the fundamental difficulty of deciding whether confidence in Election is God-given or self-induced, are illustrated by both Spark and Jenkins. The suggestion is that electing oneself to some kind of chosen position of superiority to one's fellows is an enormously dangerous and potentially destructive thing. The habit of mind inculcated by the original theological doctrine can survive a very minimal acceptance of the creed, such as Miss Brodie's, or full repudiation of it, such as Fergus Lamont's; and it is a habit that can produce monsters. Monstrous pride has a kind of counterpoint in a sense of unabsolvable guilt. We argue that George Mackay Brown's critique of Calvinist attitudes in *Greenvoe*, expressed through his treatment of Mrs McKee, concentrates on the pervasive guilt in the psyche experienced by a character brought up in a tradition that says man is totally degraded, wholly unworthy.

The prominence given to this kind of treatment must not blind us to other religious topics or emphasis. We find explicit or implicit condemnation of the bitter religious divide between Catholic and Protestant in Scotland, particularly in the industrial west central belt. We argue that Tam Docherty, for example, renounces his father's Catholicism because he finds it an inadequate account of his own experience and a narrowing element in his father's. Even young Dunky Logan in *From Scenes Like These* can see that the myths he has been fed about Catholics are likely to be at the least exaggerated, and when Fergus Lamont begins to distrust his grandfather he begins the hard process of discarding his anti-Catholic prejudices. Happily, we have no sectarian novelists. Oddly, there are few believers to be found in *Docherty*, *From Scenes Like These* and *Fergus Lamont*.

There is also a wider concern in many of these novels which can be described as quasi-religious or spiritual, although in no sense Christian. This 'spiritual' dimension is apparent, for example, in *Docherty*, where Tam is a good man, supporting and supported by the warmth of a close-knit neighbourhood but searching for a new faith commensurate with his experience and aspirations. It is evident too in *Lanark*. In that dark world, the very possibility that there might be a God could be construed as an appalling, sick joke. Yet something of an idea of a godhead, as lifegiving and hopeful, perhaps as something human beings have to bring into existence (rather than the other way round) does remain a saving attraction. And a religious or spiritual element is unmistakably present in *The Silver Darlings*. Finn's youthful exploration is not confined to the personal development of a particular individual in a specific place and time: it involves intuition of the past, apprehension of intangible continuities and aspiration beyond himself.

The story of Finn McHamish is, indeed, a good example of a very individual and essentially Scottish treatment of a very old and popular situation for fiction: the growth of a central character to maturity and self-knowledge. Seven of our novels make interesting use of this basic situation. It has obvious attractions to any writer. It can illuminate the encroachment on a child of social, environmental or ideological factors which will affect his development, and thus open out an understanding of his whole culture, or as much of it as the novelist wishes to treat. It can develop further, as in *The Silver Darlings*, where the subject is not just Finn's maturing, but a central quest involving not Finn only but the destiny of an entire people. What is striking about *The Silver Darlings* in this context is that the quest is successful and the ending is happy and hopeful—and in this respect the book is unique. For all we found an abundance of comic, witty and ironic elements in the telling of their stories, most of the central characters in these novels head towards grim or equivocal endings.

In *A Scots Quair* Gibbon traces Chris Guthrie's development, her search for fulfilment in love, relationships and work; but there is something deeply sombre, even defeated, in the picture of her final isolation. If we see Sandy Stranger's growth to maturity as a central aspect of *The Prime of Miss Jean Brodie*, as it surely is, there is no conventional—or conventual—happy ending: the book stresses her lack of repose and peace too much for that. *From Scenes Like These* is almost a kind of anti-quest novel: Williams overturns the traditional literary expectation of the lad o'pairts in a ferocious exposition of a society and culture that seems to leave no room for shared human values or quests for personal fulfilment. And young Conn Docherty, despite the altogether warmer social environment in which he grows up, arrives at a state of chronic bewilderment, while Fergus Lamont's much heralded return to his native town is at best an ironic, partial and ambiguous victory of the spirit, which leads to an isolated and misanthropic old age. Lanark finds no unequivocally hopeful answers and accomplishes nothing by his deeds of heroism: personally, he makes a kind of peace-at-a-distance with Rima; politically he is used as a tool by malevolent operators and comes to an anguished understanding of the full economic and political horrors of the world. He dies with some relief.

So these quests for personal satisfactions and dependable, hopeful values rarely issue in positives. And the other novels have similarly dark endings, with perhaps the very much qualified exception of *Greenvoe* where there is long-term hope that provides some counterbalance to the 'atom-and-planet horror'. *And the Cock Crew* ends with the always inevitable eviction of the people and the death of the minister who failed to protect them, and *Tunes of Glory* with the suicide of Barrow, the near-suicide of Jock and his descent into madness.

Happy endings, evidently, are not what these modern Scottish novels are all about. It's a grim old world on both social and personal levels. Socially most of the novelists point up class division as a central feature of Scottish society, often finding some of the cruellest class divisions within the working class, as we find in *From Scenes Like These* and *Fergus Lamont*, where there is a well-understood class hierarchy depending on what street you live in, or even which end of the street. All the novelists dealing with twentieth-century situations do demonstrate class awareness and class antagonisms through their characters to some extent; but it is interesting to note how few important characters after *A Scots Quair* become political activists. We can point only to relatively minor characters like Mick Docherty or Mary Holmscroft, or to the doomed, futile and manipulated efforts of Lanark.

Socially, then, a characteristic motif is community ridden with conflicts. What about personal relationships? In the nineteenth century, a favourite shape for the novel was the novel as courtship dance. Frequently, it ended with wedding bells. Much popular fiction still does. But although novelists generally are now prepared to investigate the question, is there life after marriage, and are happy to consider the doings of men and women without the benefit of matrimony, the male-female relationship remains a central subject.

In view of all that, it might seem strange that in no fewer than four of our ten novels the male-female relationship is remarkably unimportant. It matters nothing in *And the Cock Crew*, and it is side-stepped in *Tunes of Glory* (unlike in other Kennaway novels) and in *The Prime of Miss Jean Brodie*: these latter two investigate basically single-sex institutions. And it is hardly central to *Greenvoe*, although that novel contains both happy relationships and predatory ones.

So, when they *do* focus on male-female relationships, are our novelists as sombre as they appear to be on wider social issues? There are some mutually satisfactory relationships, to be sure. We recall Chris Guthrie and Ewan Tavendale before the Great War. Then there are Roddie and Catrine and Finn and Una in *The Silver Darlings*, all of whom appear to be happy enough with their respective partners in the end, however much we complain about Gunn's wraith-like idealisation of women. Tam and Jenny Docherty are a convincing couple in a mutually supportive partnership. Fergus Lamont has ten years with Kirstie in a satisfactory but less equal situation. It is not a lot, especially when we remember Chris Guthrie's less happy marriages and her son's failure with Ellen, or Kathleen Docherty's unhappy marriage, or Fergus Lamont's inability to relate contentedly to any woman not feeble-minded. The macho culture of *From Scenes Like These* ensures the failure of relationships. The only hope for Dunky and Elsa lies in the possibility of escape to Canada; but that is an impossible dream for them at the age of sixteen; and, while Mary O'Donnell succeeds in acquiring a legitimising father for her baby, no one would point to Mary and Willie Craig as a model of a 'mutually satisfying relationship'. The search for such a relationship is central to *Lanark*; but the novel seems to suggest that the characters' prospects are inherently blighted by fundamental divergences of interests, personalities and even perceptions. At best, we might sum up the affair of Lanark and Rima in Iris Murdoch's phrase, as 'a fairly honourable defeat'.

There is no dodging the fact that most of our novelists find very little to cheer about. The extraordinary thing is that so often the writing is so obviously not that of cheerless people, nor is it fundamentally about cheerless people. We have found repeated emphasis on conditions of unhappiness, inequality, injustice and failed personal relationships in families, streets and communities. These novelists have also repeatedly highlighted dangers or failures in traditional ideologies, both religious and political. They offer none of the certainties of the Kailyard and, of course, they reject its unctuous tones of self-congratulation. But what most of all distinguishes them from the Kailyard tradition is their insistence on avoiding cliches in language or situations, their openness to innovation, their sense of human resilience that will yield neither to despair nor spurious consolations: their sense of comedy and irony in the bleakest of circumstances and above all their verve and vigour. These are the qualities that testify to an ongoing Scottish Renaissance in fiction.

FURTHER READING

There is necessarily a wide variety of Scottish fiction of the last fifty years which is ignored in the present volume. The booklist below may offer some guide to interested readers. New and reprinted fiction is quite widely reviewed, by academic journals such as the *Scottish Literary Journal*, by literary periodicals such as *Cencrastus* and *New Edinburgh Review*, and by newspapers such as *The Scotsman*, *The Glasgow Herald* and the *Press and Journal*. Douglas Gifford does survey reviews of new fiction in *Books in Scotland* and in *Studies in Scottish Literature*. Since 1969 *The Bibliotheck* has published an *Annual Bibliography of Scottish Literature* which is extremely helpful, for criticism or reviews as well as primary texts, but it is not all-inclusive in this regard.

Interested readers should find food for thought in some of the following.

Alan Bold, *Modern Scottish Literature* (1983)
Cairns Craig, 'The Body in the Kit Bag: History and the Scottish Novel' in *Cencrastus* 1 (Autumn 1979) 18–22
— 'Fearful Selves: Character, Community and the Scottish Imagination' in *Cencrastus* 4 (Winter 1980–81) 29–32
Douglas Gifford, 'Scottish Fiction since 1945' in Norman Wilson (ed) *Scottish Writing and Writers* (1977)
— *Neil M. Gunn and Lewis Grassic Gibbon* (1983)
Francis Russell Hart, *The Scottish Novel: A Critical Survey* (1978)
Joy Hendry (ed) *The State of Scotland—A Predicament for the Scottish Writer?* in *Chapman* (July 1983) 35–6
David Hewitt and Michael Spiller (eds) *Literature of the North* (1982)
Maurice Lindsay, *History of Scottish Literature* (1977)
Edwin Morgan, *Essays* (1974)
— 'Literature in the Twentieth Century' in David Daiches (ed) *A Companion to Scottish Culture* (1981). See also some individual authors.
Trevor Royle, *The Macmillan Companion to Scottish Literature* (1983)
— 'A baker's dozen of best Scottish novels', in *Glasgow Herald* (28 Nov 1983) 7
Kurt Wittig, *The Scottish Tradition in Literature* (1958)

Neil Gunn's 1929 essay, 'The Scottish Literary Renaissance Movement', was reprinted in the December 1977 number of *Scottish Literary Journal* (vol 4 no 2)

CHAPTER TWO

Lewis Grassic Gibbon:
A Scots Quair

Before the publication of *Sunset Song* in 1932, the Scottish literary scene had been largely dominated by novels and stories of the Kailyard type, static pictures of country life characterised by cosiness. The Kailyard had produced stereotyped communities with predictable relationships and accepted class divisions—minister and dominie, for example, held in great respect. Ian Maclaren's *Beside the Bonnie Brier Bush* (1894) serves as a perfect example. And perhaps the single greatest cause of the cosiness was that these stories tended to be set in the (recent) past, safe to contemplate, generating a mild and pleasant nostalgia.

In their different ways George Douglas Brown and John MacDougall Hay wrote vehemently anti-Kailyard novels. Brown's was *The House With The Green Shutters* (1901), a very angry novel which pictured Scottish country folk as nasty, spiteful and capable of endless malice: he asserted it was 'a greater compliment to Scotland, I think, than the sentimental slop of Barrie, and Crockett, and Maclaren'. And his novel was much concerned with social change. John MacDougall Hay's *Gillespie* followed in 1914. Again it is concerned with social change, the advent of a manipulative capitalist economy masterminded by Gillespie himself, which transforms a traditional fishing and farming community. And again it is concerned not with cosiness but with evil: it is vast and epic and metaphysical, as well as realistic and detailed and documentary.

Arguably, Brown and Hay had done enough to break the Kailyard mould, had freed Grassic Gibbon from the need to fight it, left him able to pursue his own interests. Certainly *Sunset Song* was seen as coarse and shocking by early Scottish reviewers who preferred and yearned for the Kailyard. The *Kirriemuir Press* declared: 'The Kailyard writers of a generation ago gave us pictures of Scottish life at its best. The tendency today is to go to the other extreme . . .'. The reviewer complained of Gibbon: 'He is for ever calling a spade a spade, when there is no need whatever to refer to the implement at all.' Gibbon was very conscious of the inevitable comparisons—thus the drunken mutterings of the ironically named Reverend Gibbon about the trials of living ' 'tween a brier bush and a rotten kailyard in the lee of a house with green shutters' (*SS* 83). But some fifty years on it has become possible to read *Sunset Song* itself as more than a little cosy, nostalgic and safely past: immersed in the vital and attractive character of young Chris Guthrie, the reader can miss or unconsciously undervalue the novel's bitter treatment of change, the destruction of Kinraddie, the effects of the war and so on.

So it becomes even more important to read *A Scots Quair*, as Gibbon intended it, as essentially one novel. It was conceived as a whole, and produced in three volumes to suit the convenience of the publishers. When we look at the whole trilogy, it is impossible to miss the themes of change and destruction. Grassic Gibbon is not celebrating what is safely past, he is recording the vicious effects of recent history and the present situation of his country, even projecting his characters into the future, as Ewan Tavendale set off for London on the hunger march at the end of *Grey Granite*. And in so far as the personal centre is the story of Chris Guthrie, Gibbon's achievement is in no way confined to *Sunset Song*: the transformation of the vivid adolescent of the early part of that novel into the bewildered and hurt woman whose marriage fails in *Cloud Howe* is crucial, as is her emotional retreat into herself as *Grey Granite* proceeds.

It is not our intention in this book generally to give an account of previous criticism: on the whole there has been very little anyway, and our concern is to engage with the texts. But it seems to us necessary to start here with a *caveat*, because of the critical line on *A Scots Quair* which seems to hold a lot of sway and which in our opinion is becoming harmful to the reading of the book. We would like to see much less attention paid to Diffusionism and, much more importantly, to the 'symbolic' or 'allegorical' meaning of the *Quair*. For convenience, we can point to the two appendices to J T Low's edition of *Sunset Song* (Longman, 1971, pp 293–6), where these ideas are summarised.

Diffusionism is a notion of limited usefulness in the study of *A Scots Quair*. Certainly, it was an interest of James Leslie Mitchell, English writer. Certainly, he looked back to a Golden Age when man was a hunter, natural, gentle and instinctive. The theory is that corruption begins with agriculture, tilling the soil, and civilisation and its institutions follow, especially religion, all harming man's natural, instinctive self. But it is not a central concern of *A Scots Quair*. It is arguable that Diffusionism is a creed that attempts to explain the distant past, but has little relevance to present or future: in so far as one *can* extract from it any kind of message about how we should live now, Gibbon does not seem to preach such a message in *A Scots Quair*. Indeed, it would be difficult to reconstruct the theory from the trilogy—it only surfaces when old Mr Colquhoun, Robert's father, makes an unsuccessful bid for the pulpit of Kinraddie in *Sunset Song* (53). It also comes through, we are told, in feeling for the past, Chris's refuges at the

Standing Stones or the Kaims, young Ewan's passion for flints or his later identification of himself with suffering people throughout history. But no one need know anything about Diffusionism to appreciate the way these characters feel about the past.

Essentially it seems to us that Diffusionism is no answer to the kinds of problems Gibbon is investigating in the trilogy, and that he does not offer it as such. Gibbon's Marxism is a more relevant 'ism' here: the boy who spoke from Communist platforms before he was seventeen became a writer who was still considering that option seriously (and critically) in *Grey Granite*. Diffusionism, then, is something of a red herring—and the main danger is that people should feel incompetent to read and respond fully to the *Quair* because they feel ignorant about this 'philosophy'.

Over-emphasis on the symbolic or allegorical understanding of the trilogy is a much more serious barrier erected by criticism between reader and book. It seems to us increasingly baneful, doing real harm to the experience of reading the book. This is inevitable: realism and allegory are essentially at cross purposes. The more Chris is seen as 'Scotland herself' or 'the land', the blander and more two-dimensional she becomes. Eventually the reader, trained to see Ewan Tavendale as 'the Gael' or 'the original Celtic settlement of Scotland', and Robert Colquhoun as the Protestant Kirk and Jean Guthrie as Woman personified, fails to perceive the complexity and individuality of these characters in the texture of the work. It was not the Protestant Kirk that was gassed in the War: it was a very honest and puzzled man who fought an epic battle to keep his religious and political beliefs integrated, and lost, partly because of that very gassing. It is not Archetypal Woman or Mother Eve that commits suicide in *Sunset Song*, but a very tormented, individual woman, worn out and desperate with too many pregnancies. Jean Guthrie is essentially an individual who decides to kill her two youngest children also, presumably to save Chris from the cares of a ready-made and totally demanding family.

So the insistence on allegory blurs the realistic impact of the trilogy: patterns of this sort imposed on it (often, alas, in schools) mutilate the reading experience. And so much is made of so few passages—Robert Colquhoun, dreaming excitedly about his wife's pregnancy, exclaims, laughing, '*Oh Chris Caledonia, I've married a nation!*' (*CH* 145). Frog-faced young Mowat, attempting to charm Chris, finds her taller than himself, cool and unimpressed, and says later that 'he felt he was stared at by Scotland herself' (*CH* 110). Such phrases can too easily be wrenched out of context and misapplied to the whole trilogy. Similarly, when the teenage Chris sees herself as two Chrisses, one Scots and one English (*SS* 32), it is a vivid way of expressing the tensions she is aware of in her schooling and her home life; but it is a local explanation, for that stage in her development. It is idle to speculate whether the Scots Chris marries Ewan and the English Chris Robert—and which of them survives it all and welcomes solitude at the end of the trilogy. And in what sense can we talk about 'the land that is Chris'? In a highly emotional state after the emotional turmoil of her father's funeral, Chris comes to an insight, that nothing endures (*SS* 117). She goes on to except the land: 'the land was forever.' And so she has been equated with it. But her basic insight was the first one, that *nothing* endures: *that* is what she serenely accepts at the end of the trilogy, that Change is unstoppable, 'Deliverer, Destroyer and Friend in one' (*GG* 220). When she first returns to Cairndhu and the Barmekin (*GG* 45–6), she finds 'nothing, nothing but change that had followed every pace of her feet', and she realises the chance and impermanent nature of her attachment to this croft:

> So the whirlimagig went round and on: Father, now Ewan, the hill little to either, only to her who came in between and carried the little torch one from the other on that dreich, daft journey that led nowhither—
> But, standing up there, with the wind in her hair, the thought came to her that THAT didn't much matter—daft the journey, but the journeying good.

The presentation of Chris in the trilogy is meticulous and essentially realistic. She develops from a highly physical, sensuous adolescent into a post-menopausal woman, finished with men and child-bearing and on the whole glad of it, despite some wild regrets. She moves from a happy acceptance of life and relationships to a state where she is increasingly unable to believe in anything or anyone—and this is greatly accelerated by the tragic failure of her most important human relationship, the marriage to Robert Colquohoun. And none of this movement is simple: her characteristic emotional state is still some degree of turmoil, swither, indecision.

So in *Cloud Howe* she retreats, hurt and angry when Robert sneers at her. She is flushed, tempted to angry retort, bites it back, determined: 'She would keep to herself, she was nobody's serf' (173). But it isn't so easy—the next paragraph shows her aching for kindness, making sexual advances to Robert, and responding hurt and angry to his rebuff, weeping, trying to rationalise. All of this is behind her longing to be sure of herself, like young Ewan:

> Were she sure of herself as Ewan was of himself, she might go her own way and not heed to any, have men to lie with her when she desired them (and faith, that would sure be seldom enough!) do and say all the things that came crying her to do, go hide long days in the haughs of the Mounth—up in the silence and the hill-bird's cry, no soul to vex, and to watch the clouds sailing and passing out over the Howe, unending over the Howe of the World; that—or sing and be glad by a fire;

or wash and toil and be tired with her toil as once she had been in her days on a croft—a million things, Chris-alone, Chris-herself, with Chris Guthrie, Chris Tavendale, Chris Colquohoun dead!

Notice that this longing for serenity which certainly points to her eventual retreat to Cairndhu comes from a torrent of pain and involvement, and that it is clearly no simple yearning to get back to the land.

Chris is presented with equal complexity in *Grey Granite*, unable to attain the emotional equanimity, the coolness, she longs for. A typical emotional battle begins on page 112, when she is disturbed over Ma Cleghorn's approaching death, and can't sleep. She moves through 'a cold no-thought', experiences 'terrible loneliness', fears Ewan may be dead and has to listen for his breathing, is tempted to wake up Ellen to talk. She faces the future 'alone and desperate': what will she do when Ma dies? Here she hates growing old, and remembers her first marriage and 'the daftness of being young': she weeps over the croft in memory, 'afraid and afraid'. She is attacked by 'a sudden wild woe' that defeats her rational arguments:

> things would redd up in time, she wasn't hungry or starved, she had friends, she had Ewan . . . SHE HAD NOTHING AT ALL, she had never had anything, nothing in the world she'd believed in but change, unceasing and unstaying as time, light after light went down, hope and fear and hate, love that had lighted hours with a fire, hate freezing through to the blood of one's heart—Nothing endured, and this hour she stood as alone as she'd been when a quean in those wild, lost moments she climbed the heights of Blawearie brae.

Similar emotional complexity is central to the success of the passage on pages 141–2, when she remembers Robert's death a year before and resolves not to marry Ake Ogilvie for financial security. There is peculiar pathos here: for the only time she articulates the central 'if only'. After this it seems inevitable that she will retire from the battle, but here she considers that she and Robert might have found some path of commitment together:

> . . . Oh, less kind to you than I might have been. And I can't help it now, that's by and put past, nothing helps now, as little as you can I ever see a way out of all the ill soss. Not that I think I would look if I could, I've no patience with crowds or the things they want, only for myself I suppose I can plan. And I stand in the bareness, alone, tormented, and you . . . Oh, Robert man, had you stayed to help somehow we might have found the road together . . . .

These passages are crucial, deeply felt and realistically presented. They are not about 'Scotland' or even 'the land'. So we would indicate some of the limitations imposed by the symbolic or allegorical reading. The general charge is that it has been taken too far, that it simplifies and renders banal what is most effective and specific in the novel. Even these few examples suffice to indicate that Chris does not 'equal' Scotland: she is a complex and very individual female character. And Chris does not 'equal' the land, or love of the land, although indeed she loves the land. It is hard not to conclude that Kurt Wittig started criticism of the trilogy off on a wrong foot when he wrote in 1958: 'The story moves on three distinct levels: personal, social, and mythological . . . .' We shall stick very deliberately to the first two.

The personal and social levels certainly exist, but it is part of the artistry of the novel that they are not 'distinct', as Wittig has it, but inextricably intertwined. The trilogy is concerned centrally with Chris and with the three communities, village, town and city, that she lives in. A summary of central topics and themes will perhaps usefully indicate the directions in which the work is moving.

The Chris of *Sunset Song* is at her most attractive, vital and outgoing. We see her in adolescence, first love, marriage and motherhood, and very briefly as a widow. The society she inhabits, the village of Kinraddie, is a small, integrated, secure, known community. This is true in spite of coarse gossip and uncharitable attitudes; and the basic events of the novel are social occasions for the whole community, such as John Guthrie's funeral, the wedding of Chris and Ewan, and the fire at Peesie's Knapp. There is no employment problem: only Pooty and the 'dafties' are more or less unemployed, and the community's matter of fact acceptance of such social inadequates is an index of its strength. Religion is not seen as of any great attractiveness: it is represe ted by the 'curly bull' of a minister, over given to sexual dalliance, and by the harsh and repressed John Guthrie, and it is opposed by Long Rob, a highly attractive character, especially to young Chris. She is not a believer, and the news of her engagement to a minister at the end of the novel is rather surprising. The other key figure of Chris's youth, Chae Strachan, carries the political interest: his Socialism is serious but indulged rather than taken seriously by the community. The Great War is the crucial outside event that affects Kinraddie: it destroys Ewan, Chae and Rob, takes the heart out of the community, and the tree-felling ensures the subsequent impoverishment of the land.

The Chris of *Cloud Howe* is less open, gradually more self-protective. We see her move from an initially happy second marriage which warmly includes young Ewan, through the loss of her baby and the slow failure of the marriage to a second widowhood. The society, the small town of Segget, is always divided, at the least into an opposition of the spinners and the rest. The gossip and nastiness are more serious, the community feeling goes. Arguably the town operates as a community on the occasion of the

Segget Show, but more typically it is divided and mutually hostile, as on Armistice Day. Unemployment has become a real and increasing problem, with both the mills closed by the end. Religious interest centres on Robert's struggles, and any religious hope in the trilogy dies with him. Chris is not involved, except in her love for her husband and her shrinking from his desperate mysticism. The political situation of the times is reflected, with easily identifiable historical elections and the rise of Fascism: everything is getting uglier and more threatening. The effects of the Great War are still everywhere, endlessly destructive—especially destroying Robert Colquohoun.

The Chris of *Grey Granite* is mostly stoically alone. She marries Ake Ogilvie for Ewan's sake, and knows it is a mistake: throughout the novel she is withdrawing until at the end she is alone, but in no sense lonely. Society, the city of Duncairn, is hopelessly divided, and events tend to involve only one class or only another. The employment situation is terrible, the only upturn represented by an armaments contract. Religion is no longer treated seriously, and instead the emphasis is on left wing politics, the developing Communist faith of Ewan seen against the backcloth of the continuing rise of Fascism and the desperation of the times. The Great War by this time is mainly a bad memory, but the next war is already a threat, as Ewan perceives: meantime the central war in *Grey Granite* is the class war.

It seems impossible to overstress the inventiveness and flexibility of the narrative technique in the trilogy. One main movement is from personal to impersonal narration, to anonymous or fragmented presentation. Chris Guthrie's is the main narrative voice in *Sunset Song*, though events and attitudes beyond her experience are often supplied by a more knowing kind of community voice, still very personal. This becomes much more defined, more explicit in *Cloud Howe*, where the narrative is divided on the whole between Chris and a Segget voice. She is confined, generally, to life at the manse and the increasingly unhappy married life she shares with Robert. The Segget voice tells long gossipy stories, like the tale of how Dite Peat put a slaughtered pig in Jim the Sourock's bed; and it also covers most of the action. The poignant intensity of *Sunset Song* is lost: it was the product of the brief time when the vivid youth of Chris Guthrie revivified the dying community of Kinraddie. She did not experience it as dying: there was no real difference between the events of Chris's emotional life and those physical or historical events that happened round her: she experienced both with the same intensity. Very occasionally in *Cloud Howe*, other voices intrude: young Ewan reflects on life at the manse: Else has a section too. And by the beginning of *Grey Granite* Chris has become peripheral to the action and the plot: still a centrally important character in one sense, she is also importantly marginal, uninvolved.

But the real fragmentation of the narration occurs in *Grey Granite*. It sets out to be different from the first two parts of the trilogy from the start. In *Sunset Song* the main narrative, the lyrical 'song' that mainly reflects young Chris Guthrie, was framed by Prelude and Epilude in a more compressed Kinraddie voice. The Prelude gives a historical sketch of Kinraddie from Norman times to the decay of the Kinraddie estate by 1911, preparing the reader for the further decay the book must chronicle. Then it goes round, croft by croft, introducing us to all the inhabitants, giving a knowing, village account of them before the advent of Chris Guthrie, to whom it is all both new and natural. The Epilude reverts to the village account, and amounts indeed to an accounting. For all the money Kinraddie made out of the war, when the crofters get their chance to buy their land, the results are varied, as the voice inexorably sums each up. We learn too of the deaths of Rob and Chae, and the desolation of the empty croft buildings. There is also the new minister, according to old Brigson the only decent thing that has come to the village, with his Socialist tendencies and his engagement to Chris Tavendale.

The effectiveness of this framing device is dependent on the size and cohesiveness of Kinraddie, so its disappearance is inevitable. There is an introductory Proem to *Cloud Howe*, but no balancing conclusion: the book ends starkly and abruptly with Robert's death, the mills closed, the town ruined, nothing to sum up. Indeed the Proem only attempts one of the two functions of the Prelude in *Sunset Song*: we get the historical account of Segget, from the time of King Kenneth the Third, with the establishment of the owning Mowats and the Victorian boom in jute-spinning. But significantly we are not introduced to the present inhabitants: there are of course too many for individual attention but in any case the Segget voice is not willing to differentiate them—'the spinners', 'that dirt'.

The city of Duncairn is not a community, has no coherent history, and so *Grey Granite* has no framing introduction: the city is fragmented and the characters are displaced. Even in the body of the novel, we do not see many dwelling places—and Ma Cleghorn's boarding house is an image of something very different from a home. Its inhabitants are displaced middle-class people, with limited function in both city and story. Paldy Parish, where Meg and Alick Watson live, is a poor slum area of town, and it is used to illustrate division again: Chris goes looking for Meg and meets the man to whom she'd given sixpence—and we have another extension of the class war, when he sees her as 'boorjoy and stuck-up': she sees herself as sturdy peasant still: 'My class? It was digging its living in sweat while yours lay down with a whine in the dirt. Goodbye' (32). Significantly, the parts of the city we return to most frequently are not houses but factories, in particular Gowans and Gloag's, and the streets where demonstrations are held.

One technical feature which remains constant in the three books of the trilogy is Chris's retreat at intervals to a place by herself where she can review her life since her last meditation. In *Sunset Song* her refuge is the Standing Stones at Blawearie loch, and much has been made of their age and their importance to her. Most essential, however, seems the isolation she finds here: significantly they are high up, so that Chris can look down from them. In *Cloud Howe* her refuge is another historical monument, if a more recent one, the ruined castle of Kaims, again upon a high hill, and again most importantly a place where she can be alone. In Duncairn she dispenses with ancient history and its associations, pausing on the Windmill Steps, looking down on the city and relishing 'the blessed desertion of the Windmill Steps so few folk used in Duncairn toun' (*GG* 3).

Fragmentation is the essence of the narrative in *Grey Granite*. The 'voice' can still be that of Chris, of course, or of Ewan, who takes a much more important part in this novel—or it can be Ellen, or Meg or Alick Watson, or the chorus of the Unco Guid that intervenes to comment, Baillie Brown, the self-righteous man, the Reverend MacShilluck, the Chief Constable, the Provost, the press. Most interesting, perhaps, is the development of anonymous voices of the workers or the unemployed. These can be slightly differentiated—it is an old worker, by his own account, that describes the killing of Johnny Edwards, while it is a young one called Bob who reflects more often on his reactions to industrial strife or political involvement. (Bob is killed in the explosion at the Works (200–1).) For the most part Gibbon does not give obvious signals to indicate change of voice—or at least he does not announce who the new speaker is; we have to work that out.

So the reader again masters another set of conventions unique to the trilogy. In *Sunset Song* a double space between paragraphs can mean a shift in time, space or mood for Chris, or a shift to a community voice. In *Cloud Howe* it usually indicates a move from Chris to the Segget voice or vice versa, although exceptionally we find the new voice is Else's or Ewan's. In *Grey Granite* more is required of us. Like Faulkner in *As I Lay Dying*, Gibbon refuses omniscience, but wants to avoid undue weighting to any one character. Faulkner divides his narrative between the different members of the family pursuing their bizarre and repellent journey to bury Addie Bundren according to promise whatever the cost, and he gives the views of some appalled onlookers as well. He points up his method with a new page for each speaker, and the announcement of the speaker's name at the top of the page, and he is sufficiently unconcerned with realism to give one section to the defunct Addie herself. So a considerable range of voices is woven into one story. Gibbon's method is similar in some ways, but in some respects more demanding: we know less about his characters, even when we have identified them—but it is important that we have to work at identifying them each time. This technique stresses the random loneliness of city life, the lack of relationship between the characters, the lack of any identifiable community.

The whole complex of narrative methods we encounter in the trilogy is very far from any simple or conventional realism which we may seem to have asserted in dismissing the allegorical readings of the *Quair*. All realism is of course only qualified realism, and the main point we argue about Chris is that her character convinces as real, true to life, individual, while she experiences credible emotional tensions and swings of mood. But the narrative method of the *Quair* involves our accepting some very non-realistic conventions. Framing sections apart, for example, the whole trilogy seems to depend on Chris going to 'some place wherever she bade to which she could climb by her lone for a while and think of the days new-finished and done' (*GG* 67). Increasingly as the trilogy progresses and the other voices take up the tale this is unconvincing or even preposterous on a strictly realistic level—Chris 'remembers' things she surely never knew—but we are easily persuaded, unawares, to accept the unique conventions of the trilogy.

The narrative, then, is some kind of reflection or meditation on experience. It certainly does not depend on any conventional narrative understanding of time. In the course of any section, time can expand or contract amazingly: the course of the narrative depends more on associations Chris makes in her own experience—a person, a phase, or a day—so that for example in *Cloud Howe* Armistice Day is one peg around which memories and reflections are organised. Time is a deceptive medium in the trilogy, and Gibbon isn't always too careful about his planning, and some references can mislead. For example, in *Grey Granite* (173) Chris looks back from Cairndhu to 'her forty years in the distant Howe': she left Cairndhu at fifteen, so this would make her fifty-five—impossible, unless the end projects her well into the future! Other inescapable and more persuasive arithmetic urges that she left Cairndhu at fifteen in 1911, and that *Sunset Song* covers the next years to (approximately) twenty-three in 1919. *Cloud Howe* begins with two more years in Kinraddie, then the move to Segget. At the beginning of *Grey Granite*, six months after Robert's death, Chris is thirty-eight in Duncairn. Thus the action of *Cloud Howe* must cover 'ten full years' and more in Segget, perhaps a surprising notion. *Grey Granite*, on the other hand, covers very little time. Chris is thirty-eight at the start in 1933, and so only thirty-eight or thirty-nine at the end in 1934. Again we may be startled, this time that so much has happened in so few months. This arithmetic reinforces the startling idea that the marriage to Ake Ogilvie is of very brief duration indeed: it is late May when we see Chris dressed for the wedding (122), and late June when we encounter her again, alone, at Cairndhu (173). The novel becomes bewilderingly quick—even before the marriage, Chris thinks: 'What a reel of things in a few short months, what an antrim world that waited tomorrow!' (172).

Our insistence on the local interest of the narrative, its changing texture, can in the end only be furthered by examining short sections of the three novels in some detail. We have emphasised the unity of the trilogy, but this emphasis must be balanced by an awareness of the different narrative methods used in each volume, which makes the *Quair* what Douglas Gifford calls 'one great novel with three massive movements.' We have selected sequences from each volume to examine the variety of voices employed, the themes, the effectiveness. We have not looked for the most central episodes, but rather for passages wholly typical of the concerns of each novel, and we want to show how Gibbon in each case can fairly clearly indicate his response to the issues raised, without intervening in any clumsy way in his own voice. So we see the down to earth, animal nature of most of the 'harvest madness' in *Sunset Song* in contrast to Will Guthrie's caring for his Mollie; the respectable, God-fearing congregation at Armistice Day in *Cloud Howe* is shamed by the marching spinners who actually fought in the war, and the cowed unemployed man who joins the unemployment march in *Grey Granite* is restored to dignity and community, while the powers that be are effectively if crudely satirised out of their own mouths.

The part of *Sunset Song* we have chosen to examine is the 'harvest madness' sequence, from 'Drilling' (66–81). It would surely be cynical to suggest that part of the universal appeal of *Sunset Song* is its awareness of sexuality, but certainly both the subject matter of the early parts of the novel and the consciousness of a fifteen-year-old girl becoming aware of her own physical sensations and sexual emotions make this awareness dominant. So the harvest madness sequence does not particularly stand out. Sexual concerns have dominated 'Ploughing'. There is Marget Strachan's attempt to instruct Chris in the ways of men (46), and the day Andy the daftie suffers spring fever, and approaches a number of women and girls, including Chris herself (47–51). There is John Guthrie's rage over this (52). There is the minister's sermon on the Song of Solomon and his congregation's vicarious enjoyment of it (54–5), and there is trouble when John Guthrie finds Chris, stripped, treading the blankets and she sees 'a caged beast peep from her father's eyes' (60). This climaxes tragically with Jean Guthrie's desperation and suicide because of her new pregnancy.

Similarly, the subject is not finished with in the pages about to be examined. When Chris meets Ewan, she thinks immediately of the harvest madness story about him and old Sarah Sinclair; eventually the encounter has to be talked out in detail, and the developing relationship with Ewan is physically very aware. And sadly John Guthrie's sexuality will also be obscenely evident when he tries to tempt Chris to incest, quoting the Old Testament precedent of Lot.

But the harvest madness sequence (66–81) is very interesting. This is something that affects people closely in touch with nature and natural rhythms. Necessarily, it only occurs in this book of the trilogy. Although this is the only account, we are informed (66) that it hits John Guthrie every year. Most of this sequence is told by Chris, and for her the harvest itself and the hard work involved are at least at first the major topics. It is almost an aside that 'every harvest there came something queer and terrible on father', so that he sings hymns 'with a queer, keen shrillness that brought the sweat in the palms of your hands'. The next few paragraphs are supposedly concerned with the work of the harvest only, but the imagery has more to say. The reaper driven by John Guthrie has blades that 'flashed and brightened like the teeth of a beast and snarled in a famished freedom'. The tink arrives and is given a probable start: Chris's personal harvest madness begins when he almost pulls her down into the hay, and he offers to relieve her of her virginity. Her reaction is very physical, very puzzled. She feels 'sick and not angry, something turned in her stomach and her legs felt weak'. She cannot stop washing her hands and face (69). Later, she is very physically aware of the tink and his offer, and for a second she contemplates going down to the barn. Instead she undresses herself and stares in the mirror, as she will do again (for example, just before her marriage to Ewan, *SS* 144–5, and *CH* 84–5, 196–7, *GG* 40). She assesses her looks and anticipates a lover with whom she can share not only her body but all her dearest thoughts.

It is not entirely clear whose voice sums this up (71): 'So that was the harvest madness that came on Chris, mild enough it had been, she fell fast asleep in the middle of it.' It could be her own later musing: certainly it is one of her paragraphs, which goes on to regret that Will won't do night work, but is off to Drumlithie every evening. This, like Will's blush over his future hopes about Canada, helps prepare us, if not Chris, for Will's own version of harvest madness (75–81).

Before the narrative widens to examine harvest madness all round Kinraddie, Chris has a frightening night, when she hears her father padding about like 'a beast that sniffed and planned and smelled at the night'. The effect of the description of Chris's fear is partly dependent on her inability to verbalise it, and the reader's assumption of greater knowledge. 'And once he came soft down the cowering creak of the stairs and stopped by her door, and she held her breath, near sick with fright, though what was there to be feared of?'

The Kinraddie madness is conveyed in a community voice, whether or not we assume Chris would have heard it like this. In contrast to Chris's, it is both knowing and occasionally coarse. And it is introduced by a happy warning that any sexual adventure will be celebrated by delighted gossips. 'The speak' deals first with Sarah Sinclair and Ewan Tavendale, seen by Alec Mutch coming out of the larch wood. He has a powerful agricultural turn of phrase, and describes Sarah's face as 'raddled with blushing . . . like the leg of a tuberculous rabbit when you skinned the beast', and as for Ewan: 'hang-dog he looked as though it was his mother he'd bedded with, said Alec, and maybe that's how it had felt.' The story continues in coarsely comic vein, from the Kinraddie voice, with Chae fighting Ewan and his bothy lads over Ewan's intentions.

The Kinraddie voice continues with Cuddiestoun's story of disturbing the minister and the maid in the garden of the manse. It reflects on Cuddiestoun himself as well as the scandal: 'maybe the poor brute's big sweating feet were fell sore already with a hot day's stooking' (73). The narrative is detailed and circumstantial, and the imagery and language more indirectly effective than a sight of the pair *in flagrante delicto*. It is initially a question of sound, 'a rustling and squealing' like young pigs rootling, maybe 'dogs in heat . . . set for mating'. Then comes the maid 'with a glazed look', 'daftlike', 'as though she walked half-asleep', and whistling and laughing uncannily: the pig metaphor is continued in 'like the face of a pig below the knife of its killer'. Apparently the Reverend Gibbon has something of the inexplicable sexual attractiveness later credited to Dalziel of Meiklebogs. The Kinraddie voice continues the story and how it grew in the telling, but an interesting phenomenon occurs when Long Rob relays his version to John Guthrie. Two paragraphs here, beginning with 'It seemed like enough to John Guthrie', appear to voice the inner thoughts of John Guthrie, never otherwise opened to us. His thoughts are bitter, and not part of the harvest madness: the land is coarse, the day of the crofter is almost gone, and he sees his wife's suicide as a sign of the times, an attempt to bring *him* into public disgrace. The short monologue is bleak and forceful: his reference to his wife seems crudely heartless and self centred, but his short vision of doom ends with 'a darkness down on the land he loved better than his soul or God'. A strong comparison, that, because his religion is so important.

The last part of the harvest madness is the only one that has any real relation to ordinary literary considerations of plot or action. It is the story of Will and his Mollie, and is told by Chris from her experience, although she makes us aware of the gossip as well (75–81). When Chris visits Drumlithie, Galt the gardener begins the 'sly hinting and joking' we by now associate with local gossip. Chris resists his mischievous questions, as she knows she must, but even she wonders: 'Whatever could Will have been doing; and what had he done to his quean that he'd left her?' (76). Next Chris encounters Mollie Douglas herself, and Mollie overcomes her inhibitions enough to send a loving message to Will via Chris. The impressive thing here is the shared social shame of the two girls, their shared blushes: Mollie seems to read a question in Chris's eyes and accuses her of thinking '*THAT, like all of them*'. Chris is still young and innocent, but no fool, and she knows all the village stories: she 'found she just couldn't speak up and deny THAT was indeed what she'd thought, what else was a body to think?' (76). If *Chris* can misconstrue the situation we should not be surprised to find her father and the Reverend Gibbon doing likewise and interfering in the affair. But before that Will returns to Drumlithie, encounters Galt's hints and tries to demolish him, thus himself becoming 'the laughing-stock of Kinraddie'. So the sequence ends with John Guthrie's coarse questions and the danger of violence between father and son, complicated by the intrusion of the minister and Will's angry exit. It is quite unnecessary for any authorial voice to point out the inappropriateness of John Guthrie's and the Reverend Gibbon's setting themselves up as inquisitors on sexual propriety: the treatment of the two, even inside this sequence, has implicitly done that already. And Will's final reassurance to Chris that '*I'd as soon cut my own throat as do hurt to—HER*' is refreshingly different: this is the only point in the whole sequence where someone subject to sexual desires sees his partner as more than a sexual object, but a person to be respected.

It is interesting to turn from the harvest madness of Kinraddie in *Sunset Song* to Armistice Day in Segget in *Cloud Howe*. It is in the section called 'Cumulus', which covers the first six months the Colquohouns spend in Segget, and it brings to a climax the war consciousness and disunity apparent from the first. We recall Robert's appalled reaction to the Segget war memorial, and his dream of a 'League of the willing folk of Segget' (47), and the launching of his campaign (62). The day and night of the Segget Show precede Armistice Day, and indicate a very tenuous unity of the townspeople, fragmentary and undependable with at best tentative relations between the spinners and others.

After the Show comes the painful private experience for Chris when she has planned trying to start a pregnancy. Her joyful response to Robert is shattered when her fingers touch a war scar—she lies crying later, for Robert's past danger, for her dead first husband, and at the notion of bearing another child to die in another war. And so, appropriately, we come to Armistice Day (90). But then the Segget voice, more of a contrast in tone and content to Chris's than was the case with the Kinraddie voice in *Sunset Song*, chimes in with the seven page story of Jim the Sourock. It seems a diversion, but it is very deliberately placed where it is, and the date,

November 10th, is repeatedly stressed. *Cloud Howe* contains many examples of what the Segget voice sees as comic tales and the reader tends to find rather grim ones: this is one such. Dite Peat decides to put the pig he has slaughtered in the wife's place in Jim's bed, before he comes home inebriated as usual. It works, and in reactive horror Jim 'gets religion', and cleaves to MacDougall Brown. But the story unpleasantly sets the mood for Armistice Day. It is a tale of bloody slaughter, and Dite Peat thinks Armistice Day an appropriate time for butchery:

> *Fegs, mistress, I've seen humans carved up like pigs, like bits of beef in a butcher's shop, and it fair looked fine, as I often thought, you couldn't wonder at those cannibal childes*—(91)

The unpleasant, ratlike Dite, we learn, had enjoyed the war and the dismemberment: 'there was something in blood and a howling of fear that kittled up a man as nothing else could' (92).

The Sourock tale does not only refer us on to Armistice Day. The Sourock's wife sees Dite Peat as a rat in the ree, intent on murdering the pig which was frightened of rats: we are being prepared for the terrible incident near the end of *Cloud Howe* when the Kindness family has to find shelter in a pig ree and the baby's thumb is eaten by rats (212). As Jim lurches home his drunkenness is measured by his sight of the war memorial angel Robert so much disliked, and the fact that he can see two of them. The rest of the story is grim comedy, but we never forget that it centres on a 'red corpse' (97).

The events of Armistice Day proper indicate social disunity at every level, and the first part, including the service, is related by the Segget voice that perpetually criticises the spinners. The voice warns of the outcome: 'by the time Armistice was out, it was less proud than ever of its spinners, Segget' (97). Dissension is the key here: Ake Ogilvie has a verbal battle with the Provost and his son, so that there is nearly 'a fine bit fight on the go, right there by the angel in Segget Square, folk round about looking shocked as could be and edging nearer for a better look' (98). The fight is only avoided by the entry of the minister and the choir. We remember Robert Colquohoun's impressive war memorial service at the end of *Sunset Song*, and his use of the Standing Stones as memorial: now the Segget voice resents his badgering, and concludes: 'he'd soon have all Segget on his hands to fight.' The voice reflects on Robert's sermon, and on his wife, and his congregation, indicating their occupations and their (significantly limited) war experience. We're told MacDougall Brown is 'well to the fore, not that he'd fought in the War, but he'd sung': Peter Peat is a 'terrible patriot', and the congregation contains the teachers and the 'decent folk', some general representatives.

Now come the interruptions. At eleven o'clock the solemn silence is
spoiled by 'a great car': we are not surprised to learn later (109) that it was
Stephen Mowat's car. Then the singing is interrupted by a crowd of
spinners. Something like this has happened before: the spinners interrupted
a service MacDougall Brown was holding in the Square with their mocking
rendition of 'WHITER than—the whitewash on the wall!' (53). But this
time the Segget voice has more reason to become embarrassed. The
interruption is described with the usual dislike and contempt, but this time
the hymn is drowned by 'The Red Flag'. When Feet the policeman faces
Jock Cronin, we find the spinners:

> were all of them men who had been to the War; except the three women, and they
> wore medals sent on to them after their folk were dead (101).

The combined Segget consciousness is staggered,

> especially as you had no medal yourself, you hadn't been able to get to the War,
> you'd been over-busy with the shop those years, or keeping the trade going brisk
> in the Arms, or serving at Segget as the new stationmaster.

This is more effective than any authorial voice which might hint at social
inequality in the working of the Conscription Act and the system of
reserved occupations. The spinners win a moral victory, and Robert's
sermon is balanced by Jock Cronin's, urging concern with the living, and
membership of the Labour Party, and inviting Robert to join first. The
morning ends as it began, with another near-fight, this time between Ake
Ogilvie and Jock Cronin, but Robert checks Ake and 'most decent bodies
went over to the Arms and spoke of the things they'd have done to the
spinners if they'd stayed behind in Segget Square' (103).

The narrative now switches to Chris, as she runs back to the Manse for a
middle-class social situation, where she and Robert are to entertain the
teachers to lunch, and he will try to form his League. Chris has been
impressed by the spinners, their red flag and the song: 'it caught you
somehow, there was something in it that you knew was half-true' (103): and
Robert is also swayed by their belief in '*a war of the classes to bring fruit to
the War*'. The social events of the rest of the day, lunch with the respectable,
educated middle class and tea with young Mowat, will have both of them at
least temporarily on the side of the spinners.

There is plenty of comedy in the lunch scene, much of it in the
descriptions Chris later remembers Else or Ake giving of the different
characters. But young Ewan's reaction when Mr Geddes breaks his

wooden horse is direct, and he produces a fine comic effect by starting to sing 'The Red Flag' as the teachers sip their sherry: he thinks it's 'a bloody fine song'. But there is clearly no hope here for Robert's League. The dominie Geddes sees no hope for the Scots, while his wife sees the WRI as quite sufficient. Only Miss Jeannie Grant looks to the Labour Party (and she will lose any social respect she has in Segget when she marries the spinner Jock Cronin (182)). Jeannie Grant interprets Chris's dislike of 'good works' by saying she's a socialist, but it is a simpler dislike of prying patronage, and a memory of her father's contempt for '*your dirt of gentry*' (109).

The tea with young Mowat is given in Chris's voice, with a deft intervention in mid-paragraph of a non-Chris voice, relaying the gossip of Mowat's 'shover' (chauffeur) about war memorials and Mowat's queans. This is explained as repeated afterwards by Else, who is simultaneously entertaining Dalziel of Meiklebogs in the kitchen. Similarly, Mowat's reaction to Chris, including the critically overstressed phrase about 'Scotland herself', is inserted here although not heard by Chris until later. But even before their conversation, the events of the day have sharpened Chris's class awareness: 'Funny that the like of him for so long had lived on the rent of folk like hers' (111). While Robert begins his crucial talk with the laird, Chris's voice is again unobtrusively pre-empted by Else and her mirthful reaction to Mowat, and her rueful reaction to Meiklebogs.

The ensuing conversation is officially between laird and minister, but Chris eventually feels impelled to intervene. Mowat has returned, he says, 'to look after the mills and Segget in general', and to 'buck up the village'. But his answer to Robert's plans is inspired by his admiration for Mussolini: 'The thing that was needed everywhere was Discipline, hwaw? and order, and what not.' He has seen it in Italy, and by analogy he wants to restore nationhood to Scotland. Chris's intervention is dismissive—and more: she denies Mowat's sentimental picture of a past, harmonious Scotland, and finishes: '*If it came to the push between you and the spinners I think I would give the spinners my vote*' (112). This aspect of Chris, the political or social animal, is to die away, apparently destroyed in the unhappiness of her marriage with Robert. But even a year after Robert's death, in *Grey Granite*, as we have seen, she mourns: 'Oh, Robert man, had you stayed to help somehow we might have found the road together' (*GG* 142). Here she goes on, thinking of the suffering of the people throughout history (as Ewan will later, *GG* 149),

her folk . . . dying . . . chaving . . . harried and . . . spat on . . . tortured and broken . . . and this snippet of a fop with an English voice would bring back worse, and ask her to help!

Robert too makes a stand. He has looked for help from '*the middle class folk and the upper class folk, and all the poor devils that hang by their tails*', but to no avail. Now the scene in the Square seems highly portentous: Robert is willing to align himself with the spinners: '*if in Segget are the folk of the mills, then, whatever their creed, I'm on their side.*' Robert is still, after all, the minister who shocked Kinraddie by chumming up with ploughmen, storming at farmers over the low wages they paid, and helping the ploughman's Union, the minister who in his first sermon took his text not from the Bible but from the *Agricola* of Tacitus. The words 'They have made a desert and they call it peace' are put by Tacitus in the mouth of the defeated Caledonian chieftain Calgacus.

It has indeed been a full day: on the face of it, their encounter with the full range of social class in Segget has begun to persuade both Robert and Chris of a political way forward, but it is not to be. Robert's political and religious convictions cannot be held together, and his war-torn body and mind cannot survive, while Chris is individualistic by temperament, and the long years of the steady failure of the marriage encourage her withdrawal into herself, to the eventual isolation of Cairndhu.

In choosing an appropriate passage of *Grey Granite* to examine in close up, we have deliberately looked for the new kind of narrative voice, the 'you' that speaks as a constituent part of a united action, less individual even than the near-anonymous Bob who works with Ewan and whose attitudes to Ewan fluctuate typically. So we will look at the unemployment march organised by the Communist Big Jim Trease for contingents of unemployed from all parts of the city (58–67). It is appropriate again, given the pace and deliberately fragmented nature of the narrative in *Grey Granite*, that this passage is considerably shorter than the harvest madness and Armistice Day ones, and also much more violent. It is also appropriate that the narrative contains far more voices, for the fragmentary amorphous society of Duncairn to be reflected.

Politics and unemployment are of course major concerns in *Grey Granite*, and before this Broo march we have seen Ewan's various fortunes and fights at Gowans and Gloag's, Chris's visit to the slum parish of Paldy where unemployment is rife, and the arrival at Ma Cleghorn's of Ellen Johns. Ellen seems a reincarnation and development of the Jeannie Grant of *Cloud Howe*: she is a teacher and a socialist, and captures Ewan's interest. The last part of Chris's narrative before the Broo march concerns the scandal over Ellen: reportedly she has taught the children facts about excretion, and spoken dangerously of the Bible: already she is reprimanded by the authorities, and we are prepared for the paper she is later made to sign (207), choosing between Party and job.

It is not surprising that in her withdrawal Chris has very little part in the rendering of the march: only her concern for Ewan links her to the book's central action at all. The voice that opens the account is that of an anonymous marcher, a composite, '*Will*! or *Peter*! or *Tam*!' (58), 'Peter or Andrew or Charlie' (65). This typical marcher has not intended to march. Jim Trease is doing the organising, the Communists are calling to people to join the march and face the Provost over the PAC (Public Assistance Committee) rate. The unemployed man is self-conscious: he looks 'shame-faced' at others and does not join the march until Big Jim calls him by his name—'you couldn't well do anything else but join—God blast it, you'd grievances enough to complain of' (58). He lines up sheepishly, despite the frightened protests of his wife, reassuring himself that it is only a march.

When the march begins a new spirit gradually enters the narrator. Despite the jokes of others he carries a banner with the slogan: 'DOWN WITH THE MEANS TEST AND HUNGER AND WAR.' Behind the Red leaders comes a Red drummer and a united group of men, and already the narrator notices the sun shining on wet roofs: 'queer you'd never seen it look bonny as that.' The unity of the march affects them all—'now all the chaps were lifting their heads', and hiding whatever qualms they felt (59). Another unifying factor is hostility to the police—'Bobbies . . . a birn of the bastards, fat and well fed, coshes in hand', and Feet himself. And the singing also helps: it is initially old songs rewritten for topical issues, against gentry, king and country. Stite? Perhaps, reflects the narrator,

> but it gave a swing to your feet and you all felt kittled up and high by then and looked back by your shoulder and saw behind the birn of the billies marching like you, you forgot the wife, that you hadn't a meck, the hunger and dirt, you'd alter that. They couldn't deny you, you and the rest of the Broo folk here, the right to lay bare your grievances. Flutter, flutter, the banner over your head, your feet beginning to stound a wee, long since the boots held out the water, shining the drift of the rain going by.

The column is now confidently in step: it pauses easily to be joined by other contingents who draw in and form fours. Not surprisingly our typical marcher remembers his army experience, like the spinners of *Cloud Howe*. Gradually he resolves—'by God, you would see about things!' The increasing confidence of the march and the repeated attempts of the wife to intervene are woven together in the marcher's consciousness, more and more moved by the overtly political singing, more impatient with the wife.

Suddenly the scene is dominated by mounted police, truncheons at the ready, and the column is stopped. As the word comes back that the police are turning the procession back into Paldy, with no opportunity of seeing the Provost, the column reacts like a savage animal: the marchers have become part of something else:

And then you heard something rising about you that hadn't words, the queerest-like sound, you stared at your mates, a thing like a growl, low and savage, the same in your throat (62).

The men are determined to fight—they dismiss Trease's call to keep the line as lack of guts; and they find themselves facing a line of charging mounted police. It is interesting that Gibbon makes no more of the violence: characteristically here, the section ends with a dash (—) and reliance on the reader's imagination. The narration is now taken over by Ewan's consciousness, as his individual part in the riot, as spectator and leader, is economically sketched: and his part also ends with a punctuation device that breaks off the description and leaves the rest to the imagination of the reader.

Ewan may not in the last resort be a very successful character, not sufficiently rounded for the weight he has to bear, but this turning-point in his political development is very vividly rendered. He, the toff, has been in a bookshop: the shopman calls him '*Sir*'. He registers five distinct pictures. First there is Feet's absolutely unprovoked attack on a young keelie with his baton, dramatic and fearful. Second, the bobbies charge, the Broo men go mad and Ewan sees Big Jim 'mishandled and knocked to the ground under the flying hooves of the horses'. Thirdly comes the counter-attack: Ewan sees a man attack and unseat a mounted policeman and hears himself shout, 'Well done, well done!' Fourth, in the general mêlée, when both column and police have gone mad, Ewan witnesses one bobby hitting an old man who goes down, and 'the hoof of the horse went plunk on his breast—'. Finally he sees a brewery lorry full of empty bottles. As much as the typical marcher he is in the power of another force: 'something took hold of him, whirled him about, shot him into the struggling column' (63): at his instigation, the unemployed men supply themselves with weapons.

The reactions of a society portrayed as corrupt and hypocritical are mirrored in the next few paragraphs. First the press. The *Runner*'s story of a pitched battle between unemployed and police is quickly transformed into 'Reds' fighting with bottles and the 'poor police' punished merely for trying to keep the peace. Then religion. The Reverend MacShilluck has no doubts as to where his sympathies are owed. He wants to call out the army, but is confused by his housekeeper referring to the old man dying in hospital— was he a policeman? He hurriedly returns to his main interest, the sexual exploitation of the said housekeeper. Labour politicians who in some sense 'sell out' are a constant target in the trilogy: Jock Cronin was criticised in *Cloud Howe* for becoming a union organiser. Here Baillie Brown's respectability is stressed even before his Labour allegiance. His message is that the unemployed must wait three or four years for a Labour government, and not be led astray (by Communists). He asserts that the Council *cannot* change the PAC rates, and hurries Mr Piddle off the premises so that he can change for dinner. Gibbon has little difficulty here expressing some basic attitudes, although he does not speak in his own voice! The Lord Provost predictably blames the Reds rather than the working class, but nonetheless threatens obscurely, and resists pressure to alter PAC rates. The Chief Constable denies that the police had to retreat, claims the arrest of Jim Trease, and blames the death of the old man, which Ewan had witnessed, on one of the rioters.

We turn back now, briefly, to the men returning, often wounded, to their homes, reliving the fight, impressed by Ewan's leadership. Already they are thinking about next time: the wives typically oppose violence, but the husbands are still angry: ' 'twould be worth while doing that if you kicked the bucket with your nails well twined in a bobby's liver—' (65).

A one-sentence paragraph gives the *Runner*'s announcement a week later that the Council has raised the PAC rates. No comment, again, is necessary.

The postscript to the whole affair is provided by a return to Chris. She tells Ma how Ewan saw Feet beating up a helpless youth, and Ma has a confrontation with Feet in which she not only sends him packing (literally), but manages to convince him that he is in the wrong. Chris is less worried about the loss of Feet's rent and the empty room than about Ewan. As always, Ewan's feelings have a deep effect on her. Feet could not have stayed, because of 'Ewan with a pale, cool angry face, stirred as she'd never seen him stirred' (67). It is apparently only a convenient accident that she now gets a letter from Ake Ogilvie wanting a room in Duncairn. But by this time we see that the trilogy is very little dependent on accident, that the narrative method is extraordinarily flexible, creative and sure.

FURTHER READING

Our page references are to the one-volume Pan edition of 1982, where the novels are paginated separately.

Lewis Grassic Gibbon was born James Leslie Mitchell in 1901 in Auchterless, Aberdeenshire, and died in Welwyn Garden City in 1935. In his short career he was a newspaper reporter and served in both the army and the RAF before becoming a full-time writer. See the biography by Ian S Munro: *Leslie Mitchell: Lewis Grassic Gibbon*, 1966.

As James Leslie Mitchell he wrote a number of books, including several novels, the best of which is probably *Spartacus* (1933). *The Thirteenth Disciple* (1931) is an interesting novel based fairly closely on his own experience.

As Lewis Grassic Gibbon he collaborated with Hugh MacDiarmid on *Scottish Scene: or the Intelligent Man's Guide to Albyn* (1934), and the short stories and other material he contributed are available in *A Scots Hairst*, edited by Ian S Munro in 1967. An unfinished Scottish novella, *The Speak of the Mearns*, was edited by Ian Campbell (1983).

A full list of Gibbon criticism would be daunting, and time might be better spent re-reading the novels than surveying the whole field of criticism, but the following all contain vigorous and interesting criticism, and suggest the major directions of criticism so far.

Angus Calder, 'A Mania for Self-Reliance: Grassic Gibbon's *Scots Quair*', in Douglas Jefferson and Graham Martin (eds), *The Uses of Fiction: Essays on the Modern Novel in Honour of Arnold Kettle*, 1982

Ian Campbell, 'Chris Caledonia: the Search for an Identity' in *Scottish Literary Journal* (December 1974), 45–57

Cairns Craig, 'The Body in the Kit Bag: History and the Scottish Novel', in *Cencrastus* 1 (Autumn 1979), 18–22

Douglas Gifford, *Neil M Gunn and Lewis Grassic Gibbon* (1983)

Francis Russell Hart, *The Scottish Novel: A Critical Survey* (1978)

John T Low, *Commentary and Notes to Sunset Song* (1971)

William Malcolm, *A Blasphemer and Reformer: a study of James Leslie Mitchell* (1984)

Isobel Murray, 'Action and Narrative Stance in *A Scots Quair*', in David Hewitt and Michael Spiller (eds), *Literature of the North* (1983)

CHAPTER THREE

Neil Gunn:
The Silver Darlings

The Silver Darlings presents us with one of the most powerful stories to be found in modern Scottish fiction. It has strikingly drawn characters and the working out of their personal dramas is interwoven with a larger historical theme: that of the survival of their entire people. It is a book of blockbuster length, yet it is perhaps the most accessible and engrossing of Gunn's works.

The setting itself is poignant and dramatic enough by any standards. It is the aftermath of clearances and evictions which have forced people to leave their inland homes and pastures and cling precariously to life along the shores of the Moray Firth. Although they are not a sea-going people it is to the sea they must increasingly turn. By 1815 they already have the makings of a herring fishery and in astonishingly few years it will bring them unprecedented prosperity.

The story which Gunn creates in this setting is told in a prose which flows along with beguiling clarity, as befits the stuff of legend. The question of how far *The Silver Darlings* is a 'legendary' treatment of a historical theme is one to which we will return. Two things are immediately worth establishing about the book's intentions and its reception.

There can be no doubt, from the evidence of its construction, tone and tempo, that Gunn intended this novel to be effective and gripping as a story. It is in that sense 'a good read', well seeded with action and adventure and altogether calculated to absorb the reader as to 'what happens next' to individuals, crews and communities alike. Also well to the fore are Gunn's skills as a social chronicler and commentator, and his ability to evoke the very smack of a wave on a particular boat's prow, the fragrance as well as the flora of a particular landscape. And at the heart of it, in the character of young Finn, we are given an extraordinary recreation of the experience of childhood, boyhood and youth, a subject of abiding fascination for Gunn. These are formidable assets for any book seeking a reasonably wide, intelligent and appreciative readership. Since it was first published in 1941, judging by its history of re-prints, it has established for itself a sufficient and enduring appeal.

Certainly, there is also no doubt that Gunn's publishers were pleased and relieved to receive it in the first instance. As Gunn's biographers, F R Hart and J B Pick, put it: 'This was the book Faber had been hoping for—a solid mainstream novel, rich with emotion, character and incident, without intellectual conversation or philosophising, ideally suited to follow *Morning Tide* and *Highland River*. Neil's reputation was seriously in need of it' (*Neil M Gunn: A Highland Life*, 172).

Gunn's reputation did duly benefit from it—among a number of reviewers and a wider readership. Nor should one discount the extent to which the book has become appreciated by critics prepared to let Gunn's work stand comparison with other major figures of twentieth-century literature, such as Joyce, Conrad, Lawrence and others. However, that kind of critical recognition has been slower to develop and has in some respects remained more tentative. One reason for this is that Gunn was, as he knew very well, out of sympathy with the somewhat sombre mood considered essential at the time (the 'thirties onwards) for a novel to have in order to be accepted as a serious work of modern—or Modernist—literature. Another reason was that for a book to achieve success and reputation as 'a solid mainstream novel' was a pretty sure way of deflecting critical attention. The very idea suggests something for 'middle-brows' at best.

At least one of Gunn's aims as a writer was probably also suspect, considered possibly rather naïve or at least old-fashioned. And that was his straightforward intention to give readers the feeling of being in real places with real people, sharing real experiences. Paradoxically, on the other hand, he could be accused of an unacceptable kind of artificiality. In *The Silver Darlings*, for example, he might be said to have contrived some of the characterisation and the dénouement in order to produce an ending congenial to himself: and a happy ending at that, of all things. The first complaint (about his 'naïve' realism) would suggest that he lacks anything like the right degree of self-consciousness as a writer, the second that he has far too much of an outworn kind.

Questions about the nature of Gunn's self-consciousness as a writer and his attitudes to genres and conventions are in the end unavoidable. So are questions about some of the characterisation and the ending of *The Silver Darlings*. However, in the beginning they need only serve notice that it would be an over-simplification to describe *The Silver Darlings* as 'a solid mainstream novel' or some kind of rattling good yarn, although fortunately it has some of the attractive qualities of both. Here is another instance of a writer using 'the novel' as a vehicle for a variety of preoccupations and for various kinds of writing too. One of Gunn's preoccupations here was with evaluating the period of history he selected.

He had already dealt with the onset of the Highland Clearances in *Butcher's Broom* (1934). In turning to part of their aftermath, from about

1816 to about 1838, the period when the Moray Firth fisheries developed, he had to come to terms with something integral to the history of his own family as well as of his wider community. What he produced is, certainly, a story of tenacity and achievement. But the fact that he was able to see the past in that light and could give that account of it so convincingly does not mean that he found the subject an easy one to contemplate. Between the publication of *Butcher's Broom* and his settling down to work on *The Silver Darlings* there is a gap of five years. We know that during those years he did from time to time consider doing something about the history of the Moray Firth. But he kept putting the project off.

Part of the explanation for this is entirely practical. He was aware of the enormous amount of work that would be entailed in researching and organising the material he needed. In order to write this story adequately he recognised that he had to work from a factual basis as accurate and as detailed as possible. One major problem was that in the 1930s there was much scholarly research still to be done; there was no comprehensive authoritative work to turn to. Fortunately he did have to hand the pioneering books on fishing boats and fishermen by Peter F Anson. Anson furthermore persistently urged Gunn to get on with the job and do what research he needed for himself. It was partly Anson's doing that in 1939 Gunn got down to studying such sources as the Helmsdale register of fish-curers. Gunn's need for authentic (and authenticating) material soon had him poring over much raw material as yet unsifted by professional historians. He also spent considerable time talking to fishermen and fish-curers from both east and west coasts and tracking down old men who could tell him what conditions had been like before the days of steam and diesel. Some priceless material he came across by accident, such as a doctor's careful record of an outbreak of cholera in Caithness which provides one of the major incidents in the novel. Other vivid details, like the sailor who had a silver plate set in his skull after having been press-ganged by the Navy, were also acquired in this way.

Gunn's research, then, was painstaking if in some respects inevitably haphazard. What is important is the kind of care and effort he put into finding out what he possibly could. *The Silver Darlings* is most certainly not fictionalised documentary: it is a very different kind of fiction. His preoccupations included his concern for the nature and power of legend, fable and myth. However, he had equal respect for hard fact. And he was also interested in that rather different thing, folk memory. Even in investigating his roots he had to try to take account of the various kinds of material of which they were composed: facts, memories, records, fables, myths, yarns, symbols, images and legends.

All these complications apart, the stronger reason for his prolonged hesitation appears to have been the nature of his personal involvement, what he had at stake: his beliefs and hopes about *living* traditions of individuality and community rooted in the history of his part of the world. He had to explore a complicated set of feelings about the beginning of the modern era in the north of Scotland. He was very well aware that, if brought up to date as of 1939, recent history was no pageant of triumphs and no realisation of the way of life and values he so much prized. It could rather be read as a story of reverses, of those values under threat (although he would not have regarded them as extinct). The period chosen for *The Silver Darlings* could legitimately be regarded as a period that gave him something to celebrate. Even so, it was not quite the same thing as a Golden Age. Intractable facts of history might well suggest it contained the seeds of later economic and social decline. The extent to which Gunn managed— legitimately or otherwise—to get round the latter conclusion remains one of the most interesting points at issue especially about the ending of the novel. But Gunn clearly foresaw, at all events, that in dealing with the relatively recent past (rather than, for example, remote Pictish times) he was putting his ideas to a great test. Partly for that reason *The Silver Darlings* marks an important stage in his own quest for a combination of philosophy, art and way of life to set against the prevailing values of the wider society in which he lived.

When one takes into account these reasons for hesitation it is all the more remarkable that there is so little sign of hesitation in the way the story unfolds. Gunn's treatment is almost unwaveringly confident and sure-footed. The opening passage at once provides us with an example of a subtle Gunn blend in the way he can describe the simplest and most apparently ordinary kind of incident.

As Tormad tried to flick a limpet out of the boiling pot, he burnt his fingers, upset the pot, and spilt the whole contents over the fire, so that there was a sudden hissing with a cloud of ashes and steam. Fortunately the fire was outside, round the back of the cottage, where Catrine boiled clothes on her washing day.

'Did you ever see the beat of that?' he asked, hissing through his teeth and flailing his hand in the air.

It was so like him, and she so loved him, that she turned away.

He kicked the smouldering peats apart and began retrieving the limpets, which, being hot, stung him frequently. Holding one in the corner of his jacket, he gouged out its flesh easily with his thumb-nail. Whole and clean it came, and he cried: 'They're ready!' delighted after all with his judgement. 'I'll put the fire on for you,' he said, 'in a whip,' as he scraped limpets and yellow ash together into a small rush basket.

'I don't need it,' she answered. 'Never mind. And what's the good of blowing the ashes off that, you great fool?'

'Because I always like,' said Tormad, 'to leave things neat and tidy.'

As he had probably never left anything neat and tidy in his life, Catrine turned from him towards the house (9).

Catrine's deeply affectionate amusement at the hapless eagerness of her bullish young husband is, surely, the first set of impressions we get from this: swiftly and economically sketching a portrait of them. He doesn't show their faces; there is nothing about their ages; but they could hardly be anything other than a young couple. Into that neat little picture Gunn slyly inserts other elements the significance of which we need not pick up at once but which will become noticeable when we have reason to remember their happiness and Catrine's perceptiveness.

Tormad is boiling limpets. Limpets do not suggest the richest of diets. Limpets cling to rocks, but even they can be prised off. Tormad, Catrine and the other people of Dale are clinging to a rocky shoreline. Tormad is about to go off somewhere having, by his way of it, left things neat and tidy. . . .

Tormad accidently puts out a fire. 'Fortunately the fire was outside. . . .' It is a much more serious business, as we will learn, to go putting out the fire in the hearth in such a community. Nonetheless, it is Tormad's instinct to get his fire going again.

Gunn tends not to waste words. If they will lightly carry a hint, an allusion, a metaphor or a joke as well as their plain meaning, so much the better.

Having introduced us thus deftly to Tormad and Catrine (married only some four months, Tormad being twenty-four and Catrine only nineteen), Gunn widens his angle to take in the general plight of their people; and here again there is economy of description and understatement, to which he adds the driest of tones.

They had come from beyond the mountain which rose up behind them, from inland valleys and swelling pastures, where they and their people before them had lived from time immemorial. The landlord had driven them from these valleys and pastures, and burned their houses, and set them here against the sea-shore to live if they could and, if not, to die (12).

The same landlord has, to be sure, thoughtfully provided a harbour and advanced money to those who can afford to repay him at $6\frac{1}{2}$ per cent interest so that buildings can be erected for the new fishing trade. However, these are early days: there are no fortunes being made as yet in Dale where, besides, they don't know much about fishing. Tormad has managed to buy a boat, but at the very great price of selling off his 'second beast'. Tormad's 'heels sank into the earth. He was a heavy broad fellow, a little above the average in height, with black hair that sometimes glistened' (13). To such a man, so visibly of the land, the cost of that risky transaction is not to be counted in monetary terms. Apart from the as yet unproven asset of his boat, Tormad has really only one other. 'In his twenty-four years he felt full of a great competence' (10). But, as we have already been given cause to suspect, the competence he feels so full of is potential rather than actual.

Daily life, then, for the likes of Tormad and Catrine is at least as harsh as it is hopeful and it is Catrine who is the more aware of its harshness. Memories of burnings and evictions are still fresh in people's minds anyway. Their early days by the sea-shore have been characterised by disease, starvation and death by drowning. Catrine especially hates and fears the sea, however, for an uncle has already been drowned. She fears most of all for Tormad, of course: the husband whose impetuosity she loves but appraises so clearly. She knows she can't prevent him going to sea. But her fear and the strain of waiting for him to leave flares into a violent and hysterical rage and for a moment the way she looks at him is like 'an enemy, deliberately calculating, cold as greed' (11).

Catrine has a further specific reason for anxiety. She is pregnant. The child she is carrying will be called Finn; and it is his development from childhood to early manhood as a hunter-fisherman and legend-maker that is the core of Gunn's entire concern.

It is Tormad's peculiar fate, however, to suffer a kind of double jeopardy. Already a victim of the clearances, sheer inexperience and a certain lack of caution on his fishing trip make him fall prey to the net of a Navy press-gang. By land and sea such people are at the mercy of powerful forces: including forces which until very recently have supposedly been defending them, as a people, from the threat of the 'anti-Christ', Napoleon.

Tormad is reportedly captured alive, but he vanishes forever nonetheless. For twenty years Catrine doesn't know for certain fact that he is dead. However, shortly after his disappearance she has one of her dreams—this one having something of the force of second sight—and as a result profoundly believes that he is dead. So, almost as soon as he is introduced, Finn's father is swept off the face of the earth: but not out of the story. His memory, as the *ghost* of love, lost love, haunts and spellbinds Catrine for many years. It intensifies her loathing of the sea and drives her to seek refuge again in a life on the land. It makes her determined to steer young Finn away from life at sea by any means at her disposal: emotional blackmail, money, the promise even of university—anything! The terrible ghostliness of Tormad and her love for him, rather perhaps than any residual belief that he might be alive, also helps to explain her long resistance to the love of another man, a master fisherman called Roddie Sinclair.

Part of Catrine's immediate reaction to Tormad's disappearance is to hate Dale and the very croft on which they had lived. There is, somewhat conveniently for Gunn's purposes, perhaps, an alternative home for her to turn to: that of Kirsty Mackay, a friend of Catrine's mother. Kirsty lives with her seventy-year-old father further north in Dunster (Dunbeath), Caithness.

For Catrine even to contemplate handing over her man's croft to anyone else when he might still be alive is an extraordinary thing to do; and it horrifies her mother. Nonetheless, that is what she does and she makes her way on foot into a strange new landscape (flat and neatly cultivated, not wild like the one she has known in Sutherland) in search of the Mackays. On the way she meets, among others, Roddie Sinclair. He it is who finally guides her to the Mackays' croft. Just before they reach there, however, it is also Roddie who explains to her about a ruin which happens to catch her attention. Reputedly the site of an old monastery, with perhaps an even longer history as a holy place, the local people call it the House of Peace, although in fact they avoid it out of fear of the ghosts by which they believe it to be haunted. Only Roddie, it seems, isn't scared: that kind of thing seems not to bother him. The significance of the House of Peace, especially to young Finn, we will learn more of as the novel develops.

Having been made welcome by Kirsty and her father, then, Catrine settles down to what she regards as an entirely new life. She can count herself fortunate. For the Mackays have been, and still are, a little better off than most people in terms of furniture and other comforts. (They had worked a comfortable holding down in Sutherland until the landlord refused to renew their lease.) With Kirsty Mackay and with Finn (to whom she gives birth, it is worth noting, precisely as Kirsty's father dies) she is to know years of security, happiness and peace.

But, of course, she has not really been able to flee far from the sea. Nor does she realise how closely their lives will become intertwined with that of Roddie Sinclair. The novel, nonetheless, turns sharply from Catrine's arrival at her place of refuge to the story of the early development of the herring fisheries and to the leading role young Roddie Sinclair has played in that development at Dunster. By the end of this next phase of the book, chapters IV–XIII, Gunn has not only implanted and somewhat developed all his major themes; Catrine's stubborn hopes of being able to shut the sea out of her life have certainly been shattered.

The successful pursuit of herring—the 'silver darlings' of the title—has always required shrewdness and cold calculation as well as endurance and daring. Roddie Sinclair has what it takes in these respects; by implication,

Tormad had not. (Later, Catrine is to reflect on the contrast between them: Tormad strong and instinctive; Roddie strong and reasonable.) The successful creation of a fishing industry requires something more besides: money and organisation onshore. We are therefore introduced to Mr Hendry, the innkeeper known as 'Special' after a whisky he reserves for certain occasions. Mr Hendry might be compared with Gillespie Strang in John MacDougall Hay's *Gillespie*. Both seize opportunities for money-making presented to them by the expansion of fisheries and changes in terms of trade and law. However, whereas Gillespie Strang embodies the spirit of materialism in the form of a malevolent greed for power as well as wealth, 'Special' is acquisitive in ways that leave room for others to flourish, with any luck. He is quite prepared to persuade others to risk everything, including their lives; but he'll cheerfully toast their good fortune too. In so far as his activities spread life and hope, he is happy enough for all concerned. As for the rest of it (his undeniable greed, self-seeking, craftiness), Gunn seems to imply that even what enhances life can have decidedly ambiguous sources.

Mr Hendry has spotted Roddie Sinclair's prowess at the very beginning, in 1815, and stakes him in a boat called *The Morning Star*. By the time of Catrine's arrival he is the youngest skipper in Dunster, but already their star: a man others look to and depend upon. He is also a man capable of violence, especially when just occasionally he gets drunk. His explosive strength is essential to them as well; and fortunately that strength is normally concentrated and channelled in effective ways in a real war of liberation, freeing them from the power of landlords. Here the double meaning of 'silver darlings' becomes clearer. What they pursue is, of course, herring; but it is also silver itself, money by which they all seek their independence.

Against this background theme (about the re-shaping of the community) we are immediately presented with some of the most important themes concerned with the development of Finn in chapter V, 'Finn And The Butterfly'. Finn is about four years old: young, perhaps, for a hunter-killer. But that is the first of two important motifs to appear. The other is his fascination with beauty and magic, embodied in this instance in butterflies which he pursues and one of which he kills—near the House of Peace. Fascination with and pursuit of beauty can, it seems, have its ambiguous aspects and outcomes too.

Finn's pursuit draws him 'away from that place where his mother was' (91) and into a 'strange world', a wood. Strange woods and forests are to crop up from time to time again. This one is coupled with a 'strange mood that was near to tears and yet far from them.' On going deeper into the wood, Finn experiences 'the feeling of one fated to go away' (92). Having

killed his butterfly there, he also has his first experience of a sense of guilt
(94). He tries to shake the feeling off, and keeps on going until after 'his
loneliness came upon him in a great fear' he falls asleep, exhausted. He is
found by none other than Roddie Sinclair who then unintentionally upsets
Catrine by promising the boy a trip on *The Morning Star*. Catrine, already
terrified by Finn's disappearance, moreover now recognises that her son
has stumbled on 'the terrible knowledge of good and evil' (100) and that the
'meanings' and 'terrors' in life have started to take him away from her.

The economy of Gunn's methods is amply illustrated by this one episode.
His account of little Finn's adventure is enjoyably humorous and light-
handed. For example, to Finn the thought of his mother crying for him,
presuming him to be drowned, 'made him feel sorry for her, but it also did
him a lot of good. He would be greatly missed' (92). The tone delicately
catches that peculiarly innocent cunning young children sometimes have.
The same child is easily distracted from his pursuit of one butterfly by a
tempting trout. What Gunn does not do is heavily underline the point that
this represents the temptation of the sea. He describes how the trout easily
eludes Finn's comically inept attempts to catch it, adding that: 'To tell the
truth, he was also just a little afraid of the trout, for it was a monster of four
inches . . .' (90). Gunn is careful here not to lay anything on too thick. It is
all the more impressive that he is able to give notice of so many of the main
lasting features of Finn's character (including its darker side) and to give
fore-warning, too, of clashes impending between the three central characters. Nor does the chapter simply end there.

Roddie, fortified by some of Mr Hendry's 'Special', decides late that
evening to pay a call on Catrine, it being the eve of his departure for the
fisheries off Helmsdale. 'In the deep twilight of the summer night Catrine's
home looked quiet and still.' There we have Roddie's general impression:
straightforward and convincing enough as an indication as much of his
state of mind as of the cottage in its setting. Roddie then proceeds to
contemplate:

> The land, the quiet land, which for ever endures, threaded by women and children,
> in the bright patterns of their lives. Remote from the sea, from the turbulence of
> oncoming waves, from the quick movement, the excitement, from the mind of a
> man like Special, with his flow of silver herring that changed into a flow of silver
> crowns (101).

With the first few phrases, Gunn perhaps smuggles into Roddie's mind
thoughts rather more abstract than we might expect to find there. But then,
coming up to the cottage window:

> He saw her features against the red glow, warm and soft, not only with her own

beauty, but with all women's beauty. It was a picture a man might glimpse once in a lifetime, and have a vision of women afterwards in his mind that time or chance, good or evil, would never change. Like the still landscape that had troubled him a moment, when he first looked up at the cottage.

Here Gunn's writing, especially in comparison with earlier parts of the same chapter, surely does become rather forced. Roddie's picture of 'all women's beauty' is precisely not really like his troubling sense of the still landscape: it lacks that specificity, that heightened intensity of place, thought and feeling which characterises the most telling moments of illumination which mean so much to Gunn in the development of character and personality. To Wordsworth, such were 'timeless moments'. To Joyce, they were 'epiphanies'. Gunn usually refers to them as moments of delight or integration. And *The Silver Darlings* provides us with substantially more persuasive examples of them than this. It is as if, here, those wretched bright threads have drained Catrine of the very blood needed to account for her passions or Roddie's subsequent passionate loyalty to her. Here she has suddenly been blanched and monumentalised and one can almost see the pedestal slide under her feet.

That is all very unfortunate for a number of reasons. For one thing the moment marks a crux both in the opposing attractions of land and sea and in the tension underlying the relationship between Roddie and Catrine. Secondly, it indicates a tendency in Gunn to idealise his women, particularly those he would have us care most about, in a way that weakens the vitality of his characterisation of them—of Catrine in this case. Thirdly, Roddie is as a result doomed to a love which will look rather too much like glassy-eyed devotion to a plaster saint.

'The Land And The Sea' is the title of the next chapter (chapter VI), and there we find Kirsty indulging herself at length and expertly in one of the most popular and abiding of Highland pastimes, genealogy and family gossip: these are altogether more convincing threads, the more so as Catrine, ever so slightly bored with them, lets her mind wander. There is a splendid comic diversion when the cow gets into the corn and the dog proves worse than Tormad in its best efforts to be helpful. The incident provides Catrine with a moment of intense feeling of closeness to Finn. But only a week later, Finn, secure though he is in his mother's care, proves strangely susceptible to fears of the Bad Place 'in the hushed hour, the queer hour of stories and strange things.' There is a gust of wind from the sea which makes him cry out in fear. Catrine bars the door. Then we learn that some of the fleet that has gone to Helmsdale is in trouble. *The Morning Star* is late.

Of course, Mr Hendry's 'talisman', Roddie, does turn up. Catrine is among those anxious enough to be on hand just to be sure that he is safe and sound. But before she or anyone else has a chance to see him, the money-intoxicated Mr Hendry has already excitedly propounded to Roddie his vision of the greater ventures and fortunes yet to come.

'Even geography was enlarged' (132). Indeed it was. Their world has expanded from pitiful and vestigial strips of land along their own coasts to touch the coasts of the Baltic in what seems next to no time at all. Expansive in other ways too, the population enjoys its harvest celebrations and autumn becomes the time for a regular spate of marriages. Roddie Sinclair heroically explains away his apparent immunity by proclaiming: 'I have married the sea.'

For young Finn on his first visit to the November Market what matters is not the growth of trade but his first experience of being part of such a crowd and all the fun of the Fair. What matters most of all is a trumpet. Quick to recognise his fascination, Roddie buys him one as a present: 'and the trumpet sounded loud and high, clearing a path for itself over the world' (139). There is a certain legendary Celtic hero who is supposed to have had a great curved horn; but Finn knows nothing about this hero as yet. A little later, though, at a catechism lesson he is surprised and interested to learn that a trumpet could bring down mighty walls such as those of Jericho (150–1). He even has a dream (and, hearing him scream, Catrine again wonders what dangerous journey he has been on all alone) which prompts him the following morning to run out to inspect the state of a dry-stane dyke. The dyke for the time being stands as it ever did (whether we consider it literally, or as his mother's confining love) (158–9). However, we have now seen a different Finn: someone whose 'wits had run away' because of the spell-binding potential of hitting precisely the right high and piercing note. The young pursuer of natural beauty and magic in the form of the butterfly (which will be destroyed if he 'holds' it) now realises how he might possess for himself the power that comes from the right musical pitch, having a little earlier sensed the power that lies in stories.

As Finn grows into adolescence, Gunn manages to reconcile a vivid evocation of an individual's boyhood with his need to tease out the elements of character, drama and environment essential to the formation of the archetypal figure he intends Finn to represent.

So when Finn (again, the hunter-killer) catches a rabbit (160) it is a boyishly daring thing to do, considering the penalties 'the estate' is still liable to exact on an entire family for the most trivial offence and, even more to be feared, the risk of incurring 'granny' Kirsty's terrible wrath. However, when he compounds his crime, giving in to his passion for hunting by going along with his pal Donnie to do some fishing, events take on another and more terrifying dimension. A huge eel which 'moved like the father of all serpents' (167) lures them after it. The Biblical allusion is obvious but not overstressed. There is also a hint of the Celtic serpent symbol. However, what Gunn concentrates on so exactly is how in their excitement the lads fail to see that they are becoming marooned. Donnie is more disturbed by the fact than Finn. The eel slips deeper into a 'forest of seaweed'; and we may note again an allusion to strange worlds of woods, here transposed from land to sea. Even as the eel slips into this refuge Finn discovers that 'the pull on the line, pulling at his hunting instinct, his courage' dispels his panic.

As in the incident with the butterfly, it is a case of Roddie to the rescue. Finn is furious with Roddie for rescuing him on this occasion and at his mother for scolding him. His anger is both adolescent pique and a portentous assertion of self-discovery: for it takes root, his withdrawal from Catrine is something more than mere sulkiness and (despite being somewhat tearful come bed-time) he defies Catrine's fear of the sea and her attempts to cajole him as regards his duty to the croft. The moment marks a breaking point between earth-mother and Finn-the-adventurer. For Catrine it is the 'beginning of the new loneliness' (174).

Other features of Finn's character are developed, sometimes complementing those we have already seen. For example, we know the Finn already steeped in local nature-lore. Now, (177 ff) we see that he has a mind well capable of adapting to modern bookish knowledge and he will be urged to take his talents to university. No Scottish novel with a background of poverty would be quite complete without its 'lad o' pairts', the bright boy who is chosen as a member of a secular elect to rise in the world through education. The special twist here is that Finn is capable of embracing both ancient and modern culture; and, besides, he turns down the chance of choosing the latter at the expense of the former. He is becoming more and more attuned to traditional songs he hears. But if he is in a benign sense bewitched by song, he is also unreasoningly afraid of those reputed to be witches. Despite that boyish fear, he becomes increasingly attracted and sensitised to places with strong associations with the remote and dim past, even if they have the reputation of being haunted. Such a place, of course, is the House of Peace.

Gunn has to take care in the way he threads together the strands of Finn's developing association with the House of Peace. It can readily be allowed to have much the same symbolic associations as Grassic Gibbon's Standing Stones in *Sunset Song*. Much beyond that and there is a danger that the writer may leave us with an unconvincing theatrical prop and a few late tricks of the Celtic twilight.

At first, then, Finn appears to think of the place mostly as other boys in the area do: as a spooky place that is supposed to be haunted by the likes of

some monk who was murdered by Vikings. Readers of *Sun Circle* will recall
the very similar death of the missionary monk Molrua in chapter 4.
However, readers are reminded that Finn killed his butterfly near the place
and that Roddie found him sleeping in it afterwards. This can easily explain
why Finn is not so afraid of it as others are. He takes advantage of that fact
to hide things he has caught there; and he begins to find it an oddly
comforting place to retreat to when he wants to be alone. Even Finn,
though, generally steers clear of it in the dark; only Roddie does not.

The 'haunting' of the House of Peace is given an ingenious and very
human twist when, one dark night, Finn happens to pass near it on his way
home. He has just been listening, rapt but unobserved, to Anna the singer,
daughter of Lachlan the storyteller; and he has been thinking about some
of the creepy stories people tell. Suddenly a dark figure appears. Finn is
frozen to the spot: the more so when he recognises this apparition to be
Roddie. What troubles his adolescent mind at this juncture is a dark fear
and suspicion as to where Roddie might have been, and what he might have
been doing there with Catrine. This is not the first dawning of that
disquieting thought. Rather it is the moment when it sinks in deep enough
to make him lie 'in the trance of his own horror'. It is also a neat
materialisation of subconscious fears which along with other 'ghosts' Finn
must get on terms with: to master them, dispel them, or feel at one with
them.

Simple hero-worship for Roddie is definitely a thing of the past. His
relationship with Roddie must now be complicated by jealousy and rivalry
partly on account of his mother. But in addition his relationship with
Catrine is itself complicated by suspicion, possessiveness and the need to
escape the over-constricting circle of her love for him. Gunn has stirred up a
rich witch's brew of emotions in Finn. There is to be little peace for Finn in
any house for years to come. Troubling thoughts about Catrine and
Roddie coincide with his first fleeting encounter with Una, a girl who
singularly attracts or, more precisely, disturbs him. And things that plague
the mind are soon counterpointed by an all too threatening exterior plague:
an outbreak of cholera.

The events connected with 'the plague' cover four chapters, X–XIII.
These events, as we would expect, are highly consequential for the central
characters. However, *The Silver Darlings* is also in part a story of a people
struggling to master their own conditions and circumstances, to stop being
victims of 'fate' or landlords or seeing themselves simply as victims of
God's Will. In that larger context, 'the plague' comes in more sense than
one as a set-back.

Gunn has already, in the very first chapter, noted a growing scepticism
that calamities such as the clearances could or should be explained as a

'visitation of the Lord' due to their own wicked doings or those of Napoleon (12). However, what were people to make of this unprecedented disease whose nature and origins were equally mysterious to them? There were influential evangelists around, such as one Sandy Ware, to tell them that the ships which brought money and 'merriment' were now, by God's judgement, bringing the 'flapping of the wings of the black bird of corruption and death!' (193). There could be something in that somewhere. 'Their dread of it went beyond reason.' Their response was one of 'pure horror'. Victims were promptly shunned and the houses of the dead burned, as much an act of unreasoning self-defence as any kind of remedy; for, although a drastic form of purification, it neither identified nor tackled the cause of the problem. People's use of the word 'plague' itself evokes a pre-modern era and their lack of scientific medical knowledge.

Yet, as Gunn takes care to demonstrate, they were not far—either literally or intellectually—from a source of that knowledge. What was needed was the will to seek it out and to trust it; and someone had to lead the way. That role is duly performed (a little improbably, perhaps) by young Finn who has heard of a doctor up by Wick, walks there and returns with medicine. It saves his mother. People can stop burning down houses too.

'Scientific' knowledge clearly has its part to play in freeing people from their terror of the unknown and the bogeys they create to account for their fears. But a recurrent theme in Gunn's work is the need for other kinds of sensitised awareness and knowledge to complement the analytic intellect. The problem about the former, of course, is how to distinguish between states of consciousness and awareness that induce mere fantasy, bogus apparitions and cock-eyed nonsense and others that bring genuine illumination and thereby gains in terms of general sanity and the ability to live life to the full.

We are on the verge of two specific problems others have found in Gunn's work (especially its later stages): an allegedly cloudy 'mysticism', and an arguably wilful tendency to find and idealise 'evidence' of a lost-but-retrievable integration of man and nature, body and mind, intellect and emotion. We have already suggested that on occasions when Catrine is depicted as somehow 'all women' or (cf. the way some people regard Chris Guthrie in *A Scots Quair*) as symbolising the values of The Land, we are being invited to contemplate an 'essence' and find instead a wispy outline containing nothing to hold onto. The same problem arises with Roddie in so far as his stance towards Catrine is depicted as that of eternally patient and spotlessly chivalric protector (and happily it isn't always so). The problem becomes worst of all, we would argue, with the etherealised Una, Finn's Great Love. These are portraits rendered in hot air, and in this kind of thing, wherever else it may be found, we do find a depressing cloudiness.

It is the very opposite, in fact, to the extraordinarily heightened sense of presence, of actuality, which Gunn can convey so well. It is abstraction.

That apart (and this is not the place to explore the wider issues raised by Gunn's philosophical inclinations), one of the interesting things about *The Silver Darlings* is that it shows Gunn's awareness of the need to sift and subtly evaluate sources either of genuine insight or mere superstition, true knowledge or bogus lore, revelatory states of consciousness or pure fantasising.

While Catrine tends the cholera-stricken Kirsty, for example, she reflects on her sense of the God, the spirit, of Sandy Ware's version of the religion compared with other 'ghosts' or spirits. Although she doesn't doubt the existence of God, the spirit of that religion seems to her properly to belong to a remote hereafter. 'Better not to think about it, to keep it away, and meantime to have life' (229). She thinks this in the face of death, her love of life all the more intense. Thus she puts that 'God' firmly in his place. Other ghosts, however, she perceives as part of life. She can find some room even for 'the superstitions and wild irrational fears that were in such mysterious fashion part of the core and quick of life'. But, most of all to the point, has 'Sandy Ware ever met—the ghost of love?' Tormad's ghost is still real to her, of course: and by this time, we believe, Gunn has established him as real to the reader. In Gunn's book, so to speak, this kind of perception is not to be lightly dismissed as fatuous or wrong-headed, especially when it is compared with the dismal hollowness of the spirit offered by Sandy Ware.

Folk beliefs and customs also figure during the episode of the plague, including a purification and regeneration ceremony (featuring the extinguishing and rekindling of fire in the hearth) which suggests that some of the men, at least, have a residual belief in the efficacy of white magic. Interestingly enough, Roddie plays a prominent part in the ceremonies: he who is apparently impervious to the spooky reputation of the House of Peace. Gunn's description of these goings on is touched by some wry humour, except that it is clear that the ritual still has force as an expression of and an act of faith in solidarity with each other. Although Roddie's crew are elaborately secretive about it all, it is also clear that others are in the know.

Finn himself, of course, is granted his moments of illumination and vision. Throughout the book, these occur in a state between sleep and wakefulness, when there is a mingling of light and dark, of conscious and unconscious thought processes. Gunn himself proceeds with great care in dealing with this, seeing the half-awake state as a time for adolescent fantasies more often than it is a moment of truth. Nonetheless, Finn is permitted early on in adolescence to see more than most: 'Somewhere between dreaming and waking there was a world that came or went by the flick of an eyelid . . . this in-between dream was clear as light' (216). He has an important early experience of this kind at the House of Peace as the plague strikes all around (214). He sees the figure of an old man (and will see such a figure again). He experiences great peace. As a result he realises that 'The great thing was not to be afraid.'

It is a version—not quite fully formed yet—of an epiphany, a 'timeless moment', a moment of delight and integration. It is especially worth noting that Finn has this experience at a time of terrible public and personal distress. The gifts of calmness and wholeness of vision and of fearlessness are crucial to Gunn's view of the sources of hope and strength whatever appalling turn human history might take.

After 'the plague' the time comes for Finn to accompany his mentor, Roddie, on voyages into strange and unknown waters, voyages which will expose them to dangers—and in some instances to enchantments—as weird and wonderful to them as any encountered by Odysseus and his men. For, after Finn's sterling medical work (and Kirsty's advice to Catrine from her deathbed) he earns Roddie's respect and an amnesty from his mother. He joins the crew of Roddie's new and bigger boat, *The Seafoam*, the first out of Dunster to attempt to sail round the north of Scotland to the West Coast fisheries. From the time they set out until they return (chapters XIV–XVIII) the novel fairly boils along with a mixture of adventure, tales of endurance and comradeship, comedy, social and historical observation—and, of course, further developments in the relationship of Finn and Roddie both to each other and to their personal daemons. They are (among other things, and especially Roddie) reincarnations of the Vikings. 'Finn looked ahead . . . and again had the impression that the peak of the stem, in a dream of its own, was searching out the far distance with invisible eyes' (286).

This voyage takes Finn especially, but the others too, into a world where dream and reality are apt to merge: sometimes ambiguously, misleadingly or fantastically, but sometimes in a way that implies clarity of vision and insight. Again, Gunn is careful to provide for the whole range of these possibilities. It is a world in which men may lose themselves, literally and metaphorically speaking. They do, in fact, overshoot Lewis and head out into the Atlantic until set back on a proper course by a friendly Shetlander. By that time, they are desperately low on both food and water; cue for a mighty deed.

There is nothing unreal or, fortunately, over-written about Finn's leap onto the rocks of the Flannan Isles and his triumphant return to the boat with three puffins, twelve eggs and two bottles of water. Through Gunn's suspenseful and economically descriptive writing we watch Finn climb the sheer cliff face—and imagine his plunge from it—as Roddie does: in slow-motion and freeze-frame. It is a legendary, a fabulous moment which young boys will subsequently try to re-enact in action replay. By now Gunn has only to slip in a few code words, like 'extreme horror' and 'nightmare' to convey not only Roddie's anguish as guardian of Catrine's son but echoes of the people's recent horror at the plague and a contrast with other life-giving dream-like moments (315–16). Up on top, Finn is youthfully irresponsible, clowning around riding a sheep (320)—there's a hint, no more, of a derisive allusion by Gunn to the sheep of the clearances. Finn wanders around, curious, exploring. He comes across a strange little building where a 'feeling of remoteness came over Finn, as if he stood on the last storm-threshed outpost of the world' (317). He learns later (362–3) that he has stumbled across a chapel dedicated to Saint Flannan: representing a Celtic Christian culture which found both refuge and natural shrines to *its* spirit on such wild outcrops of Europe; and he confesses (363) that he half expected 'an old quiet man' to appear. This entire sequence, comprising action, drama, high emotion, comedy and (still incomplete) disclosures and realisations—is an excellent encapsulation of Gunn's approach.

Finn's feat may have been fabulous, his moment of half-illumination formative, but things don't go well at the fishing. Dreams are at risk. Although he describes Stornoway as a thriving port, Gunn also pinpoints the uncertainties afflicting the entire fisheries business: the need for new markets, the vagaries of Governments, the dangers (even in those days) of taking immature fish; and locally the fishing is very poor this season. Roddie doubts his own dream, becoming intensely depressed: a mood which triggers in him an explosion of violence in a pub. Finn, however, has the most remarkable good fortune to be tipped off that there could be herring down Loch Odhairn way. *The Seafoam's* crew—having fraternally passed on the word to some others—survives a suitably legend-like encounter with a whale to land a fabulously large catch. Roddie, the mad Viking, is now looked upon with awe.

In the meantime, Finn suffers between sleeping and waking recurring images of Una: they are always an 'affliction' to him, whereas he can lie in the boat of a morning pleasantly enough dreaming of a Lewis girl called Catrine (the significance of whose name Gunn rather needlessly points out). To compensate for his trouble with these turbulent and contorted sexual emotions and his wildly veering attitudes to Roddie, Finn is drawn into and fascinated by the life and culture of his Hebridean counterparts. Drink and religion are given due place in his rites of passage. But it is the ceilidh house—where the songs are charged with affection, flow with the goodness of life and have the rhythm of the sea-tide—which proves the deeper and enduring influence. And having also learned much from the comradeship—and rivalry—of fishermen, it is a rapidly maturing Finn who returns in triumph with Roddie to Dunster, both of them great heroes. Moreover, Finn has an ear by now finely attuned to music, a mind attuned to stories and an ability, already intimated on the voyage out to Lewis, to hold an audience with what he has to say. He is on the point of discovering the full extent of his artistry as a narrator of great stories. He is both man of action and artist.

He makes this discovery during a visit to relatives in Dale where he is asked to give an account of the expedition. The power of his story-telling makes a deep impression on everyone who listens to him and in particular on a drover who happens to be present, prompting this incident at the end of the night: 'Out in the dark, beyond the door, the drover put a finger on Finn's breast. "You gave me a vision—of the youth of Finn MacCoul himself"' (449).

And there we have it: the key to recognising the archetype which in Finn Gunn was re-creating. For Finn MacCoul was, according to legend, both a slayer of monsters and a magician. He was a poet, too; and he was chief of the Fianna of Leinster, a leader among a nomadic people—hunters!—in the heart of primitive forests, the strange bewitching world of trees, foliage, fronds. The legendary Finn had a great curved horn to rally his people; little Finn had his trumpet. Finn MacCoul figures in the Fenian sagas which are common to both Ireland and Scotland; and there is even a suggestion that he was an incarnation of the Breton god of the Beyond, Gwyn ab Nudd; so his provenance is in a mingling of peoples and myths. In North Uist an old story-teller, Finn-son-of-Angus, will say this to young Finn, complimenting him on his story-telling: 'You brought us into the far deeps of the sea and we were lost with you in the Beyond where no land is, only wind and wave and the howling of the darkness' (540). The last phrase is an echo of Finn's sense of desolation as he stood in Saint Flannan's chapel, half expecting an old man to appear; and another link with another archetype and culture is thus made. Finn brings Viking and Celt, pagan and Christian, old world and new world together.

The voyage Finn makes all the way down to North Uist and his encounters there with an older and still untouched culture (rather like that of his own people, perhaps, prior to the clearances) in what at least approximates to a Tir-Nan-Og, the Celtic paradise, completes Finn's youthful immersion in the old culture (chapter XXIV). It is one kind of culmination of his development towards manhood. Another necessary culmination is already under way: the resolution of his stormy emotional development, hinging on his relationships to Roddie and Catrine on the one hand and Una on the other.

There is a natural enough explanation for part of Finn's feelings of resentment at Roddie and Catrine's decision to get married: 'Folk realized it was an odd joke for Finn right enough! What grown son or daughter liked a mother to get married?' (501). Besides, the reader knows even better; for we are aware of the intense and troubling emotions present particularly in the relationship between this mother and this son and the inevitability that another man's intrusion would be painful. However, Finn's jealousy and fury goes well beyond reason; and his revulsion at the idea of these 'old' people having sex together not only carries over into a revulsion against poor Una: it is a revulsion deeper and more comprehensive than any of the causes Gunn appears to supply. Be that as it may, the effect of this feeling is to drive Finn into a bitter, desolate state of solitariness and alienation. Perhaps that is simply what Gunn requires: another trial for his hero.

He comes through this test by way of three stages. First he has to become harder and more acquisitive; so, having initially wrathfully rejected the bequest of Kirsty's (and now Catrine's) croft and money, he takes them to himself: 'He felt them surround him and gave him power' (502). Secondly, he has a revelation, another moment of epiphany: Finn 'sees' Una properly for the first time when he appreciates her beauty in distress after having (with Roddie's help, of course!) saved the life of her brother (519).

Actually, this is one of the less convincing epiphanies, largely because Una has been allowed only fleeting appearances in somewhat mannered symbolic postures and circumstances. She is the most spectral of Gunn's characters in *The Silver Darlings*: consequently we find it difficult to see her at all. Her name, like Finn's, belongs to legend: in her case that of the pure and beautiful lady-love of the champion, the Red Cross Knight, in Spenser's *Faerie Queene*. Such an association does not enlarge her, it diminishes her almost to vanishing point. More's the pity, since Gunn is more than capable of drawing closely observed and lively young women, as we see in the Catrine of the early chapters, the Catrine Finn meets in Lewis and Finn's cousin Barbara.

The final stage of Finn's emergence from his, so to speak, interior darkness follows on the achievements of his expedition to North Uist. He has indeed become hard—and can afford to be generous. He has discovered his strengths, one of which is (an artist's) self-conscious detachment: he can therefore, with a little smile on his face, allow himself to be reconciled to others and to take part in everything. The leader and poet of a people whose lives are based on hunting and who must face appalling risks and take change in their stride: such a man must approach life with generosity of spirit yet, in a curiously detached way, be prepared to accept all the strange—and even terrible—things life may cast up. Such a man has two selves: the one open, social, active, convivial; the other is reflective, private and yet the self capable of the greatest sense of the unity of everything in time and space: capable of moments of delight and a sense of integration.

So, Finn the hunter has—in finding others, including Una—finally tracked himself down and, not altogether intentionally, taught his contemporaries how to follow him: even to his most precious sanctuary, the House of Peace. There he retreats on the eve of his marriage to Una, performing the 'mental act of describing the circle of sanctuary around the ground on which he lay' (580). It is a sign that he will always have a need (that of the self-conscious artist) to withdraw somewhat from others, to be temporarily alone: but to be alone in order to experience a state of heightened consciousness of everything his culture and experience means to him, past, present and future.

He also simply wants to escape certain customary ribald pre-nuptial rituals his mates have in mind: and again, Gunn neatly combines Finn's meditations with this element of comedy. For a little while he feels safe: his 'hunted look caught a gleam of cunning relief. They would never find him there. They would never think of looking for him in this haunted spot. He would escape them yet.' But he is wrong; and he soon realises and accepts that too. 'The hunters in their primordial humour were closing in. Life had come for him.' So the book ends.

Such an ending, with a young man decisively and positively facing up to the challenges of life after a problematic initiation, has its distinguished counterparts in modern—and specifically 'Modernist'—fiction. D. H. Lawrence, for example, has Paul Morel in *Sons and Lovers* reject the allure of the darkness into which his mother has gone and turn instead 'towards the city's gold phosphorescence'. Even more notably and aptly, Joyce's Stephen Dedalus has this to say to himself, in his diary, at the end of *Portrait of The Artist As A Young Man*:

Amen. So be it. Welcome, O life! I go to encounter for the millionth time the reality of experience and to forge in the smithy of my soul the uncreated conscience of my race.

Pretentious stuff, of course: but young men are apt to be like that on such occasions. Gunn, in fact, alleviates any solemnity with his touches of 'gaiety' and his sense of comedy. However, if we widen our angle to consider the ending overall and not only as it concerns Finn, there is an implicit but nonetheless striking optimism about it that seems to say 'All's right with the world' and, specifically, these people have it made. There is peace all round: harmony and apparently nothing but well-founded hope for a merry and prosperous future. It's not a little like the ending of a fairytale: and they all live happily ever after. Finn has taken over, painlessly in the end, from Roddie as acknowledged leader of the fleet. Roddie is happy on land as much as amidst the freedoms as well as perils of the deep; Catrine is therefore happy with Roddie; their marriage in middle-age not only furthers the unity of Viking and Celt but, through their child, produces a new breed; and their marriage parallels Finn's. So what we have is not only optimistic but remarkably tidy and symmetrical. The standpoint of the 'Modernist' writer has been described as typically concerned with 'a lost past and a sour present'. This is not necessarily so, as novels ending with brash and challenging young men illustrate. But Gunn is astonishingly cheery in the context of 'Modernist' company.

Of this he was well aware; and his sense of being out of sympathy with the prevailing mood deemed necessary for a serious modern novelist grew throughout the 'forties with his later work. Here is part of a letter he wrote to his anxious publisher, Geoffrey Faber, in 1950:

> Where most novels of the more ambitious kind today deal with violence and material leading to negation and despair, I thought it might be a change if I got a character who would wander among his fellows looking for the positive aspects of life.
>
> Is it possible to pierce the negative husk, the dark cloud, even for a few moments, and come on the light, the bubbling well at the end of the fairy tale? Do folk still do it, ordinary people? can this feeling be conveyed, the moment of wonder, of integration? . . . For this the principal character must appear to have a wide knowledge of life actual and historical, so that the whole may not seem merely naive. And it must be carried through in the spirit of comedy because of a gaiety at the heart of the notion . . . (F R Hart & J B Pick: *Neil M Gunn: A Highland Life*, 230).

He then goes on to defend the idea of books which do not have conventional plots but which describe the unfolding of a man's quest.

We do not want in any way to misapply these later observations to Gunn's work and viewpoint as of 1939–41; yet the extent to which one can fairly relate those comments to what we have described in *The Silver Darlings* is surely quite obvious. We would certainly argue that Gunn himself was not naïve: about history, or novel writing, or life in general.

First of all, Gunn's self-consciousness as a writer and intellectual might be compared with Finn's. Even Finn, integrated in the end with his own community though he is, recognises a need to remain somewhat detached: part of all and yet a man apart, amused, critical, knowing. Finn could and did choose to reserve that right to detachment. Gunn's own rather more distressing situation was that he had little choice: the *extent* of his detachment was in part much the same as that of modern writers in general in relation to society as a whole; but it was also a measure of the distance between the kind of community Gunn would have liked to have around him and the much more fragmented modern industrial society in which he actually lived. He was sadly aware of that.

However, he applied his self-consciousness to the task and aims of writing most ingeniously too. He believed that a writer could, and should, bring to life at least in the imagination something of those moments of wonder and integration: 'to pierce the negative husk, the dark cloud, even for a few moments.' In order to do so, the writer must know a lot: including knowing the differences between the strands of thought, awareness, memories and forms of expression that constitute the fullness and variety of experience. Gunn could have produced, no doubt, a quite straightforward, a 'solid mainstream' novel: or, indeed, a conventional historical 'romance', in which writers are allowed a bit of lee-way to indulge themselves with fantasy and other such frivolities. Instead, we believe, he produced a much more subtle and probingly perceptive blend of elements of fact, myth, fable and legend. In constructing his tale and drawing it to a conclusion, he is not saying, 'Things were like this exactly'. He is celebrating what there was to celebrate about that phase of history. That is surely legitimate enough. But on that basis he is also presenting a vision of how even more remarkably and wonderfully life and culture, reality and dreams, deeds and awareness could come together, be experienced and live on as a source of hope. Finn's role is to be a carrier of that vision and hope which survives but does not deny the realities of history, including the fact that the history of his own people would soon take another downturn. That view of Finn's role certainly seems to us to provide a reading of the ending consistent with the actual later history of the north of Scotland and with Gunn's well-earned reputation for taking a realistic view of public affairs.

Gunn is not presenting us with a legend and hoping that somehow we will be taken in by it and confuse it with historical reality. He knows his history, and readers, too well for that. Nor is he arguing for some idealised and ideally static community. On the contrary, these are characters who understand risk and drastic change but are the better able to face up to such things through a collective awareness, on many levels, from that of the artist to crewman, of recurring signs and sources of strength in their culture. We may object that the harmonies and reconciliations Gunn arranges for his ending are altogether too contrived, unnecessarily so. We could make further criticisms of other aspects of the book (for example, that minor characters—although often enjoyable and vividly enough drawn—are suspiciously content to be a supporting cast and play a willing second fiddle first to Roddie and then to Finn). However, these are not reasons for misunderstanding the spirit and intentions of this 'fabulous' tale or its ending. Nor would they be good reasons for rejecting that spirit.

FURTHER READING

Our page references are to the Faber paperback edition of 1969, reprinted 1978.

Neil Gunn was born in Dunbeath, Caithness (the 'Dunster' of *The Silver Darlings*) in 1891 and died in Inverness in 1973. The Gunns were an old Caithnessian family and Neil lived much of his life in those parts of Scotland in which the novel is set. As a very young man he spent a short period as a clerk in London, but returned to Scotland at eighteen. For twenty-six years he was a Customs & Excise officer and consequently his early writing had to be produced part-time. Nonetheless, by the time he resigned his post as supervisor of a Highland distillery in order to become a full-time writer in 1937, he already had a substantial body of published work to his name. Besides, he had become an authority on whisky.

He was to produce twenty novels in all. Apart from *The Silver Darlings*, some of the most memorable are *The Grey Coast* (1926), *Morning Tide* (1930), *Butcher's Broom* (1934), *Highland River* (1937), *Young Art and Old Hector* (1942) and *The Green Isle of the Great Deep* (1944). See also his autobiographical book *The Atom of Delight* (1956). His other writings indicate the variety of his interests, expressed through journalism, reviews, essays, short stories and plays. He took an active interest in politics, notably Scottish Nationalist politics in the 'thirties. His strong streak of practicality is exemplified by his admiration for the effectiveness of Labour Secretary of State, Tom Johnston: to Gunn the nationalist it was more important to promote policies that would bring benefits to Scotland than to fight, perhaps uselessly, for a purist goal of independence. His concern that he should remain a practical man of affairs and not only a writer is well attested to by his work for Government Commissions. For further reading about Neil M Gunn and his work we recommend:

Douglas Gifford, *Neil M Gunn and Lewis Grassic Gibbon* (1983)
Francis Russell Hart, *The Scottish Novel: A Critical Survey* (1978)
F R Hart and J B Pick, *Neil M Gunn: A Highland Life* (1981)
Alexander Scott and Douglas Gifford (eds) *Neil M Gunn: The Man and the Writer* (1973)
G. J. Watson, 'The novels of Neil Gunn' in David Hewitt and Michael Spiller (eds) *Literature of the North* (1983)
Kurt Wittig, *The Scottish Tradition in Literature* (1958)

CHAPTER FOUR

Fionn MacColla:
And the Cock Crew

Arguably, Fionn MacColla is the most individual, idiosyncratic writer represented here. The adjective eccentric might well also be used. MacColla had some very strong views, on politics, religion, history and nationalism, and saw no reason to disguise these in his writings. He thought it part of the proper function of fiction to debate large issues, to be contentious, to attempt to persuade, and he is singular in the extent to which he does this. His novels progressively take up clear stances: in the first, *The Albannach*, the hero's rejection of the joykilling Calvinism of his parents and much of the community is clearly approved of by the author: he saw Calvinism as a denial of life, a 'naysaying'. The same opposition is central to *And the Cock Crew*, most obviously in chapter 7, where Maighstir Sachairi and the Poet Fearchar consider the human condition, and Maighstir Sachairi claims that only 'pagans and papists' value the natural man and this life in themselves and for themselves, while the true Christians 'have been converted from the world and the life of fallen man on earth, and can cherish nothing here'. MacColla clearly agrees with Fearchar on the importance of man and his life in the world, although he presents the minister with delicacy and sympathy. *And the Cock Crew* thus includes this distaste for Calvinist Christianity, and also, through Fearchar, argues MacColla's intemperate belief in 'England our Enemy', and England's sustained attempt, over hundreds of years, to overcome and subdue Scotland, especially the Gaels.

There is no reason why we should object to a writer's having a clear point of view, and attempting to persuade us of it, unless his polemic attitudes destroy the balance of his imaginative picture and harm his novels. We would argue that this is not the case in either of these novels, but that some of MacColla's later work, including his novel *The Ministers* and the published portions of a large scale novel about the Reformation, do tend to resolve themselves into static intellectual debates rather than the stuff of imaginative fiction.

Elsewhere, in his autobiography *Too Long in This Condition*, and his aggressive polemic book *At the sign of the clenched fist*, MacColla is very outspoken and extreme in his beliefs. He rejected the Plymouth Brethren beliefs of his parents and as an adult embraced Roman Catholicism. He made himself as much at home in Gaelic as in English, and adopted a Gaelic pseudonym and persona, and he identified himself passionately with what he saw as a Gaelic culture being deliberately extinguished. He responded to music as strongly as Fearchar, calling it 'of all influences perhaps the most dangerous', and he responded fully to the arts and the natural life of man. He became a Scottish Nationalist also, his trenchant expression of extreme anti-English views often an embarassment to more moderate Nationalists. But moderation is not a charge to be levelled against MacColla, and *At the sign of the clenched fist* is a remarkable and in its animus often an unpleasant book.

So: surely all these beliefs are going to overbalance a novel about that most emotive of subjects, the Highland Clearances? You need share none of MacColla's dogmatic opinions to react with a traditional mixture of anger, outrage and compassion to the circumstantial accounts of a helpless community evicted from its time-honoured home to make way for sheep, evicted often with brutality and generally without compunction, and left to scratch a precarious living on a bare sea shore. Historians argue about the larger causes of the Clearances, and most suggest that some change was inevitable, that the Highlands were not able any longer to support the traditional population in the traditional manner. Be that as it may, novelist and reader are entitled to choose to concentrate on the terrible actual experience of a people as outlined above.

MacColla is only one of a number of writers who have used much material. Neil Gunn used it in *Butcher's Broom* (1934), a fine novel which readers of *And the Cock Crew* will find an interesting comparison. Gunn concentrates much more on the community than MacColla: he establishes firmly its traditional nature, its values and its continuity, especially through Dark Mairi, the personification of traditional wisdom, before it is destroyed by the 'improvers'. And he chooses to be an omniscient narrator, explaining and expounding the inarticulate characters or ancient ways, not confining himself to one main consciousness, as MacColla tends to do with Maighstir Sachairi. From that point of view MacColla's novel has more in common with Iain Crichton Smith's *Consider the Lilies* (1968). Crichton Smith chooses a very small canvas, 'only the story of an old woman confronted by eviction'. Issues such as fear of the factor, lack of support from the minister, increasing dependence on a freethinking neighbour, are seen almost exclusively from her point of view. The personal impact of the novel persuades, despite various historical anachronisms: as in many of his finest poems, Crichton Smith is masterly in his portrayal of the old woman's mind, and this makes the novel, while imperfect, a notable fictional achievement.

In a way the most interesting literary treatment of the Clearances to compare to *And the Cock Crew* is John McGrath's ceilidh play *The Cheviot, The Stag and the Black, Black Oil* (1973). It was written for a socialist theatre company, 7 : 84 Scotland. The title comes from a claim of gross inequality, that seven per cent of the population owns eighty-four per cent of the wealth, and the play was written from a socialist standpoint, above all to alert the Scottish people, and Highlanders in particular, to the likely impact of exploitation following the discovery of North Sea Oil. But it begins with a passionate account of the Clearances, well documented and truthful, but deliberately contentious, intent on persuading the uninitiated and reminding others of the history of exploitation of the people of the Highlands, especially in regard to land and its ownership. McGrath's beliefs are clear and strongly argued, and it requires strange criteria of criticism to argue that this in any way inhibits the success of the play.

But we asked of MacColla: surely all these beliefs are going to overbalance a novel about that most emotive of subjects, the Highland Clearances? It is a loaded question, for a start: not all MacColla's dearest beliefs are given full rein in the novel. But more importantly, in this instance MacColla retains balance by centring his novel with great imaginative sympathy not on a Dark Mairi, a Fearchar or an ordinary member of the community, not, in other words, on a victim, but on one of the ministers, the characters often singled out for blame in helping to implement the Clearances against the interests of their flocks, and to their own financial advantage. So MacColla does not, like McGrath, straightforwardly present the case against the 'improvers' and for the people: he has chosen to be a kind of devil's advocate and present the case of a good man genuinely in terrible doubt about the appropriate attitude to take to the Clearances, and his own personal convictions are generally only voiced by the Poet Fearchar, who is mild in his behaviour, if extreme in his hatred of the English.

So MacColla has here avoided the problem of simply arguing his own most passionate convictions, and his dislike of Calvinist Christianity is only expressed indirectly, in the agonies of Maighstir Sachairi and instances of his past harshness, or briefly, in the pictures of Maighstir Tormod and Maighstir Iain, the ministers who acquiesce in the plans of the Black Foreigner, and are to gain financially from them. In an unexpected sense a key to the whole novel is in Maighstir Sachairi's moment of illumination in chapter 7, when he first perceives that an honest and sincere man (here Fearchar) can in all sincerity and in good conscience hold views different from his own (129). MacColla, with that understanding, has himself chosen to portray such a man. Maighstir Sachairi then is the centre of the novel, and if his beliefs are to be found wanting, or he is to fail his people, he is not easily to be accused of cowardice. But we might be forgiven for assuming something like this from the title.

The title and the epigraph of *And the Cock Crew* refer us very specifically to the night of the Last Supper, when Jesus foretold that Peter would deny him three times before cock-crow. The epigraph quotes Luke chapter 22, verses 31, 33 and 34:

> And the Lord said: Simon, Simon, behold Satan hath desired to have you, that he may sift you as wheat. . . .
> Peter said: Lord, I am ready to go with thee, both into prison and to death.
> And He said: I say to thee, Peter, the cock shall not crow this day till thou thrice deniest that thou knowest me.

Interestingly, MacColla omits verse 32, which is more hopeful in its tenor: 'But I have prayed for thee, that thy faith fail not: and when thou art converted, strengthen thy brethren.'

As the gospels all tell the story, Peter has boasted his readiness to follow, but denies Christ in the event out of fear, and repents at once at cock-crow. It is quite difficult to relate all this to the situation of the novel. True, the Poet Fearchar tentatively puts it to Maighstir Sachairi that he sees a resemblance here:

> They are the brethren of Christ, Maighstir Sachairi. And when you do not protect them it seems to me—forgive me speaking plainly—that you are doing the same thing as Peter did when he three times denied the Lord (137–8).

But Maighstir Sachairi is untroubled about the suggestion: 'It is between my soul and God'; and Fearchar does not press it. It is as if the suggestion was a last desperate try to shock Maighstir Sachairi into changing his mind about not opposing the clearance of the glen. Certainly no one in the novel, the narrator, Fearchar, even the scrupulous minister himself, accuses Maighstir Sachairi of simple cowardice. If he does deny Christ or the people, it is because of a genuine bewilderment of conscience. The ironically named Master Wiseman is paralysed and unable to act. Certainly the minister who puts himself forward as protector and defender of his people in chapter 1 may be said to have failed them by chapter 8, when he finds himself unable to preach to his desperately anxious congregation, but Maighstir Sachairi shows no such simple fears as Peter, fear to share prison and death with his Lord. Maighstir Sachairi torments himself, indeed, precisely because he cannot fully share the suffering of the people he loves and has devoted his life to. So the title seems to point to a denial not really seen in the book.

Peter denied Christ—but went on to be the rock upon which he built his church. Denial does not equal betrayal. Denial smacks of timorousness, fear to share suffering, but betrayal is positively evil, a deliberate and secret breach of accepted loyalty. At the very worst Maighstir Sachairi denied Christ and/or his people by his failure to maintain their defence, but the book does not urge this. On the other hand the people were betrayed: there are many examples of this in the book, and they help us by contrast to judge Maighstir Sachairi. The people are not betrayed by the Factor, the Black Foreigner, because there is no situation of trust or loyalty here. But they *are* betrayed by their chief. Mac 'Ic Eachainn by Fearchar's account betrays his people partly because he has learned to speak and think in English: being in a real sense a foreigner helps him to indulge his greed, and he betrays his time-hallowed relationship with his clan for material gain, the profits from sheep. Similarly the ministers, Maighstir Tormod and Maighstir Iain (again both English speakers), accept bribes of material gain to persuade the people that the Clearances are God's judgement for their sins and must be accepted. They are to have two more farms each, new roads, and a new manse for Maighstir Tormod (89). Their case is very hard to defend, although Maighstir Sachairi in his confusion and humility takes back his previous harsh judgement of them (37). Fearchar argues generally that people who learn to speak and think in English cleave to the adopted culture and betray the Gaels, the Albannaich.

Most clearly of all, Lachlan betrays Maighstir Sachairi and identifies himself with Judas thereafter. As Judas betrayed Christ for thirty pieces of silver, Lachlan betrays Maighstir Sachairi to the Black Foreigner for land. The Judas comparison is telling. Jesus was betrayed by Judas and denied by Peter within a few hours. The novel's title and Fearchar at least attempt to suggest that Maighstir Sachairi like Peter denied his Lord, but Lachlan's betrayal and repentance suggest a situation where Lachlan resembles Judas and Maighstir Sachairi Christ himself. So the religious dimension is not clear cut.

The essential form of MacColla's relatively short novel is a presentation of impending catastrophic happenings to the community of the glen, as a backdrop, almost, to the soul drama of Maighstir Sachairi, but a backdrop of intense concern to the major characters, the author and the reader. Let us look at the actual novel now, and see how this larger drama of history and the internal drama of one man's conscience are interwoven and presented, and with what success.

The novel is divided into ten chapters, and is very economical, very pared down. Each chapter is concerned with one main topic, whether the gathering at Dùn Eachainn in chapter 1, or the mental processes of Maighstir Sachairi (chapters 2 and 6), or the confrontation of Maighstir

Sachairi and another character, be it the Factor (chapter 3) or the Poet Fearchar (chapter 7). There is no padding, no softening of the harsh lines of the story, and when chapters are subdivided this again clarifies stages in action or argument.

The gathering at Dùn Eachainn in chapter 1 is prefaced by a short section in which a minimal amount of information is conveyed to the reader, along with a strong sense of atmosphere and impending doom. Nature itself is apparently hostile: in the very first page the searching, cold wind dominates: 'A wind out of the north-east narrow and bone-seeking and with an icy tooth blew at once into their faces.' The wind continues, 'keen and thrusting', and the first words spoken in the novel are: 'This is cold.' A bleak world, the only named colour grey. The two men who discuss the situation here are apparently strangers to each other, and contrary to conventional expectations at the beginning of a novel we never learn more of them, or after this hear of them at all: we are to have no individuals to identify with at the gathering. They are apprehensive: one says to the other: 'Great are your troubles, poor man. And maybe you are only at the start of them' (8). Old customs and standards no longer suffice. Duty is no longer a question of fearing God and going about one's business:

> Something else has come among us, something from altogether outside our way and our life. . . . Only the Black Foreigner yonder knows it. . . . Nowadays a man has to honour God and the Factor (8).

The brief conversation tells very little—that is all the people know: but it sums up the situation we are about to witness. The Factor has summoned all the people to Dùn Eachainn, the chief's castle, and the minister explains the summons and interprets it as God's judgement because the people have sinned and resisted God's will. One old man, 'some bard or other', Fearchar, sees it as the coming of the Law.

Now the two men have served their purpose, and as if we were watching a film the scene moves to shots of the arrival in the glen of an irregular procession of people of all ages: it is an early indication of their togetherness in community that they are 'all moving on at the pace of the weakest and most infirm' (9). The cold wind greets them all—'cold . . . bitter . . . icy . . . penetrating'. And they are on the whole silent. Soon another procession is sighted, 'crawling' towards the meeting place. Vivid emotion and action only begin when yet another band of people is sighted approaching Dùn Eachainn from the south. The anxious watchers gradually realise that *this* band is marching, not crawling, and excitement turns to panic when an occasional shaft of sun lights on the arms the soldiers are carrying. A babel of sound bursts out—since the failure of the

Jacobite Rising of 1745, the 'red soldiers' have been objects of fear to the disarmed Highlanders—and the people try to retreat. But here is a short but unforgettable picture of our first minister, Maighstir Tormod, who has been riding at the back, herding the people on. Now he waves his arms 'as one heads a straying flock', and urges them on to meet God's judgement. Since Jesus described himself as the Good Shepherd and his followers as sheep, the image of the pastor in charge of his flock has been traditional. But it takes on a terrible irony here, where the hireling shepherd has sold out to those who want to run four-legged sheep where the people have lived time out of mind. Tormod pitilessly waves and threatens and shepherds them: 'On! On! It is the will of God! . . .' (12).

The scene at Dùn Eachainn takes up the rest of the chapter. It begins with an image of two colours which will haunt the whole novel. The 'dense and obscure greyness' of the first page is still there:

against the level hardness of stone-grey sky the roofs and turrets of Dùn Eachainn were knife-edged. The scene was everywhere an equal grey,

but there is another, extra bright colour:

where the tunics of the soldiers made a line of vivid scarlet along the castle front (12).

The effect is of aggression on the landscape, towards the people, even when the 'red soldiers' are simply waiting.

MacColla shows remarkable skill in rendering this scene, and mixing various literary tones or modes. The people are described economically but with sympathy: their predicament is tragic, and they are treated appropriately. The Factor, the Black Foreigner, is taken seriously, and his cruel character and psyche are carefully analysed. The most famous, or infamous, factor of the Highland Clearances was Patrick Sellar, factor to the Countess of Sutherland, who most notoriously cleared Strathnaver in 1814: the Black Foreigner has some relation to this universally execrated figure, as his name, Byars, punningly indicates.

MacColla's literary tact is remarkable when he deals with the 'small legal personage' who reads the indictment, or the 'stout, purple-faced officer' in whom corpulence and military manner are ridiculously at odds. These are simply comic, and rendered as such, without disturbing the tense atmosphere of the people's expectation. So in one paragraph the 'small legal personage' keeps an eye on the helpless people as if they might ignore the bayonets and loaded cannon of the soldiers and rush him—and in the next the people are 'silent, awed and defenceless', understanding not a word of the indictment, which is in English, and waiting only to be murdered by the legendary red soldiers. There are multiple ironies here. As it turns out the indictment itself accuses several men of 'having threatened (a) strange gentleman with violence, pursued him, and put him in bodily fear' (20). But when Maighstir Sachairi produces the commonsense and clearly true account of the incident, we find that the Highlanders were genuinely trying to help a stranger, believing him to be lost, and he took fright at them because he was conscious of his own hostile intentions towards their livelihood and continued residence in the land of their fathers. Small wonder that the 'small legal personage' is similarly nervous!

This 'small legal personage' is a fine vignette of character. His nervousness is his main characteristic, and it is accompanied by quick, nervous motions, as when he reads the indictment to the anguished people, and before the end, almost 'skipped down from the little knoll and scuttled behind the military, where he incontinent took snuff' (13). And at the end of the scene, having sheltered behind the soldiers, occasionally peeping out, until the confrontation of Maighstir Sachairi and the Factor is over, he reads the Riot Act 'at the pitch of his thin voice'—to no one at all: he has waited too long. The corpulent officer in his pomp is also the subject of MacColla's ironic raillery: 'It was clear that if the people did break out in rebellion the military at least were ready to face the conflict without flinching' (14). And the other butt of humour here is the pair of ministers. In one paragraph their true allegiance becomes clear to the naked eye. They begin by 'standing a little in front of their flocks', but gradually seem 'not so near the people': the distance increases, and 'in the end they were some twenty paces distant and almost half-way to the military' (15).

All these characters are diminished by MacColla's cutting comedy, so that only the people and the Factor are presented seriously. The people's plight is desperate. They have no English, do not understand the indictment, and to them the English soldiers mean only one thing: 'They had no protector. They merely waited for the massacre to begin' (13). The Factor, a Lowland Scot, is presented now and later as hating the people, the more in proportion as they are defenceless. He is momentarily tempted to the very order the people fear. He begins to dominate the scene, and stretch the people's nerves to breaking point by making them wait and wait. Then follows the absurd but unpleasant scene when the Black Foreigner, assisted by Maighstir Iain, interrogates Domhnall Meadhonach. It is unpleasant enough because of the bullying of the Factor and the bullying self-importance of the minister, but doubly so because of their victim. Domhnall is even at first sight 'a little peculiar' in movements and appearance, and his confused reactions of smiles and fear and submissiveness are pathetic. Gradually the reader begins to realise—although the bullies apparently do not—that Domhnall is not a fully mature adult. He seems to have a minor fit (19). When Maighstir Sachairi intervenes, he calls him a 'poor body without his share of sense' (22).

Maighstir Sachairi's intervention is a great relief to the reader: the power situation in the scene has been intolerable and promised to be virtually unending. But now a voice is raised up in anger in answer to the Factor, to the people's amazement—and it is the voice they perceive: 'There could be no doubt about it, an angry voice was making its way to the front!' (20). When we see Maighstir Sachairi, he is a vivid figure: he shares in the colour patterning of the novel, grey and red. Here he is red and dominant: later Peigi will notice his turning grey as he is helpless and acquiescent (97); and at last he will emerge as champion again, and face the *Black* Foreigner with 'snow-white hair' and a 'look of doom' (173). But in this chapter he is the self-appointed champion, and the description emphasises his strength and aggressive anger:

> It was a strong-looking reddish man, wearing his bonnet. He was about the middle size, but looked both larger and redder because he was buzzing with rage (20).

His challenge to the Factor is effective, and provokes the Factor's rage. He suggests that the Factor has seriously exceeded the Law. The 'offence' of frightening the sheep man Reid was no offence; and the charge was no kind of excuse for the Factor's reaction: he deliberately uses it to terrorise the glen for his own purposes:

> Ye send for cannons and regiments of sodgers and get ready for a ceevil war. Ye're no a fule, Maister Byars. Ye dinna do sic things without ye have your reasons. Ye maun admit this is a byordinar' way o' doing, and ye canna wonder if it starts the question what would be your reason for seeking to put this haill countryside in terror o' their lives (24).

MacColla does not always stick to realistic presentation, and here Maighstir Sachairi makes an unrealistically long and fluent speech, to which the Factor offers neither interruption nor reply: this kind of thing will often happen again. Unrealistic it may be, but it clarifies the situation admirably. He asserts the Factor's intention to uproot and terrorise the people. He will not here pronounce on whether the coming evictions represent, as his brother ministers suggest, the judgement of God, but he seems to imply the contrary:

> It is no' my place to be putting my brethren right, and I will say therefore that it *may* be the judgment of God. But I will say further and on the other hand that it

may *not*. And if so be it is no' the judgment of God, Maister Byars, then it can be nothing more nor the oppressions of men (25).

He ends by invoking all the traditional Biblical images of good shepherd caring for his flock and wolves breaking into the fold (see, for example, Acts chapter 20, verse 29). And at this stage he has no doubts: 'In the day of bloody men *I* will be their protector!' (26). Both the minister and the Factor understand: '*Battle was joined*!' The Factor leaves, and Maighstir Sachairi gently dismisses the people in their own language.

The general impression of this chapter has been the establishment of an intolerable relationship of oppressor and oppressed, abruptly broken by the advent of a hero to protect the oppressed: habituated to traditional fairy tales or tales of chivalry, or to Western movies, we recognise such a heroic champion and anticipate his struggles and ultimate victory. But MacColla is not writing a book like that, and deliberately gives us one set of expectations here to deflate them hereafter.

The second chapter moves abruptly to Maighstir Sachairi's consciousness, and its formal division into three sections underlines the stages of his unsettlement and disturbance. In his disquieting interview with Mairi, the self-confident leader and protector has become fundamentally puzzled, and subject to unexpected and uncontrollable swings of mood and opinion. MacColla is again very economical in rendering Maighstir Sachairi's past certainties, his harsh drive against 'sin' on his arrival in Gleann Luachrach, and the disturbance he now experiences in learning that Mairi, who *looks* the epitome of 'pure and modest womanhood', can be guilty of 'so scandalous an instance' of sin. We see that he considers all 'the popular forms of vanity' as truly sinful: throwing the hammer and running races, playing the chanter, singing, dancing, contests of wit: all these for the new minister represented the extreme of 'contempt of Godliness' (28). Now Mairi's admission of her pregnancy is a new extreme—and apparently the actions and behaviour of the Factor and the ministers in the previous chapter are less striking. He is totally astounded by Mairi's news, and intensely confused: her composure and lack of shame, 'the serene front of virtue conscious of itself' (30), is so far from the stereotype picture of the shamefaced fallen woman, that he becomes uneasy in his role as judge and accuser. We learn that the hand of the Black Foreigner is at work here too. Mairi is only unmarried because the Factor has forbidden marriage to the people of Gleann Mór:

if any man marries a wife his land will be taken away from him and his house will be pulled down and both himself and all his family will be driven out into the world and banished from the neighbourhood (30).

Instead of new outrage at the highhanded threats of the Factor, Maighstir Sachairi feels reassurance, confident in his position as judge: this is no excuse for Mairi's sin. But again he becomes insecure, their positions seem reversed—he feels young and inexperienced; she seems more mature:

> And it was as if his view or system was suffering a silent judgment at the hands of another, less partial or superficial, which was hers (32).

It is on leaving this house that Maighstir Sachairi comes to a new understanding of his mind and its habits, the realisation that his mind loves harmony and wholeness, and has been in the habit of supplying limits to his vision so that what he sees is 'a harmonious whole'. He now begins to believe that his outrage at the notion of unpeopling the glen is caused by an attack on his own love of harmony:

> The life of the glenpeople . . . possessed in his eyes a shape and harmony. . . . To destroy it seemed an outrage and a violation, the triumph of chaos over order. . . . Maighstir Sachairi's mind had revolted from such an irruption of the meaningless (35).

Now in a moment he judges the unconscious habit of mind of years:

> Constantly . . . he had been seeking the satisfaction of an inner craving of his mind for harmonies. . . . And as the natural man is in Sin, and the natural mind seeks what is contrary to God, *he had been sinning* (35).

Because he has an 'unregenerate human mind' he sees his love of beauty as 'in direct opposition to God', and condemns himself as no saint but 'no better than a Pagan poet or philosopher' (compare a similar analysis in his talk with Fearchar, 132-3, where the total depravity of man, a basic tenet of the Reformers, is again insisted on). This sudden insight into what Maighstir Sachairi sees as years of unconscious but blameworthy sin is crucial to the novel: he is precipitated from serene self-confidence as Elect and a servant of God into a state of acute anxiety and doubt which will determine the rest of his behaviour in the book. MacColla hints his disagreement with much of this, but when Maighstir Sachairi repents his judgement of his brother ministers (37) we are confident that he is wrong.

The chapter ends with Maighstir Sachairi's return to himself, and figures of frightened men—and the perception, eventually, of smoke on the moor. And he sees the colour pattern basic to the novel: 'dense grey masses mingled and shot with the glow of flame . . .' (39). The firing of the heather is serious enough, as we will see with the starvation of the cattle, but it also foreshadows, sickeningly, the firing of the houses and the eviction of the people.

Although chapter 3 includes a conversation between Maighstir Sachairi and the Factor, the narrative is still mainly trapped in the minister's mind, and our attention is on that more than on the opposition of the two men. The Factor cannot see what advantage Maighstir Sachairi can get from defending the people—and we see a touch of MacColla's anti-Calvinist prejudice here too:

> (For not only was he in the habit of attributing self-interest to all men as their sole motive, as it was the only one he admitted to himself, but he had never hitherto encountered any exception to ministerial venality) (41).

The encounter of the two is brief, and less fiery than the last. Maighstir Sachairi sees ruination for the people and starvation for the cattle in the burning of the heather, while the Factor foresees better grass for the sheep. Maighstir Sachairi's mild reflection on the people's long-earned right to their glen is easily put aside by the departing Factor. MacColla's attention is on Maighstir Sachairi's miserable reflection on the conversation and his own helplessness: 'he had found himself deprived of all decision' (44), unsure where his duty lay, 'or whether the man ought to be opposed or submitted to'. In his reflections he swings from one extreme of self-confident defiance of the Factor to total doubt. He cannot tell how to interpret the coming evictions, from God or from man:

> If He will utterly destroy my people in just recompense for their sins and my own . . . it is for me to quell the resistance of my rebellious human mind and make humble my heart before His chastisement (45).

Once he has admitted an honest doubt, he is powerless to act or decide. He recalls the confidence of his attacks on vanity in his early ministry, his zeal, effectiveness and victory. Since then he has become gentle, and soft, and the 'comfortable curves' of his waistcoat reproach him (46). As he longs for another sharp, spiritual encounter with God, he realises with horror that the suffering this time would not be simply his own, but would include 'fire, ruin, the faces of his people transfixed with dread and horror, their doom and endless banishment . . .' (47).

It is a relief to move out of the tortured consciousness of Maighstir Sachairi in chapter 4, although some of its subject-matter will be painful enough. It centres on the Factor, and on Maighstir Sachairi's man, Lachlan. One of MacColla's skilful narrative techniques is to make the reader share as far as possible in the tensions and uncertainties of the characters, as at the beginning of the novel when our understanding of what is happening is only gradual and partial. The same technique is found here, and this time we are liable to leap to a wrong conclusion. The chapter begins with the Factor on the summit of a ridge where 'green points of grass were again pushing out among charred heather roots and boulders blackened by a recent passage of fire' (48). We take it for granted that this was his own burning of the heather in Gleann Luachrach. Up here, the Factor sees a beautiful prospect with natural colours, green grass, blue sky. And then he looks down into the glen which is quite full of smoke, a 'dense blanket'. He smiles at this, and his smile broadens as he detects 'distant shouting or shrieking'. When we see his 'triumph and satisfaction' we naturally expect that he has attacked Maighstir Sachairi's defenceless people in Gleann Luachrach. It is some time before we know for sure that this glen under process of eviction is in fact Gleann Mór.

Now the Factor meets Lachlan and the two have a short conversation in which neither shows to advantage. Lachlan has been visiting his sister in Gleann Mór, and is ill at ease, unwilling to speak about it. But when the Factor refers to a previous conversation he gains confidence, and the Factor rehearses him for a future speech about Gleann Mór and what he saw there: 'I wass see the Shudgment of God' (50), he will say. Innuendo pieced together, the reader sees that Lachlan and the Factor have a bargain, that Lachlan is to assert God's judgement and the need of submission to his will whenever possible to Maighstir Sachairi—and Lachlan reminds the Factor that he expects a reward:

'And them that wass do His will iss be rewarded,' he said as if meaningly. 'You wassna forget that, Maighstir Byars?' (50).

Clearly we are being prepared for Lachlan's role as traitor, as Judas figure. And he is the only English speaker whose accent is conveyed by a plethora of hissing, serpentine double 's' sounds, which anticipate the guileful self-interest of Tolkien's Gollum. The serpent image will continue. In chapter 5 he is described as 'crawling on his belly and calling for food', reminiscent of the serpent God punished in Genesis for the temptation of Eve: 'Upon thy belly shalt thou go, and dust shalt thou eat all the days of thy life.'

The rest of the chapter is taken up with Lachlan's difficult journey home, and again it is a process of gradual discovery, for us as well as for Lachlan, of the extent of the devastation so far. It is a dismal journey in unpleasant weather even before Lachlan hurts his ankle, and so it is understandable that he chooses the shorter road, we later learn to Srath Meadhonach. Lachlan's hunger increases as he makes his painful way, and he entertains vivid visions of the food and the welcome in store, for hospitality is a basic Highland quality. But this is what he finds:

> Gradually he knew that he saw what he saw. The house was a smoking shell. The pale moonlight went through the gaping window-holes and lay across the smoking heaps that had been the roof and the interior. The gable had fallen out. The air was filled with a sickening stench of burning. He now noticed that even the branch he was still holding on to to support himself was charred (53).

MacColla is being economical again, and refusing to exploit the horror of the situation. There was no need to let us see the mass horrors of Gleann Mór: this one house, unpeopled in the moonlight, conveys enough. Lachlan has no alternative but to try to go further, and all he finds is emptiness, ruin and the sickening smell of burning. Until he comes to the churchyard, where the moonlit scene is conveyed in terms of black and white. He hears voices from the graves; he is living in a horror movie. And it is like a horror movie, or a gothic horror novel, as he sees movement:

> A woman. The moon shine white on the deathly face, the long hair hung in disorder, through the hair the eyes looked with a wild, unearthly gleam. It raised its arm and began to extend it, slowly, in his direction, the finger pointing. His knees smote against each other. A shaking sound trembled from his lips. Suddenly the thing moved—shrieked— (54).

Instead of being a ghost, we find, she is only a woman driven out of her mind by the horrors of the day, mistaking Lachlan for the Factor—not such a silly notion, we know, because of his treacherous intent to his own people.

This incident is all we will see until the end of the novel of the reality of the Clearances; a ruined house, a churchyard with a frantic woman and her family in a shelter rigged up round a gravestone. It is enough. The desolation is spelt out when Lachlan desperately begs for food. Not only are the people also starving, but that their whole way of life is destroyed is apparent when the man has to refuse: 'Never has any man gone hungry from Donnchadh Mac-na-Ceardadh's door' (56). And the chapter ends with the desperate summing up: 'All here are wiped out.'

Lachlan's bringing back of that stark message is the starting point of chapter 5, which conveys the fear and panic of Gleann Luachrach in face of the news. Again we see individuals watching others' undue haste, fearing, running themselves. Gradually it resolves into a meeting of the men, as they try to understand the incomprehensible, 'There are no *people* in Glenn Mór and Srath Meadhonach' (63). We learn at second hand how the pitiful party in the churchyard were hunted out next day by the minister Maighstir Tormod and the 'tools of the Black Foreigner.' The fugitive family were treated with extreme brutality—and again one case is enough: the novel would be unbearable with many moments like this:

> So they went, Donnchadh Mac-na-Ceardadh walking alone with his arms tied behind him and his face covered with blood, and one of them holding the woman in front of him on a horse, screaming, and Maighstir Tormod carrying the child (65).

Now the men debate the question of God's judgement and resistance to the Factor. They all accept their turn is coming. One urges resistance, violence to the Factor and his men, and gets support, but the smith argues that their enemies are too strong, behind the Factor the chief, and the English Parliament. The debate is concluded with an unreally long and cogent speech from the miller: Maighstir Sachairi protected them at Dùn Eachainn; he told them to sow their seeds; he is strong and just and godly: '*Put your hope in Maighstir Sachairi!*' (75). United, they do, but the reader with private knowledge of his paralysis of will cannot share their excitement and relief.

We return to Maighstir Sachairi's endless dilemma in the next chapter, the first section of which consists of a long, circular meditation and self-questioning whose very circularity shows the kind of torment he has been undergoing, for weeks now. Weeks have passed: since the burning of the heather, the cattle have had time to starve, and Maighstir Sachairi has retreated from the people into his lonely self-torment. Here he is characteristically apart from the people, hiding behind the window, watching the struggles to persuade the wretched cattle to stand up. Moving away from the window and immersing himself in his thoughts does not help: his mind is dragged back to that morning's round up of the pathetic beasts:

> Maighstir Sachairi looked at the approaching drove, and at the sight he could have grat. At the same time, too, he felt revolted by something about it that seemed grisly, horrible, and unnatural. The cattle were so emaciated that many of them resembled skeletons. They walked only at a snail's pace, moving their legs slowly and with difficulty, and as they staggered along their heads drooped and lolled about, the eyes without life staring dully (80).

He is tormented by the patient acceptance of the people, remembering their humble approach to ask if they should sow their seed, and guiltily feeling that his advice to sow had been wrong. Most of all he combines total uncertainty about his duty with his insistent feeling of guilt: again and again he recapitulates events, and asks himself question after question, with no suggestion of answers. When was he right? When he opposed the Factor, or when he was convinced 'God was in this'? Why can't he be sure as he used to be? 'Why were there only warring possibilities in his mind, whose ceaseless strife destroyed his peace?' (85).

The minister's behaviour and moods now become erratic and un- controlled, in his visit to the miller and his confused reaction afterwards, culminating in his visit to Fearchar, when his mental and physical state is one of extremely acute stress amounting to illness. He sets off now to visit a dying old woman whose need he had uncharacteristically forgotten, but instead makes his way to the miller's, mulling over his distrust of Lachlan and his assurance of God's judgement, and his distrust of his fellow ministers: 'They were a strangely unlikely folk who claimed to have received the grace to discern God's purpose. . . . What do we know of ministers who take gifts from Satan for serving God!' (89). At the miller's, Maighstir Sachairi is unusually expansive, uncharacteristically paying compliments to Peigi, the miller's wife, leaving the miller with the conviction that danger is past. But Peigi sees a big change in him:

> His hair, Tormod! On his brow and temples, and here along his cheeks—it is quite grey! It was always red before, and now suddenly it is grey. Why do you think it would get grey so quickly? (97).

The change is more than physical, as the colours imply. Maighstir Sachairi was described in chapter 1 as 'reddish', and so associated with the energy and vigour of red soldiers and red flames: in his 'paralysis of nerve and will' he has become grey and insubstantial, like the dominant images of smoke and cloud.

After leaving the miller's, Maighstir Sachairi cannot be at peace: he begins to reproach himself strongly for his behaviour at the meal. Dogged yet again by uncertainty, his judgement 'all unseated', he makes hastily for the smithy, although he knows that the smith is elsewhere, and there experiences greater despondency than he has ever known, which is described in the phrase made famous by St John of the Cross, the dark night of the soul:

> He felt that here at last he was at the end of himself, his hope, his help, his strength and resources; the dark night swung down upon his soul. It flooded in upon him darkly, drowning him under a wave of fear and helplessness. . . . Choking now. Afraid of a nothingness that wanted him (101).

The image is violent and effective, and points on to what we learn later when he is dying, about the drowning of his beloved Jonathan. The chapter ends with him making his hasty, jerky way up the glen to the house of Fearchar.

Clearly the visit to Fearchar is an important turning point in the novel, and the confrontation of the two men teaches us something about both. As already indicated, Fearchar is to enunciate some of MacColla's own beliefs, and he is described with sympathy and admiration: 'What made this man outstanding was felt rather as an energy or intensity of his being, a certain vividness of the self, an essential vigour' (104). The chapter is divided in three, and the first part is a conversation between the two men in which we are constantly presented with Maighstir Sachairi's reactions and private thoughts, a constant wild distrust and detection of traps that contrasts sharply with Fearchar's calmness and possession, and keeps us alert to Maighstir Sachairi's unstable state.

Fearchar has one special question to ask: 'Can the will of God be known for certain in particular circumstances?' (107), and he elaborates it: can the Spirit 'be withdrawn from one of the Elect *without his knowing*?' (109). Although he has been tormented for weeks by these very questions and the temptation to pessimistic answers, Maighstir Sachairi responds and dismisses the questions with good traditional theology. They return to their old disagreement over Maighstir Sachairi's opposition to music and poetry in the glen, and two views of man emerge. Fearchar sees this life as important and man as susceptible to improvement by the experience of art, while Maighstir Sachairi restates the Reformers' belief in the total depravity of man and the unfathomable nature of God's justice. Fearchar returns to his original question and applies it very specifically to the present situation:

> Supposing, for instance, an event were about to take place, an event, let us say, that would be a great calamity to many innocent people, and to avert it it was necessary first of all and above everything to know whether it was the will of God or not; is it possible—I only ask in order to know—is it possible even for one of the Elect to make a mistake and suppose that event to be according to the will of God while in truth it is opposed and contrary to God's will? (116).

Maighstir Sachairi's whispered admission, 'It . . . is . . . possible . . .' precipitates a further internal crisis of nerve and feeling, so that the second part of the chapter is introduced by the perception of both men that the minister may be ill. Meanwhile Fearchar has a chance to make his case for resistance to the Clearances, in another of MacColla's unrealistic long and cogent expositions. He argues the age-long attempt of England to destroy

Scotland, relating a history in which England is all that is bad, in which the Gaels, the Albannaich, always obeyed chivalrous rules of conduct in war and the English soldiers are unspeakably brutal. He sees attacks on the Gaelic language as part of the process, and the adoption of English by Gaelic speakers as the fundamental treachery: and he wants it all to be resisted.

Meanwhile Maighstir Sachairi has had an experience of great illumi-nation, 'of more moment in his soul and spirit, if it were possible, even than his conversion itself' (127). He has been unmoved by Fearchar's historical argument: his mind acts vertically, in terms of the relation between God and man. He suffers a period of 'death-like exhaustion', and then his vision, but we are reminded before the vision how short he is of sleep or food: his 'transforming vision in a timeless instant' may not be an illumination from God. It has its attractive side: his understanding that Fearchar can be, and is, a good man (129), but his serene assurance of the inevitability of the expulsions is more questionable. It solves his previous dilemma of uncertainty and makes him eloquent, but there is something inhuman about his eloquent account to Fearchar of the way Christians are 'rapt away out of the world' (132) so that 'neither the world itself nor any of its affairs is our concern'. He sweeps away politics, history, tradition—all as much vanity as Fearchar's poetry and music, and of no concern to the Christian. If Maighstir Sachairi is not being criticised here, and we argue he is not, then by implication his beliefs *are* criticised, as inhuman and disabling. Fearchar rejects them: the people were 'as bold as lions until they got this religion' (134), and he momentarily comes to passionate denunciation:

> What use is a religion that bids us tear out our bowels in the here and now of our life for the sake of a heaven where also our humanity will be worthless and covered up, and from which after all we may have been shut out by the decree of God before our birth! A fart for such a faith: a people that got it would be destroyed by it: the Devil must have made it! (134).

Maighstir Sachairi goes on to ask Fearchar's forgiveness '*for everything*', although he does not believe he has wronged him: his consciousness is purely spiritual now, while Fearchar is still desperate over the impending destruction of his people. In his new serenity, the minister sees the arguments for opposing the evictions as proceeding from Satan, and is untroubled by Fearchar's suggestion that like Peter he is denying Christ. He pursues the question of Fearchar's resentment of his past treatment, and we learn of his destruction of a hoard of ancient and wonderful Gaelic poetry. More, Fearchar explains: 'I felt you were a poet yourself . . . I felt . . .

I felt you had *betrayed* us both' (140). Another act of betrayal, and this time Maighstir Sachairi feels quite innocent, because he is convinced that by turning from 'vanity' to the ministry he has done God's will: again, if the minister is not being criticised here, his beliefs seem to be.

Maighstir Sachairi's vision remains the subject of the start of chapter 8, and here it comes to grief, when he fails to preach his sermon to the waiting people. The episode has a certain resemblance to the last days of Robert Colquohoun in *Cloud Howe*. There, we remember, Robert's tottering faith is bolstered by a vision of Christ himself, something Chris reacts against with disbelief and distaste, and the author makes no suggestion that the vision is real or proceeds from God: quite clearly it proceeds rather from Robert's own desperation. Here Maighstir Sachairi is still protected by his 'timeless vision' which has remained with him and endowed him with a 'strange calm', a total acceptance that the destruction of the glen is inevitable, although it continues to move him profoundly. It is as if he is outside time, experiencing time like God in Heaven, 'the Simultaneous' (143).

The whole glen has assembled to hear him. It has been troubled by his transformation: 'every man on whom he turned his slow, calm glance experienced a something deeply disturbing, as if it had been a stound of dread or premonition of catastrophe' (145). The entire parish assembles on the Sabbath, in a way reminiscent of the great assembly at Dùn Eachainn. In church the people are 'troubled inwardly and disquieted', while Maighstir Sachairi is 'apart in some calm, cold fervour of his own' (146). He reads from Deuteronomy, a passage describing the miseries of the people of Israel led by God into the wilderness, 'a sufficiently notable text, and of bitter application'. It is made the more bitter by the omission, twice, of God's feeding the people with manna in the verses quoted, and of a number of verses describing the good land, paradisal in nature, to which God is leading the people, for a good life.

Robert Colquohoun's last sermon was a wild and bitter one, and he died, dramatically, in the pulpit at the end of it. Maighstir Sachairi is no less dramatic. Silence and waiting are prolonged: he looks terrifying: he utters only a broken gabble, trying to repeat his text—and then he sits down. Even yet they wait—until they hear him sob. Silently the people leave the church, and 'the huddled and motionless figure in the pulpit' (148).

Now Lachlan is to complete his Judas-like betrayal. There is a terrible irony in his behaviour here. He is going to the Factor to betray his master and collect his reward—but he lies on his bed for hours first, waiting for the day to end: Sabbath-breaking is a serious sin! Only after the Sabbath 'must for certain be over' is it 'time to do what was to be done' (150). He walks the fifteen miles to the Factor's house with good speed, considering how recently his foot was badly injured and declared broken (51, 55).

His interview with the Factor underlines the man's dominance, 'effrontery', delight in bullying and playing with victims. In his broken, jerky English, Lachlan claims that the minister has 'come till't', and tells of the unuttered sermon, enacting it to the great amusement of the Factor. He asks for his promised reward, the farm of Balivany, but the Factor hardly bothers to refuse, and counters Lachlan's 'baffled rage' with jerks of his naked big toe. He gives a long, unrealistic account in vivid Lowland Scots of how the cause of Maighstir Sachairi's submission is not Lachlan but the Factor himself. He claims he has been playing the minister as an angler plays a fish.

He now has 'things to dae' (158): there is no further need to postpone the destruction of Gleann Luachrach by so much as a minute. It is not until he tells the dejected Lachlan that he cannot go home that Lachlan begins to understand his role of Judas:

> A kind of *recognition* dawned in his look. He even drew away a step with a movement of repugnance, staring with horrified fascination at something he appeared to have that minute seen. Just as the Factor turned away he took his head in his hands and broke out in a high, wailing voice, swaying to and fro. 'Oh! I wass sinned . . . I wass sinned!' (159).

We begin to feel compassion for him, because of this recognition, and because of his treatment at the hands of the Factor. He pretends to let Lachlan go and instead locks him in a deep cupboard and leaves him there, forgetting all about him until the end of the novel.

In chapter 9 Maighstir Sachairi recovers from his indispositions and becomes again, too late, the champion and protector of the people he made himself in chapter 1. He remains in the pulpit, in a stupor and then in a healthy sleep, until daybreak. It is the last day for the glen, and we see the start of the evictions from the miller's house. No adults have slept since their return from the minister's abortive sermon, and silent foreboding possesses them. Peigi feels a new consciousness of every detail of her house and the familiar glen outside. Her understanding that it has begun is gradual; did she see smoke? 'A look of concern crossed her face as the thought occurred to her, watching, that something must be on fire yonder' (165). Soon she sees more smoke, men advancing on a house with 'a spot of fire in their midst'. The people have been presented as a community from the first, as all proceeded to Dùn Eachainn at the pace of the old or the sick. Now, characteristically, the miller and his son run to the aid of the old woman whose house is threatened, and Peigi watches so intently that she is unaware of the men arriving to burn her own house.

When Maighstir Sachairi wakes he has 'no hesitation . . . no problem': Too late, he is restored to true perception:

the world had righted itself in his perception. Now again, his horizons no longer conscience-clouded, things were themselves (168).

He rides into the heart of the fires, in search of the Factor. And now the colour pattern of red and grey which has dominated the novel reaches its height: flame and smoke have taken over:

> the whole slope he had descended was stained a bright blood colour . . . the wind . . . dying again let the grey acrid blanket thin slowly away, to reveal the red glares of a score or over of homes . . . in flames at once, each sending up one of the long living pillars to support the moving red-shot pall that roofed the whole glen over (169).

The description of the fires and the evictions is short and general, but effective enough, with the continual noise, the smoke, the heat. When he comes to a burning party at work, Maighstir Sachairi's attention is not for the evicted but the burners in their mindless orgy, as one lot catch escaping animals and laughingly throw them back into the flames, and another lot throw the stored meal over 'a pretty steep precipice that overhung the river'. But Maighstir Sachairi is looking for the Factor, and sees him at last: 'Out of the smoke, like a fiend from the Pit' (172). But it is too late. The Factor is drunk with destruction and full of triumph, now able to enjoy the destruction he was tempted to at Dùn Eachainn: he refuses the minister's command to stop: 'Never, Maister Wiseman!—I *hae* them!' (173).

The pointless confrontation is interrupted by a stampede of cattle. The Factor has one last glimpse of the minister, now white to his black, and like an avenging angel:

> Maighstir Sachairi's snow-white hair blowing, the look of doom he bent on him, the forefinger he raised above his head, seeming to appeal straight upward through the smoke-filled sky (173).

The Factor is thrown clear but the minister's horse bolts headlong over the precipice.

Unexpectedly, we are to see Maighstir Sachairi again before his death. In the final chapter he comes to, gradually and painfully, and finds himself in his own room, where Fearchar has brought him and cared for him. The present is full of pain, and anxiety about the shelterless people, and his new conviction that he was wrong:

> *It was pride, Fearchar, I understand now. I saw myself . . . in the centre . . . too much . . . in the centre* (178).

But Fearchar's sad response carries conviction: 'You did what you saw right, Maighstir Sachairi.' Before he dies, Maighstir Sachairi has two periods of some kind of delirium, dream or memory, reliving his early days, and we learn at last a little of his potential for love and affection, and of his early conditioning about sin. First is a wonderfully coloured account of a seaside scene, using all the colours that have been excluded from the account of his ministry in the novel. The picture of the sea, its movement and the familiar form is ecstatic, full of vivid movement and sound. The scene shifts to a river bank, where the future Maighstir Sachairi seems to save the life of his friend, Jonathan. Glimpses of the two and their close relationship continue, with the 'vanity' Maighstir Sachairi will later condemn, playing mock-hockey with a turnip, writing poetry, reciting it. Then the grey enters with the news of Jonathan's death, and colour drains from the picture. When Jonathan dies, the future minister is convinced of sin and punishment:

> *He had loved him more than his own soul, sinfully it seemed, not without idolatry; and how terribly the sin was punished: friendship might live henceforward, but no more the Friend—forever* (183).

And so he turned away from his youthful joys, to Duty.

His final memory is of an earlier scene, a little boy breaking the Sabbath and perplexed that his father does not know his fault, a little boy tempted by light and happiness but precociously aware of sin and '*one seeing Eye*' (184). MacColla's critique of Calvinism surfaces again here, in the picture of the little boy's terror of damnation. It is reminiscent of the auto-biographical incident he relates in *At the sign of the clenched first*, when as a tiny boy he put out a gentle hand to touch flowers he saw with adoration. At the same moment, a loud knocking came from behind, his mother rapping on the window. This early, he was being conditioned: 'I early came to realise that the law from outside tapping peremptorily on the window-pane, was *Truth*, and the inner law of my being which it interrupted and rebuked, was *Sin*.' Maighstir Sachairi's last memory is a final indication that for MacColla no blame rests with him, but much in the naysaying that reared him.

But the future, of course, is with the Factor. We see him back from the burning, washing himself, setting off on a ride which takes him past a long line of refugees from Gleann Luachrach. He continues south and meets the shepherd, and the sheep. After his return home he returns comfortably to his papers, and it is only his dog's unease that at last reminds him that he had shut Lachlan in the cupboard.

Even the Factor is temporarily discomposed when he opens the cupboard and finds Lachlan's hanging corpse, unrecognisable. Half a tumbler of whisky restores him to composure, and the reflection that Lachlan was a 'damned fule'. But he cannot recall the faint association he has with the words of his man: 'He went and hanged himself.' He does not remember that Judas repented his betrayal of Christ, and gave back his blood money to the chief priests and elders—'and departed, and went and hanged himself' (Matthew chapter 27, verse 5).

What the Factor cannot remember or understand he dismisses, and the novel ends with his impatience at the arrival of a minister from another threatened strath: 'Meenisters! As if I hadna work o' my ain!' he complains, as unaware as ever of the hellish nature of his work and the appropriate reaction of a man of God.

FURTHER READING

Our page references are to the Souvenir Press edition of 1977.

Fionn MacColla was born Thomas Douglas MacDonald in Montrose in 1906, and died in Edinburgh in 1975. He reacted against a strict Evangelical upbringing, and became a Roman Catholic, a fervent Scottish Nationalist and a champion of what he saw as a dying cause, the Gaelic language—hence his adopted name. He made himself as much at home in Gaelic as in English, and spent many years teaching in the Gaidhealtachd as a headmaster, with an interval teaching in Palestine, 1926–29. He retired to Edinburgh.

His literary output was small, partly because he was a perfectionist, and partly because his books were much misunderstood or neglected by readers, and much refused by publishers. Several books remain as yet unpublished. For all this see his autobiographical work, *Too Long in This Condition*, 1975.

Three complete novels have been published: *The Albannach* (1932), a fine picture of contemporary Highland life, *And the Cock Crew* (1945—but first planned 1930), and *The Ministers*, posthumously published in 1979. The most controversial aspect of MacColla is summed up in his polemic analysis of Scotland, *At the sign of the clenched fist*, 1967.

His work has as yet attracted little sustained criticism, but some approaches are indicated here:

Francis Russell Hart, *The Scottish Novel: A Critical Survey* (1978)
J Herdman, 'Fionn MacColla: Art and Ideas' in *Cencrastus* 13 (Summer 1983), 11–13
D Morrison (ed) *Essays on Fionn MacColla* (1973)
Isobel Murray, 'Fionn MacColla: Pilgrim of Independence' in *Leopard Magazine* 59 (February 1980), North East Review, i–iii

CHAPTER FIVE

James Kennaway:
Tunes of Glory

Tunes of Glory was James Kennaway's first novel, published originally by Putnam in 1956. By any critical criteria it is a spectacular piece of work: an explosively dramatic story dazzlingly yet tautly written. For a first novel, it was astonishing. Happily, it quickly gained the recognition it deserved. It was also turned into a successful film starring Alec Guinness and John Mills. Kennaway himself wrote the screenplay, and for that he was nominated for a Hollywood Oscar. In style of presentation, imagery, construction—in almost every respect—the novel itself powerfully suggests a film. It is as if we watch its obsessed and doomed central characters flicker in and out of shot in their haunted castle, actually the barracks of a Highland Regiment. Although it avoids the absurdities of many a horror movie, there are Gothic overtones enough in this wintry and oppressive setting: all in all, a brilliant production in more senses than one.

The dramatic outline is stark and clear. Jock Sinclair has been Acting Colonel of a Highland Battalion for some five years, having fought his way up from being a piper, from the ranks, and gained command as a result of his wartime heroism and leadership. Now, with the Battalion stuck in its peacetime home quarters, he is passed over and displaced as Colonel by a gentleman-soldier, a nervous and solitary man called Basil Barrow. Barrow has had harrowing war experiences of his own: but as a POW of the Japanese and hence out of the thick of the kind of action by which Jock measures men. His social background and his other service experience— with MI5—further highlight the contrast between him and Jock. He even prefers brandy to whisky. Trouble is inevitable.

It is already brewing when Jock, losing control of himself in this situation, strikes a corporal in a fit of rage on discovering him in a bar in the company of his daughter, Morag. Barrow feverishly seizes his opportunity and opts to put Jock up for court martial. However, it is Barrow who breaks first under the strain of processing Jock's disgrace. In part this is because, as a historian of the Regiment, Barrow admires and also envies Jock's kind of heroism. Barrow commits suicide. Jock is back in command. The incident with the corporal could, by common consent, be forgiven if not forgotten by the Battalion. Instead, Jock undergoes a drastic mental collapse as he issues his orders for Barrow's funeral, an event which he seeks to create on a grossly lavish scale which horrifes all the other officers. Jock does not actually die at the end of the book. But we are left in no doubt that he is destroyed—by himself as much as by anything else. A colossus has crumbled.

Jock Sinclair is so much larger than life yet credible, his conflict with Barrow so inevitable yet such a waste for both men, that the spectacle of their destruction has quite enough force for any novel without further ado. The other characters caught up in this central drama are sharply observed and precisely drawn for us, sometimes mercilessly so; as when, for example, the extent of the treachery and cold-bloodedness of Jock's friend, Major Charlie Scott, is suddenly revealed (111). Kennaway's concentration on crucial scenes, on dramatic shock, is intense. There is no room here for meandering or elegaic prose. Things happen swiftly and at times breathtakingly.

That being so, it is one of the most interesting and effective paradoxes of the book that he also succeeds in conveying a curious air of languor, of violence held in suspended animation, out of action. It is an impression heightened by repeated references to the cold and to the snow, softly falling, covering them and their surroundings. Men trained for violent action appear to be hibernating, and yet there is a dangerous, pent-up restlessness about too. Only one blow is actually struck against another human being. Only one shot is fired, and that when the would-be big shot shoots himself in, of all places, the mouth. One blow and one shot are enough to shatter a kind of peace and numerous illusions and dreams about shared values as well as the lives of two men.

On the one hand, then, compactness and economy of expression are oustanding features of Kennaway's skill and keys to the sheer power of this novel. On the other hand, a single action or a particular detail can be used, as the above example suggests, to create multiple effects. So it is that Kennaway is able delicately to inject into the story a great variety of sidelights on Scotland, on the peculiarities of its culture and its people, without damaging essential dramatic tensions. Critics have already noted that in *Tunes of Glory* we can find many of the themes and preoccupations that were to characterise his later work: a concern with creative energy that is also destructive energy; fear at the heart of the Calvinist ethic; people taking refuge in unreal worlds often characterised by obsessive rigidity and over-correctness. There are others too. They all bear closer examination. What we wish to do here is explore some of the highly particular forms Kennaway's insights take in this novel. One of our main reasons for doing so will be in order to suggest that Jock Sinclair is a more complex, perhaps a more subtle character than he has sometimes been supposed to be.

But first, how could Kennaway manage—as we are suggesting—to pack so much into such a highly compressed work? It is, after all, only some 190 pages long in the Mainstream edition (1980). Is it necessary or desirable to read all that much into so straightforward a story?

Kennaway's writing appears to be so effortless that we can almost imagine it flowing in well formed phrases and sentences from his typewriter like chords and runs from the fingers of a good pianist. A moment's reflection is enough to realise that it could hardly have been as simple as that. But just how far that picture is from reality has only fully become apparent in recent years and especially since the publication in 1981 of *The Kennaway Papers*, edited by his widow. There is no question, of course, that he did have at his command an elegant and terse style of English prose. However, his practice was to write a vast amount then edit and prune away until he was left with what he considered the essence of what he wanted to convey. The result could approach a kind of bareness as, arguably, in *The Cost of Living Like This* (1969); and possibly this tendency grew more marked in his later work. Nonetheless,

> James used to say that for every slim novel that he published he would write an average of a million and a half words, which was not an exaggeration. The differently coloured drafts of each novel, which led from one to another, piled up in crumpled heaps under the windows and on every shelf in his study.

Thus Susan Kennaway (*The Kennaway Papers* (12)). We needn't suppose that this method of production was fully operational during the writing of his first novel to recognise that some such method was already in use. One of the signs of it is his effective exploitation of recurring, variable images and motifs. The snow is one we have already noted and we can immediately add that the nature of the snow, or the context in which it appears, has a way of changing. Atmosphere more generally has an important part to play in defining both interior and exterior worlds: inside the barracks as well as outside, in a psychological as well as an environmental sense.

> There is a high wall that surrounds Campbell Barracks, and in the winter there is often a layer of crusted snow on top of it. No civilian rightly knows what happens behind that grey wall but everybody is always curious, and people were more than ever curious one January a year or two ago (9).

That is the very first paragraph of Book I. The atmosphere here is simply and, it might seem, innocently described. However, that passing mention of wintry conditions serves to heighten our sense of the blank inscrutability, the air of mystery, surrounding that enclosed order hidden behind its high wall. When we turn to the beginning of Book II, we see that Kennaway picks up the self-same atmospheric motif of gloomy wintriness, but now does more with it.

> It was just freezing outside and the barracks was at its worst. The high wall closed out the real world like a frame surrounding an etching. A tint of brown in the sandstone was the only colour within the perimeter, apart from the white of snow, and the grey: the grey of the slates where the snow had thawed a little and shifted in an untidy avalanche; the grey shoulders of the Officers' Mess at the end of the square; the grey figures scuttling about from block to block, the orderly corporals, the pickets dismissing, the bugler in search of breakfast, and the detention squads sweeping away the first paths through the sticky snow (99).

First impressions (those we get from the opening of Book I) are repeated and reinforced. But there is more. By now he is able to strengthen further impressions for which he has prepared us: that this enclosed order not only shuts out the world, it lives in a world of its own; and that it is an unreal world, a ghostly and haunted world. Those dimly seen figures are spectral grey. We are reminded, too, of other things said earlier on, in Book I, chapter 11. The snow created 'a white felt world that was lonely and eerie', a world haunted by memories of sorrows and privations and of a savage, fearful Jacobite soldiery destroying and pillaging as they retreated. Memories of what was experienced generations ago linger on 'like a superstition. Snow comes not as a friend.' It raises old ghosts and fears. 'And of all men Jock was the most superstitious' (91). The Colonel of the Battalion is most prone of all to be drawn into that oppressively haunted world; and the Campbell Barracks is its centre.

These are fairly straightforward examples of Kennaway's way of inserting a motif—in this case an 'atmospheric' motif—and playing on it as the action proceeds in order to add new perceptions and give more layers, more depth, to the picture he is etching. Certainly, it is not necessary to take in or pursue each and every one of these motifs with all their twists. It is one part of Kennaway's artistry that the story he tells doesn't need elaborate embellishment. However, it is another part of his artistry that he lays in such a rich store of insights about his characters and their world for us to savour on second or third reading.

Irony and paradox are what chiefly characterise these insights in *Tunes of Glory*. Their variety, rather than any univocal argument or 'statement' about these soldiers and their culture, is what gives the book its richness. We are presented with a credibly solid and forbidding barracks, shut off from the world outside. It is also an imprisoning psychological environment teeming with illusions and fantasies. The barracks is part of a make-believe world. We can also accept the fictional Scottish town around it as real enough. Moreover, both barracks and town are haunted by an overly oppressive past. The men play out fantasies but at the same time pursue very life-like ambitions. The Jock Sinclair who goes 'mad' is a coarse, tough, desperate man. He is also dreamer and artist who creates, celebrates and destroys his greatest dream. At the end of the book what we have is a real funeral: it is Basil Barrow's funeral. It is also both the apotheosis and the end of a kind of martial code and martial glory. Kennaway can make all kinds of wry and ironic comments on the camaraderie, rituals and naïvetés of this man's army; but he also conveys the pity and pathos of it. We may read the book as a reflection on the Scots' obsessive habit of celebrating deaths, massacres and other disasters, many of them self-induced. On the other hand it is a genuine, angry lament for the terrible waste of human energy and creativity past and present. Jock's tunes of glory include skirling, swaggering marches of a conquering, imperial soldiery. There are also self-deceptively sentimental national ballads such as *The Flowers of the Forest*. But the tunes of glory also include something much subtler, and Jock is a master of this too: the pibroch.

'It is a lament.' He mopped his brow. 'But it is something else as well. That's the catch. It's no just a grieving. There's something angry about it too' (30).

Thus Jock explains it to an admiring Corporal-Piper Fraser: the young man whom Jock will hit and, by so doing, bring about his own lamentable downfall.

None of these readings and interpretations, general or particular, cancel each other out. They add to the story. They contribute ironies, sometimes savage and sometimes simply sad. They are often complementary.

So when we turn to Jock Sinclair it is perfectly easy to accept as valid many of the interpretations others have placed on his role and character. He is indeed a brutal and violent man. In the peace-time army he is an anachronism: the tough and wily old street-fighter was in his element in the thick of battle. He is out of it entirely amidst the civilities and sleekit ambitions of the post-war Officers' Mess. We may be on his side against the snobberies and fopperies that so enrage him; but we can see that his restless snarling, his deliberate rudeness and offensiveness, his wild bouts of drinking will get him nowhere—other than out. He might be said to have an inferiority complex: he certainly senses that to be who he is is to be at a disadvantage. He unquestionably suffers from a kind of vanity that will partially, disastrously blind him.

His role, then, it might seem is to represent a temporarily necessary kind of vitality and know-how which has unfortunately for him been tacitly declared redundant. In view of his achievements and what he has done for others we can sympathise with him for the position he finds himself in. But then there are his flaws to be considered. There's a kind of lawlessness about him. Indeed, if his kind of cunning and violence had not been legitimised by the army, no doubt the man would have been kept locked up (as once he was, in Barlinnie prison). As it is, when the novel opens he looks like a caged beast.

> From time to time he glanced round the table, and other officers when they caught his eye quickly turned away while he continued to stare. The look in his eye was as flat as the sole of his polished boot (11).

We sense that he is held on sufferance, on a longish but fraying leash. We have also just seen that his vitality is about to turn to grossness as he begins to age.

> The Colonel's face was big and smooth and red and thick. He had blue eyes—they were a little bloodshot now—and his voice was a sergeant's. His hair, which was thin, was brushed straight back with brilliantine. It was not a bit grey. The Colonel did not look broad because he was also deep, and had the buttons on his tunic been fastened there would have been little creases running across his chest and stomach. But at times such as this he was inclined to unfasten his buttons. He had even unfastened the top two buttons of his trews this evening and his striped shirt protruded through the gap in the tartan. His trews were skin tight and it looked as if he need only brace his muscles to tear the seams apart. In his lap he nursed a very large tumbler of whisky, and he tapped his foot on the ground as the pipers played (10–11).

A certain gracelessness is imputed, leaving aside the implicitly snobbish allusion to his working-class origins and their uneradicated traces (the voice, the hairstyle). As well as pointing up these imperfections of grossness and gracelessness, the novel also raises questions about his intelligence. It seems that he lacks subtlety. It may be that his vanity and impatience with his surroundings prevent him from applying his intelligence adequately to his changed circumstances. It could be that he doesn't have the requisite intelligence. The upshot seems to be the same, either way. We may fully sympathise with his plight. But the old warrior lacks the necessary brightness and adaptability to get by. It is no one's fault—except perhaps his own—if he behaves stupidly, especially if others do their best to get him out of the hole he digs for himself. Our sympathy must be qualified a bit, surely, when we notice that he fails to observe the first law of holes: when in one, stop digging.

    That view of Jock is entirely reasonable. It is also consistent with our overall interpretation to accept it so far as it goes. What we argue is that Kennaway provides more of Jock—or more 'Jocks'—than that view might allow for.

We are told that Jock had led men in the desert, in Italy, France, Germany and Palestine, and that he had the authority and knack needed to inspire confidence—to steady them—with even a slight gesture (16). We are given only one glimpse of what he must have been like in action, and that comes from Barrow during their fateful final conversation. Barrow is making a great effort to be honest; and when he says he has great admiration for Jock as a result of his research into Battalion history, we may believe him.

> I know that desert campaign as if I'd been there myself. The night you took over, in the light of the flares. Five hundred were killed and wounded that night. Five hundred and forty-two officers and men, to be precise. Quite a battle. The wounded put their rifles, bayonet in the ground, to mark where they were. And you brought in the carriers, wasn't that it? Somebody had a phrase for you—I think it was the Pipe-Major—'Like a Bobby at a tattoo,' he said (136).

This amply testifies, of course, to Jock's self-discipline, courage and coolness. There is no suggestion that his was merely a bone-headed or reckless fearlessness. On the contrary, his authority seems to have been based on an ability to take the right decisions, on organisational skill under stress, on clear-headedness and realism. We find, as the novel progresses, that he is far from infallible in his assessment of men—or women. But he is not dumb or unperceptive either. He shows, as we shall see, greater insight into his own position than do some of the others most anxious to help him.

This capable Jock co-exists with another: the quintessential Scottish squaddie, the 'Jock' spoiling for a fight especially if he is aware of underlying dislikes and conflicts which (in his view) are best squared up to and thrashed out. He despises evasiveness and papering over cracks. However, there is an important qualification that must be made even as regards this side of his character. The street-fighter in him may bear some similarity to the roaring Scot always ready to fight anyone or anything so long as it is a good fight. But this wild man has learned how to control himself and expects proper discipline in others, however much he looks down on men who only know how to go by the book (one of the charges he hurls at Barrow (134)). This Jock can be a mercilessly hard man who 'never fought to finish with a handshake. He fought to kill' (134). He knows 'the down' of army life and is crafty enough to try a little gentle persuasion, or moral blackmail, on Pipe-Major McLean in the hope of getting the latter to forget the blow struck against Corporal-Piper Fraser. But when McLean, sadly but sternly, points out the simple reason the deed cannot be ignored (the Colonel was seen doing it!), Jock pushes no further: he accepts the code, an essential law which he readily enough distinguishes from the fussiness of army regulations (104–5).

There is another Jock who, for all his wildness, can be graceful, intuitive, artistic, and capable of a deep but flawed perceptiveness that expresses itself ultimately in the bizarre grandeur of his funereal vision of himself and the Battalion. The combination of gracefulness and wildness is established early on: in the opening scene in the Officers' Mess where we have already found him brooding like a caged animal after a full-dress supper. He has news for his brother officers and he must break the news himself, for his pride could not permit of anything else. Incredulously, they learn from him that there is to be new Colonel and that he is expected the very next day. There is a little not very well-informed chit-chat about the new man; but no one can find the right thing to say—rather the opposite. Jock remarks to his good old friend and comrade, Major Charlie Scott, that he himself is no good at talking at the best of times and suggests calling back the pipers. 'It fills in the gaps' (16); and Charlie, with what proves a significant terseness, agrees. So these men, Jock and his fellow officers, will let themselves go and celebrate their togetherness on the night of Jock's 'last supper' (15) with a dance. They will dance when they cannot speak.

> Jock danced with energy and with precision. He leapt high in the air and landed miraculously softly on the toes of his small feet. That was how he had been taught to dance and the others had to try and dance like him. They put their hands above their heads; they swung; they yelled; they hooched. Then they had a drink and they began all over again with a new dance (19).

His boorishness and gracelessness in some respects is matched by skill and adroitness in others; a ferocious boisterousness has its counterpoint in precision. Others may dance clumsily and ineptly, but not Jock. He may allow himself to be carried away by this music for which he has such a passion; but thus far, at least, it is a vehicle of self-expression over which he has control.

The second example of this side of Jock is even more telling and it occurs only a little later, after an extremely awkward interruption to these musical proceedings. Colonel Barrow arrives inopportunely and prematurely. Jock is enraged but successfully and politely conceals his discomfiture. Barrow, who clearly dislikes this noisy dancing as much as he dislikes whisky and 'whose tread was as light as his voice', soon finds an excuse to leave them to it: a diplomatic thing to do however much it coincides with his own need to escape the situation. After Barrow leaves them and the serious drinking really gets under way, Jock is melancholy. Again he tries and fails to get emotional reassurance from having a heart to heart chat with his anglified, womanising pal, Charlie Scott: who is for none of it. It is Charlie this time who remarks, 'We're not great talkers, Jock' (28). Once again, Jock calls for music, but this time for the pibroch from Corporal-Piper Fraser.

> To the unpractised ear a pibroch has no form and no melody, and to the accustomed ear it has little more. But it is a mood and a pibroch was something Jock felt almost physically; damp, penetrating and sad like a mist. It enveloped him and pulled at his heart. He was far too much the professional to be moved to tears, but the Corporal played well and it took a moment before Jock fully recovered himself (29–30).

We may note in passing that Jock has made some drunken remarks to the corporal, jokingly, on the subject of how healthy young soldiers might be expected to deal with lassies, along with a boozily solemn observation or two about his daughter and the responsibilities of fatherhood. His daughter's name is Morag. The corporal plays a tune called *Morag's Lament*. We also note how this music envelops Jock 'like a mist'; but he is not the man to be overcome, to let tears come to his eyes. Each and every one of these details, we need hardly say by now, will become sharp and vivid in retrospect as their significance—which Jock in no way suspects— becomes clear. In the meantime, blissfully unaware of some things he ought already to know, Jock demonstrates the surprisingly glorious skill he still has as a piper.

> In his trews, with his fat bottom waggling as he marched up and down the room, Jock looked comic. To begin with, he looked comic. But soon he was in the full rhythm of the tune, and he was absurd no longer. A good piper is like a rider who is one with his horse, and Jock was soon part of the music. He played some marches, with a fault or two; then a slow march; then a faultless pibroch. That is something that a man does only a few times in his life; and the Corporal was dumb with admiration (30).

Kennaway has slipped in a number of points about what people, including most Scots, commonly feel about pipe music, the pibroch especially. It seems formless, yet if one is drawn into the full rhythm of it, it can grip one like an intense mood. A performance on the pipes can sound merely noisy and look comic; yet it can become transformed into something stirring or in some other way moving. Formlessness and comicality on the one hand, an odd variety of emotional power and appeal on the other: a classically contradictory combination of Scottish qualities. Jock here makes his striking observation about pibroch being both a lament and an expression of anger. It is this combination most of all which finds its fullest expression in *Tunes of Glory* in Jock's envisaged production of Barrow's funeral. The key to Jock's dream of what that funeral should be like, what it is to celebrate and in what manner, lies in his intuition of what it is about life—and death—his favourite music conveys.

We would certainly argue, then, that in the one Jock there are many Jocks set together in a deliberately contradictory combination. If we argue, for example, that he shows more insight than he has sometimes been given credit for and that he has a kind of artist's sensibility, it is not to deny that he is also blundering and blind. There is a sense in which in the end after nearly drowning himself in fact, he drowns in his own blinding tears: the very same man who, passionate and emotional though he is, has been 'far too much the professional' to tolerate in himself the (effeminate) weakness of tears. All along, as well as being an archetypal commander, guardian and protector to his 'babies' (his men as well as his daughter Morag), he is also, as his mistress Mary Titterington repeatedly reminds him, 'a child' (147 and 149) who is apt to misconstrue what more ordinary and completely moulded adults are up to.

Later in his life, Kennaway was to see important links between the artist and the child and, more specifically, 'the baby'.

The artist is the baby. The baby is the boy I have had to protect since those first days at school . . . I'm not at all knowledgeable about clinical literature. But I'm *sure, sure, sure* other artists of awkward cut-off-your-nose-to-spite-your-face kind like myself have a baby within them to defend; and that baby is themself, but somewhere along the line the pain was unbearable and the character split, one part ruthless in defence, the other preserved in original innocence (*The Kennaway Papers*, 106).

Such a person, with an essential part of his personality thwarted as much as protected, is liable to be both creative and self-destructive, generous and malicious, highly aware in some respects and blind in others. These characteristics are recognisable in Jock Sinclair; so in him we see the beginnings—although we would stress only the beginnings—of that preoccupation which became so important to Kennaway. The important thing is what Mary Titterington recognises in Jock, the particular disparity between the child in him and the man: his 'innocence' in the sense of his failure to see through certain of his men, notably Charlie Scott.

When we consider the men surrounding Jock Sinclair one of the most conspicuous things about them is that they belong to a peculiarly exclusive order: not only that of the British army but that of a particular Battalion of a Scottish regiment. The subtle but pronounced differences in degrees of

exclusivity are emphasised again and again. The Battalion provides much
the most important nexus of relationships and loyalties. The title of Book I
is 'The Complexion of the Colonel' for the excellent reason that the
complexion of the Colonel is held to determine that of the Officers' Mess
and hence that of the Battalion (39). There is a hint of an analogy with a
clan and its chief. Indeed, towards the end of the Book II ('The Beating of
Retreat'), an egregiously fat-headed officer called Alec Rattray attempts to
explain not only Jock's misfortune but that of the entire Regiment as a
result of their desertion, as he sees it, of the ancient tradition of clan-based
recruitment and the implied weakening of the necessary loyalties. Rattray
is, of course, fatuously mistaken. (By the way, an added irony here is that
we are discussing a 'Campbell' Regiment: the Campbells of Argyll being
noted in history for their loyalty to regimes bent on destroying the old
Scottish clan system.) Nonetheless, both in the ethos of the Mess and the
trappings of the Battalion there is a bogus suggestiveness of that older
order: one of the thinner layers of unreality misting over the complex truth.

Part of that truth is that most of these officers require any psychological
props available, however artificial, to shield them from personal in-
adequacies as much as from the 'outside' world. That is one kind of
unreality which Kennaway suggests. We have already noticed his interest
in how these particular people—various kinds of Scotsman—often tend to
take refuge in excessive rigidity and correctness. Barrow himself is one of
these, Rattray another and RSM Riddick a third. Dusty Millar, the fat
Quartermaster, with his couple of tricks with a matchbox, is implicitly a
social inadequate: but he need only silently acquiesce in others' foibles to be
permitted to enjoy the musty congenialities of a venerable club. Jock
himself does not escape the charge of dubious kinds of dependence. His
very identity rests on his vision of the Battalion; his position depends in
part on his being able to exact a debt of loyalty; the Battalion loyalties he
keeps faith with prove illusory when set beside what the majority actually
feel. In reality, the Battalion is not a web of loyalties freely and generously
given; instead there is a precarious trade in mutual needs and ambitions. To
the extent he fails to see that much Jock is somewhat like a child.

The diversity of needs and ambitions lurking in these modern professional soldiers is in part real; it is also usually masked in order to maintain a
front of solidarity; and sometimes there is little more than the need to
sustain insubstantial vanities. One way and another, however, the officers
of the Mess are play-acting, their real or imagined interests at odds with the
gentlemanly and clubbish atmosphere they cultivate (and could perhaps
maintain more serenely without the robust presence of Jock). Kennaway
observes (39–40) that despite their indolent pose they 'were a set of anxious
and ambitious men, and some were extremely shrewd'. Their charade is

conducted in a setting as theatrical as a stage set complete with theatrical pictures of illustrious, 'fairy-tale' forebears. But 'the only thing they shared with their fairy-tale forefathers on the walls was their vanity, and even this took different forms'.

There is a delicious element of social comedy throughout in Kennaway's depiction of the social as well as personal incompatibilities which conflict with the pretence of cohesiveness in the Battalion. Jock sticks out, of course. But otherwise there is quite a spectrum. There is the foppish Sandy Macmillan simply waiting as elegantly and patiently as possible for a posting to a nice little UN lark. He is the nearest thing to the old officers-and-gentlemen set. Rattray is an aggressive and 'violently ambitious' Glasgow day-school boy rivalled only in his strict treatment of the men by his friend Jackson, who would not have been out of place among the Nazis whom he would so dearly have loved to kill. The two principal NCOs, RSM Riddick and Pipe-Major McLean, glower at each other through their ideological illusions from their opposing political trenches. McLean, the Highlander, an implacable enemy of patronage and snobbery, is sustained by his faith in merit and achievements and is a Liberal—or, as he endearingly reminds us, 'A Whig, a Whig, a Whig!' (54). Riddick is the perfect trusty custodian of his own conception of decent Tory order, to which the presence of Jock is a baffling affront. Major Charlie Scott is an Anglo-Scot with little left to offer the army or anyone else other than a fertile moustache, portentous silences and a fading raffish charm. Colonel Barrow's upbringing and education is actually stranger than most people suppose; but in that he has reputedly been to the right sort of places, he is instantly acceptable to 'the county' whose views on the matter are usually filtered through to us by way of *female* comments: a nice touch, this, in so male-dominated a world.

It is interesting that Kennaway selects the Adjutant, Jimmy Cairns, to be 'the least vain' of them all (41): that is, the man least swayed by ambition or fantasy. Jimmy is of the land: 'a mature farmer's boy in uniform', effective, fair-minded, judicious. For all his intelligence and because of his fairness, he has difficulty seeing some of the stranger aspects of what happens around him. And he is doomed to be much misunderstood by Jock. However, what he consistently stands for throughout the more lunatic goings-on is level-headed human understanding and sympathy. The character closest to him in that respect is Mr McLean. Like other Scottish novelists Kennaway turns to different parts of the Scottish rural landscape, lowland or highland, in search of touchstones of stability and sanity, although even the sane have their illusions (as we have seen).

These officers and men, cooped up together in their protective, regimented environment are not all what they seem. Most of them are

deceptive, or self-deceptive, or both. They are compelled to foster the
pretence, at least, of belonging to a close-knit brotherhood: the world of a
Battalion of a distinctively and cohesively Scottish Regiment. Yet they are
in a number of crucial respects 'foreign' even to each other. Their foreign-
ness to each other is something which Kennaway gently but very
deliberately underscores on a number of occasions. Corporal-Piper Fraser,
for example, comes from the southern shore of the Moray Firth.

> It is like a foreign land, and the people speak their English slowly, and with a mild
> intonation, as if they were translating from a foreign tongue (19).

Then there is the young subaltern, MacKinnon, whom Jock cruelly ticks off
early in the book for puffing at his cigarette like 'a bloody debutante' (11).
Towards the end of Book II, Jock is genuinely pleased by the lad's
gumption and sees through his own social prejudice; yet he marvels at a
strange and until then impenetrable difference between their worlds.

> Jock couldn't get over his expressions.
> ' "Thanks most awfully." Dammit, dammit,' he said, 'It's a different language
> altogether' (173).

Most crucially of all, there is a remark made by Barrow ('That's always the
way in a foreign country' (133)) during his confessional interview with
Jock. Barrow is referring specifically to the Battalion and to his wariness
within its territory. But shortly afterwards he links his return to the
Battalion with his return to Scotland, wistfully reflecting on how the
thought of such a homecoming—to a place where he once was happy—
kept him going as a POW of the Japanese. But there can be no such
homecoming to that imagined Battalion-cum-homeland. To Jock, of
course, Barrow is very 'foreign' in that he seems not to belong to the world
of men as he understands it, let alone to the world of the Battalion and its
Colonel as he has imagined it.

Kennaway, we recall, has described this world of the Battalion—this
mixture of unrealities, pretence and submerged realities—as being largely
hidden from the outside world. It is also virtually cut off from much of that
outside world, even from the conflicts going on out there. Ironically,
Barrow is the one who keeps most in touch with that exterior reality.

> He had a habit of discussing general political news, perhaps because he always
> knew more of current affairs than any of his colleagues. For the most part the
> officers lived body and soul within the limits of the high wall; Macmillan could
> gossip a little on social items, but even he was inclined to concentrate on county

news. Some of the other more earnest officers knew something of the disturbances in other parts of the globe, Malaya, Kenya or Korea, because they had friends there, but by and large they were innocent of world, and even of national, affairs (109–10).

Jock does not speak of such things. There is at least one extraordinary but crucial reason for this. Nothing going on currently in the outside world or the inturned world of the barracks can possibly be as real to him as the past and those who haunt him from the past. The most important thing in the past for Jock is, naturally, World War II and his own part in it. It is a subject which others are very interested to hear him speak about:

> . . . because he never spoke much of the days of his glory. It would have been impossible for him to recall truthfully one week of the campaign without sounding now as if he were bragging, and something made him brag about other things. They had all heard about his piping and his boxing days, the days he had told the Sergeant-Major off, and so on and on. But this was the very first time some of them had heard him speak of the war . . . (118).

But the past is present. His comrades are there: dead or alive they are more substantial in that they weigh upon him more heavily than any other living soul. As Jock's decline into his final, brilliantly illuminated madness begins, we find this:

> Exhaustion swept over him, leaving him ragged and apprehensive, too tired to think and too excited to sleep, even now. Worst of all, he knew, as he had known every night since that night in the desert, that in the morning they would be waiting for him to cope with the thing, and suddenly he did not want to cope any longer (175).

'That night' is the night he first had to take over command. 'They' are all his own comrades; but they are also all the officers and men of the Battalion that ever were, and even the men of all such armies, just as Jock depicted in his long greatcoat is the figure who:

> had moved from platoon to platoon when the snow was falling on a flatter, duller land: in every war, back and back, in every siege and trouble that same figure existed and exists: the anonymous commander in the long coat moving through the night, alone. He is the guard (92).

It is this image of himself, as custodian of the Battalion's spirit and protector of his 'babies', that Jock betrays by striking the corporal. It is the source of his vanity that he personifies the Battalion, has an intrinsic right to be its leader, and as such could not conceivably be betrayed by an old comrade-in-arms like Charlie Scott. But the Guard is solitary, more isolated than he imagines for all the bottled up tears and love of which he becomes aware. His sense of himself is only in part well founded in the deep awareness and respect he feels for the needs, fears, quirks and sacrifices of soldiers. For his isolation has bred one unreality that is a crushing burden—and another which is as much a self-deluding 'fairy-tale' version of affairs as that which his forebears created of themselves. He has been attempting to sustain this fragile, fairy-tale version of Colonel and Battalion with more and more drink, by more and more extravagant posturing and rugged conviviality. His own efforts have been undermining it.

The reasons why Jock should so hate the nervy, bookish, punctilious, unconvivial, lightly-treading and soft-speaking Colonel Barrow are fairly self-evident. However, it is not Barrow's role merely to provide a hapless foil for Jock's ferocious jealousy. He is more interesting than that as a character in his own right. He is a liar who desperately wants to be honest. He is a man seeking a home and self-fulfilment. Both of these are sure indications of Kennaway's interest in him. Moreover, again we find Kennaway's liking for counterpoint. Barrow is in his own way appallingly lonely and burdened. Also, Barrow is 'a child'. We know because the ladies say so.

> Sometimes, and all of a sudden, they felt that it was only right that he should be called Boy. In spite of the grey hair, he looked like a child at a party; looked as if he had lost his way. And that, to regimental women, is something very attractive: their own husbands are always so vehement in protesting that they know where they are going (62).

Indeed he has lost his way: or, quite possibly, he never rightly knew where it lay. He certainly has a gift for making the wrong move. No dancer himself, he gets off on entirely the wrong foot when he first attempts to assert his authority by insisting that all officers—including Jock—must have early morning lessons to teach them how to dance in a seemly, disciplined, regimental manner (42). The new Colonel appears to imagine that what he is doing will be recognised as a sign of a restoration of civilised decorum and dignity: a rejection of the barbarism and vulgarity represented by Jock. Instead, this attack on their performance on the dance floor is widely regarded by the officers as an insult to both manhood and nationality, and we note the observation (42) that the man delivers his orders without a trace of a Scottish accent. So when eventually (and, we may suppose, unenthusiastically) he responds to numerous invitations and general social pressure by permitting a regimental cocktail party, it is very easy for the crafty Jock to ensure that an innocent little dance soon becomes provocatively rumbustious. Barrow visibly loses all control of himself. Round One to Jock. Kennaway plays what is perhaps a little self-deprecatory joke by having the mouse-like doctor, a very minor character, remark that: 'It's surely significant that the quarrel should have revolved round such a primitive thing as folk dancing' (68): a remark which is at once pooh-poohed. These men have no use for fancy theorising. But the reader will take the doctor's point, regardless of how he puts it.

Meantime, the Adjutant Jimmy Cairns has rushed out after Barrow; for Jimmy, in spite of his enduring loyalty to Jock, is angered by the merciless cruelty of the trap laid for the new man. As a result of Jimmy's kindliness, Barrow unbends sufficiently to reveal at least a little of himself. He is anxious that as a result of his POW experiences he might have become 'cranky', as he puts it (72). He is divorced. He admits to having been lonely—even that that is one of the reasons he has taken this job. He is terribly afraid of ridicule, saying: 'Ridicule's always the finish. You know that?' (70). Clearly, he is in desperate need of reassurance; for he clings 'childlike' to the first brisk thing Jimmy can think of saying to put his performance in the Mess in a more favourable light.

Barrow's accounts of himself are always limited: brief and clipped. Evidently, he has the greatest difficulty when it comes to revealing anything about himself. He lacks self-confidence. He has no real outlet for self-expression. What we learn about him is fragmentary, an incomplete detail here and there. Much the most important of these glimpses concerns his upbringing. It turns out that, contrary to rumour, his sojourn at Eton or any other school has been brief. He has been privately educated, although he doesn't quite explain why. There is a very strong hint here of another aspect of Kennaway's developing concern with the relationship between childhood and self-expression in adulthood. In Barrow's case the suggestion is that a repressed, solitary and thwarted childhood lies behind the anxious adult personality much more than anything the Japanese may have done to distort it further. That much adds up. What puzzles Jimmy Cairns (73) is something that doesn't fit: an unexpected burst of confidence from Barrow at the end of their evening when he declares that being Colonel of the Battalion is far from the height or the end of his ambitions.

Jimmy is right to be puzzled. Barrow is lying. He finds it in general difficult not to lie about himself. Until their final conversation together, he finds it utterly impossible to tell the truth to Jock.

He seemed incapable of speaking the truth to Jock. He was almost like a son with a father too fierce: in order not to offend he told a half-truth, until the time came when he found it more natural to lie. It was perfectly obvious to him why he did this. Everything about Jock frightened him. His authority, his unpredictability, his bluntness. It was more than that. The very depth of his voice and the thickness of his forearm made Barrow afraid (121).

The suggested link between the personality of Jock and that of Barrow's own father is fairly irresistible.

Yet at this juncture in the story Jock is, at least in a formal sense, at Barrow's mercy. Jock has already hit the corporal. True, neither his self-image nor his fighting powers have as yet been completely undermined. But he is already seriously weakened by what he considers treachery on his daughter Morag's part and by his own remorse at striking Corporal-Piper Fraser merely for being in his daughter's company. Moreover, what with all his drinking and the nervous strain he is dangerously near a breaking point although only just managing to disguise the fact. It is a moment, really the very last moment, for parley and a negotiated peace within the Battalion. Jock is willing. Barrow dodges the issue, fearfully. He refuses a drink, refuses to talk, lies about what he is going off to do, then leaves (121).

Later the same day, when Jock and Barrow have their finale meeting (in Charlie Scott's room where Jock has been sleeping off those lunchtime drams), Barrow is in a state of irresolvable moral and emotional conflict. On the one hand, he wants to be honest with Jock as perhaps he never has been with anyone before: honest about himself and his need for a place among men, for a home, for this Battalion; honest, too, in his admiration for Jock. On the other hand, this agonisingly unself-confident man cannot function without reference to the certainties and clarities of the letter of the law. His attempts to be honest and self-revealing with Jock are rooted in a need for compassionate understanding, flexibility and forgiveness. The only way he knows how to behave (even allowing for his guilty habit of lying and self-concealment) is to be seen to follow out regulations and procedures to their conclusions. He is in an impossible bind and it shows in the way he speaks.

> 'I genuinely hope Brigade decides to dismiss the thing. I can assure you I would support any such recommendation.'
> The Colonel seemed to want to say something quite different and quite plain but his words, like his feelings, were half strangled. He turned, expecting some encouragement: some reward for his gesture. He wanted more than anything in the world the relief of a handshake (133–4).

But it is Jock who is merciless at this point. He listens implacably as Barrow rambles on 'almost to spite himself or purge himself' (136); but from his position he cannot give Barrow the fatherly absolution, so to speak, which he seeks.

And Jock's position is this. He still harbours hopes (and, as regards Charlie Scott, the illusion) that others will rally round to defend him. Nonetheless, there is enough of his old realism there for him to have realised somewhat fatalistically that he is liable to be busted. He has even confessed, to an embarassed Charlie, that he thinks that Mary was right in calling him a bore (126). Still, if clemency is not to be freely and generously given, it is not permitted in Jock's code to beg for it. The two Colonels are in a hopeless impasse.

Even when Barrow emerges into the open air the entire barracks seems to him like a prison, with the sky as a low roof. He meets Mr Riddick who, to his astonishment, suggests re-considering the matter. Barrow dithers, first refusing and then, as he is having second thoughts, he is so maddened by an Orderly's innocent reference to one of Jock's little habits that he despairs of ridding himself ever of that giant ghost. Having told Jock that he is going to shoot ducks, Barrow disappears—and shoots himself. Jock will yet hold himself responsible for that death too. He will feel that he should have 'seen it coming' (174).

However, at the time of that meeting with Barrow there is still a lot Jock has failed to understand or has reacted to mistakenly. There is a web of betrayals or merely apparent betrayals which he has failed to sort out.

Morag certainly didn't intend to betray him by going out with Corporal-Piper Fraser. Her act of deception was perhaps unwise (saying she had gone out with her friend Jenny); but it is one of the most trivial and innocent ruses anyone performs in the book. Perhaps Morag, with her common sense and her 'efficient presbyterian modesty', has been unable to appreciate the wealth of emotion which her father has invested in the security of their life together. She can hardly be blamed for that.

Then there is the tangled affair of Jock, Mary Titterington and Charlie Scott. Mary Titterington is, in this male-dominated cast of play-actors, an actress in her thirties; and the downward incline in her career has brought her north to play for a repertory company. We learn (34) that Jock has ditched her: a fact that no doubt damaged her self-esteem and increased her sense of isolation still further. So, when eventually Jock goes back to seek solace with her, it's the more surprising that his drunken advances are repulsed so kindly, if firmly; and Mary puts him to bed to sleep it off. When he awakes (having been disturbed by a 'sort of dream' (85)), he finds Charlie there. Jock doesn't mind this, really. He and his old mate Charlie have shared girls before and it has never made any difference to their friendship. What Jock doesn't grasp is that the resentment is the other way round: Charlie is upset at the thought—the realisation, indeed—that Mary still finds Jock a more attractive man than him.

Charlie Scott's cold refusal to back Jock up, or at least put in some plea in mitigation, horrifies Jimmy Cairns. In part, this is an expression of a self-lacerating pessimism which Charlie has concealed from others: 'Don't let it give you ulcers, Jimmy. They'll do the same to you and me one day' (112). Mary knows that Charlie was also acting out of sexual jealousy. Eventually, she has the courage to tell Jock three things: that Charlie did abandon him to Barrow's justice; that jealousy was a motive; and that she has been in love with him, Jock, all along. At first Jock angrily rejects the first two suggestions, then seeks 'honourable' reasons for any such behaviour on Charlie's part (146–8); and even then his mind cannot fully tolerate the possibility. For betrayal by a wartime comrade is the crucial, shattering betrayal which he dare not contemplate. It is only later, when the idiot Rattray confirms what Mary has said (158), that we see at last the first of the flow of pent up tears which, in Book III ('The Funeral Orders'), finally carry Jock away in a geat flood of emotion. (And, Rattray being an idiot, he totally unfairly implicates poor Jimmy Cairns in Charlie's treachery.)

As for Mary's love, Jock has never allowed himself to recognise it or believe in it explicitly before. It belongs to the world of 'soft' emotions which this most macho of Scotsmen fears. Even now he cannot give himself up to its (possibly saving) protection; although he does make a futile attempt to do it honour by trying and failing to arrange for them to have supper together (156): as he says, 'just for old times' sake' (152).

> But even as he spoke, and patted her, his mind wandered away. She seemed to sense this and she pushed closer and closer to him in despair while he looked over her shoulder into the long mirror at the sad soldier there (153).

The image in the mirror is mute. It is ghostly. Jock's 'fairy-tale' is destroyed and there can be no happy ending. Jock sees he is done.

Jock reaches his lowest point of depression after his failure to arrange that supper for Mary and himself, after Rattray's convincing—although muddled—confirmation of Jock's worst fears and after the pair of them have re-visited the hotel where Jock hit Fraser. There they join some sympathetic sergeants and others in a sing-song. 'Like all drunk men, they got round to the sad tunes' (161). Then they twice sing *We're no awa' to bide awa'* and *I belong to Glasgow* for good measure. But none of it is enough to lift Jock. At last, he manages to shake off Rattray, sending him with a message of apology to Mary. We next see Jock through young MacKinnon's eyes, standing on a bridge. We realise that he is on the very point of throwing himself in the river.

However, MacKinnon brings news of that other suicide, Barrow's. When this has sunk in and Jock recognises the ironic coincidence of his own intentions and Barrow's action, he suddenly says:

> Och, we'll away out of here. It's a lonely place, the bridge, neither one side of the river, nor the other (167).

They go to Jock's house and, like MacKinnon, we are astonished to find it in a shambles and are dazzled by the glittering pre-war dress uniform which Jock is wearing. Evidently, he had decided to indulge his passion for dressing up one last time.

But now, if there can be no happy ending, there can at least be a defiant one. 'A colonel does not need an arm to strike with; he needs teeth to hang on with' (176). Jock has just enough bitter determination to hang on a while yet, to create an ending full of bravado and a sombre grandeur. He has not lost his earthy sense of humour, either, as regards his own immortality. As he looks for the last time at the book of nursery rhymes he had been fond of reading to Morag, and as he unseeingly scans the lines of a fairy story he had written for her, he already feels 'as if he were looking at it from another world'. Then the opening lines of a rude barrackroom ballad occur to him. 'The thought of that gave him just a little relief and he clenched his fists together' (176).

Book III, 'The Funeral Orders', consists of a single scene only some twenty pages long. It opens with Jock very brisk, crisp and in unchallenged command of the situation, having called his Order Group—the officers and senior NCOs—together in the piping-room to hear their instructions.

> INTENTION:
> The Battalion will bury the Colonel (181).

It ends with Jock's disintegration. He can no longer hang on. He has lost the place, lost self-possession and therefore lost command. But how are we to read this last section? Has Kennaway himself gone over the top, yielding to heady Scottish sentimentality in a celebration of martial glory in a burial of Battalion, Jock and all?

There is no doubt that Jock intends, before he goes, to hurl in the faces of small-hearted and impious men a spectacular commemoration of the dead of all ranks: an expression of pity and love for them all, including Barrow, whatever the circumstances of their disastrous fall. There is also no doubt that what Jock proposes is not only out of order (a martial funeral of a kind reserved for marshals), it is preposterous in a way more likely to embarrass than it is to produce the emotions Jock understandably demands. Jock is always too much: in the way 'Jocks' are liable to be, especially when their emotions finally run riot. But discriminating people, such as Mr McLean and Jimmy Cairns, can nonetheless see something truly and harrowingly pitiable in what he is driving at, for all the superfluous grandiosity and the overblown tunes of glory. That, it seems to us, is what Kennaway is putting before the reader—in a *tour de force* of melodramatic writing, neatly punctured where need be by deflating gasps and comments.

It is an extraordinary thing that for all the importance of martial prowess in Scottish cultural mythology, Kennaway's *Tunes of Glory* is the only modern novel to confront themes and stereotypes related to that inheritance and mythology as filtered through the Officers' Mess. We have argued throughout that, within the confines of a relatively brief and very punchy dramatic story, Kennaway has managed to provide a remarkable range of insights. Part of the success of the book no doubt lies in the fact that it is so clear in its intentions and execution. When Kennaway uses and exploits stereotypes to create an atmosphere or move the action along or provide comment, then he as it were openly declares that he is doing so. There are, indeed, elements of stereotype in all the characters, including the major ones. The fascinating thing is that, given variation and individuation by Kennaway, they provide such a wealth of credible feeling and action.

FURTHER READING

Our references are to the Mainstream edition of 1980.

James Kennaway was born in Perthshire in 1928, and educated at Glenalmond and Trinity College, Oxford. He served as an officer in the Cameron Highlanders. He worked as an editor for Longmans Green from 1951 to 1957, and then became a more or less fulltime writer of novels and filmscripts. His major novels are: *Tunes of Glory* (1956), *Household Ghosts* (1961), *The Bells of Shoreditch* (1963), *Some Gorgeous Accident* (1967), *The Cost of Living Like This* (1969), and the posthumous fragment *Silence* (1972). He wrote several screenplays, including that for *Tunes of Glory*, and *The Mind Benders*, a film about brain-washing of which he wrote a book version afterwards. He also wrote a play *Country Dance*, which was performed at the Edinburgh Festival in 1967. Kennaway died in a car crash in 1968, having suffered a heart attack, at the tragically early age of forty.

Interesting light is shed on Kennaway, his life and work in a book recently edited and published by his widow, as *The Kennaway Papers* by James and Susan Kennaway (1981). Trevor Royle has produced the biography, *James and Jim: A biography of James Kennaway*, 1983. The last two works mentioned above, and the recent republication by Mainstream of almost the complete oeuvre, indicate an early renaissance of interest in Kennaway. Critical approaches so far include:

Francis Russell Hart, *The Scottish Novel: A Critical Survey* (1978)

Duncan McAra, 'James Kennaway' in *London Magazine* 18(8) (February 1978), 37–55

Allan Massie, 'The Artful Art of James Kennaway' in *New Edinburgh Review Anthology* (ed James Campbell) (1982), 124–35

Bob Tait, 'Scots Apart: The Novels of James Kennaway and Gordon Williams' in *Cencrastus* 5 (Summer 1981), 20–2

CHAPTER SIX

Muriel Spark:
The Prime of Miss Jean Brodie

Three very different novelists of our ten have one thing in common; an adult conversion to Roman Catholicism. They are Fionn MacColla, Muriel Spark and George Mackay Brown. Brown we must meantime leave to one side: his religious beliefs form an integral part of a personal vision of natural harmony in *Greenvoe*. Can anything useful be said in comparing such disparate novelists as MacColla and Spark? Well, both are concerned with Scottish Calvinism in their novels. MacColla reacted vigorously against an extreme Calvinist upbringing, and makes his critique of Calvinism central to all his novels. Spark, on the other hand, was raised in Edinburgh, with an English mother, a Jewish father and a conventionally Presbyterian schooling: perhaps like Sandy Stranger she missed having Calvinism to react against. But *The Prime of Miss Jean Brodie* also centres on a critique of the impact of Calvinist thinking, and a magnificent reincarnation of the concept of the Justified Sinner.

Both novelists manage to raise an exceptionally wide range of issues in the apparently narrow contexts of their novels, and to view them in some sense *sub specie aeternitatis*. In both *And the Cock Crew* and *The Prime of Miss Jean Brodie* there is treatment of religion, politics, history, sexuality and art—and the idea of betrayal is central to both. The betrayals in *And the Cock Crew*, as we have seen, are multiple, while the obvious case in *The Prime of Miss Jean Brodie* is the betrayal of Jean Brodie by Sandy Stranger—with a clearly arguable prior betrayal of the set by Miss Brodie. MacColla and Spark both choose a central character who is in some sense 'of' the Calvinist enemy, and each treats this central character with sympathy and understanding, so that the character is eventually seen as both attractive and misguided: we remember Sandy and Jenny completing their literary rendition of the love letters of Miss Brodie and Gordon Lowther, finding it 'a delicate question how to present Miss Brodie in both a favourable and an unfavourable light, for now . . . nothing less than this was demanded' (72). MacColla's instinct is to go for the jugular, and so in his denunciation of the naysaying qualities of Scottish Calvinism he chooses as his central character a minister of the kirk: Spark also goes for a traditionally central element, education. But the differences are clearly much more striking. MacColla expresses his central interests by writing a historical novel which demonstrates to his satisfaction the historical ill effects of the naysaying of Calvinism on Scotland, while Spark expresses hers vitally in relation to her own century—indeed, to the city in which she spent her own school days—and the most important political movements of the time. Where MacColla is making a case, fairly clearly preaching, she is very 'laid back', and refuses to intrude judgements in her novel. And of course, most crucially, she transforms the traditional figure of the dominie into an unusual woman schoolteacher at a privileged girls' school.

All the same, perhaps these two novels have more to say than the others about the nature and character of the Calvinist tradition underlying Scottish life.

Spark refuses to intrude judgements, we say, but the matter is more complex than that. Can we find Muriel Spark anywhere in her fiction? *Miss Jean Brodie* seems to have two narrative centres, the developing consciousness of Sandy Stranger, and a third person narrator who is apparently uncommitted and factual. But we should not over-readily accept this appearance: Mrs Spark has commented on this problem, in a piece called 'My Conversion', published in 1961, the year of the novel:

> With a novel, you know the dialogue. It belongs to each character. But the narrative part—first or third person—belongs to a character as well. I have to decide what the author of the narrative is like. It's not me, it's a character.

The narrator in this novel has a splendid sense of comedy, and is no respecter of persons; and the wit usually economically serves some satiric purpose or undermines a mood or attitude. Irony is pervasive. We can look at our first experience of the tale of Miss Brodie's lost lover, Hugh (12–13). We are nowhere told that Miss Brodie is being wildly romantic and self-indulgent, with apparently no awareness of the realities of the war in which her lover died. Her own prose tells us this, as she starts with an unacknowledged quotation from Keats, 'Season of mists and mellow fruitfulness', and latches onto that alliterated 'f' sound to make Hugh's death insubstantial, melancholy and beautiful: 'He fell on Flanders' Field. . . . He fell. . . . He fell like an autumn leaf.' The narrator effectively punctures the mood while reinforcing the alliteration by referring to 'the story of Miss Brodie's felled fiancé', while Miss Brodie, unheeding, goes on to describe Hugh, inevitably, as 'one of the Flowers of the Forest'.

The witty comment can be lightly satirical in a religious dimension, as when gaunt mistresses say 'good morning' to Miss Brodie 'with predestination in their smiles' (75), or it can accumulate in gentle mockery of Miss Brodie's behaviour and attitudes, as she declaims 'The Lady of Shalott' with a dedication worthy of Sybil Thorndike, and perhaps too many decibels: 'Miss Brodie's voice soared up to the ceiling, and curled round the feet of the Senior girls upstairs' (21–2). Miss Brodie enjoins composure in the full flow of her peculiar declamatory speech—'It is one of the best assets of a woman, an expression of composure, come foul, come fair. Regard the Mona Lisa over yonder!' The narrator punctures the mood again:

> Mona Lisa in her prime smiled in steady composure even though she had just come from the dentist and her lower jaw was swollen (22).

The actual narration in the novel is sometimes direct from this ironic, witty but non-aggressive narrator, and often a rendition of Sandy's thoughts by the narrator. Apart from the ubiquitous witty phrases, the narrator is usually careful not to comment. She (it is surely a woman?) stands back, never judging, and only occasionally offering analysis. We come to recognise these occasions as particularly important, from their very rarity, whether it be the context offered for Miss Brodie by the description of the 'war-bereaved spinsterhood' of Edinburgh (42), or the passages where the narrator looks closely at Miss Brodie and religion (85–6), or at Miss Brodie looking for a confidante (105), or at Sandy's attempts to come to terms with religion (108–9).

Sandy emerges as a central consciousness in chapter two, and we gradually come to accept her as a fairly reliable guide, as we outgrow our distaste for her little piggy eyes—or indeed become irritated with the narrator for such insistence on them. Although we learn fairly early that it was Sandy who betrayed Miss Brodie (60), we do tend to trust her reactions to people, events, churches, only remaining slightly uneasy about her clutching the bars of the grille—from nervous tension? a false vocation? fear? guilt?

There are other specific narrative techniques which Spark utilises to help us in our understanding of the action: Muriel Spark's refusal to judge for us does not remove the necessity for judgement, but transfers it to the reader as part of the required response. The novel can be seen as a complex problem requiring solution, arranged in both a helpful and a challenging way to facilitate the reader's exercise of judgement.

The chief and most obtrusive of these techniques is to do with chronology. Conventional chronology is continually interrupted with glimpses of future occasions, and future assessments of present issues. Thus we find terrible ironies, for example in the case of Mary Macgregor. Mary is appallingly treated throughout the novel: the description 'the nagged child' (29) is a gross understatement. But we know from the end of the first chapter that Mary will die in a fire at the age of twenty-three, and from the beginning of the next that she will look back on these days of bullying and victimisation as the happiest days of her life. This dismal irony is kept firmly in our awareness, just as Vonnegut keeps the doom of 'poor old Edgar Derby', shot for stealing a teapot in the ruins of Dresden, in the forefront of our consciousness from beginning to end of *Slaughterhouse Five*.

The departure from simple conventional chronology offers a picture of a developing scene: in the first chapter we meet the Brodie set at sixteen—and at ten. We gradually develop a double awareness, not particularly conscious or clear cut at the first reading, of the attractions of Miss Brodie to the ten-year-olds of 1930, and the dangers inherent in her and apparent to Sandy by 1938. In all this we get a lively sense of the whole of Jean Brodie's 'prime', and all sorts of ironies and insights are implicit in our early learning that Miss Brodie was betrayed (27), and that Sandy betrayed her (60), and in the retrospective conversations different members of the set have with Sandy in her convent throughout, given in 'flash-forward', as it were.

In fact, the departures from conventional chronology are fewer than at first appears, and almost always brief: the narrator employs the economy of method Sandy admires in the methods of Teddy Lloyd and Miss Brodie (101) and employs herself in the betrayal. With the exceptions noted above, the novel progresses straightforwardly enough. After the introduction to the sixteen-year-olds, chapter one gives us the beginnings of the Brodie set and our introduction to this amazing teacher and her unconventional methods, and chapter two concentrates on the first year with Miss Brodie, especially the walk through old Edinburgh. Chapter three covers the second year with Miss Brodie, in more senses than one 'the sexual year', as the little girls are preoccupied with sexuality and Miss Brodie falls in love with one master and embarks on an affair with another. This emotional situation for Miss Brodie continues in chapter four, when the Brodie set moves up into the Senior school for session 1932–3. After this, things are telescoped: three years are virtually omitted, and chapter five deals with the girls in fourth year, 1935–36, while in chapter six at age eighteen Sandy leaves school, has her affair with Teddy Lloyd and betrays Miss Brodie.

Another very effective narrative device is juxtaposition of scenes or characters so that a vivid effect of comparison or ironic contrast can be created without overt comment. Early in the novel, the introduction of Miss Brodie is interrupted by a terse little paragraph about Marcia Blaine, founder of the school, like and unlike Miss Brodie. Widow to Miss Brodie's spinster, admirer of Italian patriot Garibaldi and his 'red shirts' to Miss Brodie's celebrator of Mussolini and his 'black shirts', Marcia Blaine is economically described by reference to her 'manly portrait'—Miss Brodie is the eternal feminine. The ethos of Marcia Blaine's school, with which Miss Brodie is so much at odds, is implicit in the Founder's Day bunch 'of hard-wearing flowers' (6), as well as the Bible text underlining a traditional notion of female virtue. (Incidentally, Mrs Spark has a little joke at our expense here: Blaine is an unusual surname, but a biographical dictionary may offer us a nineteenth-century American journalist and statesman called Blain, whose first names were James Gillespie. Spark herself attended James Gillespie's Girls' School in Edinburgh, and Marcia Blaine's is very clearly based on it.)

Again, in the walk in chapter two, Sandy's understanding of the set as 'a body with Miss Brodie for the head' (30) is balanced by her vision of the queue of unemployed men as 'one dragon's body . . . the snaky creature' (40), and through her meditation we see the Brodie girls, the Girl Guides and Mussolini's fascisti as oddly similar. A final telling instance where juxtaposition lends resonance is in chapter three, everybody's 'sexual year'. After Jenny's experience with the 'terrible beast' who exposed himself, Sandy falls in love with her imagined image of Jenny's policewoman, whom she interestingly decides to call Sergeant Anne Grey, and in Sandy's fantasy the two set out, 'dedicated' (Sandy is not Miss Brodie's pupil for nothing) 'to eliminate sex from Edinburgh and environs' (68). This immediately precedes the scene where Miss Brodie and Teddy Lloyd have an implicitly charged conversation about Cramond, the home village of Gordon Lowther, and Miss Brodie puts her arm round Rose's shoulder and thanks Teddy Lloyd, 'as if she and Rose were one' (70). Thus early, and however unconsciously, while Sandy is reacting against sexuality, Miss Brodie is beginning to manipulate Rose into her own sexual fantasies. The comment through Sandy can apply to the juxtaposing technique as well as the developing relationship between teacher and pupil: it is both intriguing and forward-pointing:

Sandy was fascinated by this method of making patterns with facts, and was divided between her admiration for the technique and the pressing need to prove Miss Brodie guilty of misconduct (72).

The final specific technique we will point to here is the effect of introducing parallel situations. One central example should suffice. It is clear to most people reading the book that both Jean Brodie and Sandy Stranger to some extent lead fantasy lives, or double lives. It is made most clear in Sandy's case, where her imaginary life is a preventive for boredom (21), and is nourished for the most part by her reading—which is directed to a considerable extent by Miss Brodie. Apart from the joint literary compositions with Jenny, we are introduced to Sandy's double life in a bizarre conversation she holds with the Lady of Shalott, who bears, here, a certain resemblance to Miss Brodie (chanting in the classroom the while). Miss Brodie's choice of poem is significant, dealing as it does with a Lady who is destroyed by turning from shadow to reality. Sandy holds a series of romantic conversations with Alan Breck from Stevenson's *Kidnapped*, involved in quest and cause and chivalry, quite transfiguring the commonplace sections of the famous walk through old Edinburgh when she would otherwise have to attend to the tiresome Mary: the 'real life' fantasy here (31), of a married lady and her husband, is brief and comparatively very unsatisfactory. Later Sandy moves on to Mr Rochester (58): Miss Brodie has been reading out *Jane Eyre* during sewing lessons. And later still, after Miss Brodie's inspired teaching and a trip to the theatre, she moves on to Pavlova, and has a delicious conversation, one diva to another, soulful, melancholy, and irresistibly funny. Again Pavlova smacks of Miss Brodie, and much of the comic effect rises from that one extravagant detail, the claw:

> 'Sandy,' said Anna Pavlova, 'you are the only truly dedicated dancer, next to me. Your dying Swan is perfect, such a sensitive, final tap of the claw upon the floor of the stage . . .' (63).

The last example of Sandy's fantasy life is her invention of Sergeant Anne Grey. The interesting things to notice are that Sandy seems always quite conscious of the difference between fantasy and reality, and that we see no more such fancies after she leaves the Junior school.

Miss Brodie's double life is less easy to chart, because we see her only from outside and from her speech, and it is harder to know when she is fantasising completely and when embroidering fact (as in the new picture of Hugh after her greater awareness of both Teddy Lloyd and Gordon Lowther). It does seem clear that she gradually drifts further into fantasy, and determines to make it into reality, when she determines to use Rose to sleep with Teddy Lloyd by proxy. And of course she leads a very conventional kind of 'double life' when she combines the roles of correct Edinburgh spinster schoolmistress and weekend lover to Gordon Lowther: this seems to cause her no trouble. She lays claim to the long tradition of double life or split personality in the Scottish Calvinist consciousness (e.g. Hogg's *Justified Sinner*, Stevenson's *Dr Jekyll and Mr Hyde*) when she claims to be descended from one of the archetypes, Deacon Brodie. As she relates (88), Deacon Brodie was a pious and respected Edinburgh householder who had a conventional double life, keeping mistresses and indulging in cock-fighting, and he became a burglar by night for the sake of the excitement and danger involved, and died at last for these crimes on a gibbet he designed himself as justicer: 'it is the stuff I am made of', declares Miss Brodie. The character of Deacon Brodie for many years fascinated Robert Louis Stevenson, like Mrs Spark another notable exile from Edinburgh. He collaborated with Henley to write a play on Deacon Brodie, and this historical character lies behind his most famous novella of double life, *The Strange Case of Dr Jekyll and Mr Hyde*. Miss Brodie's double life is more subtle and much more alarming than Sandy's, and instead of growing out of it, like the little girl, she gets imperceptibly more enmeshed in a complex web of fact and fantasy, and a gradual determination to flesh out her fantasies.

But the notion of a double life does not finish with Sandy and Miss Brodie. Oscar Wilde wrote an essay called 'Pen, Pencil and Poison', about a poet and painter, Thomas Wainewright, who was also a forger and a secret poisoner. Teddy Lloyd's double life is by no means as sensational as this, but it lasts over years and bears some little resemblance to Wainewright's. Wilde quotes a Zola murderer who paints respectable people so that they all bear a curious resemblance to his victim; and he says that Wainewright put the expression of his own wickedness into the portrait of a nice young girl. Teddy Lloyd surely owes something to Wainewright and Zola, as he turns out portrait after portrait of the Brodie set, each bearing an uncanny resemblance to Miss Brodie, each secretly confessing his fascination with her. Sandy precipitates her affair with him when she shocks him by claiming that 'all his portraits, even that of the littlest Lloyd baby, were now turning out to be likenesses of Miss Brodie' (122), suggesting that Miss Brodie has completely taken over his life and art; and it is Sandy's curiosity about Teddy Lloyd's secret love for Miss Brodie that is central to her interest in him, before she is infected by his Catholicism. If we begin to see double lives everywhere, it is not necessarily just our imagination: in an interview with Frank Kermode Mrs Spark acknowledges this tendency:

> When I become interested in a subject, say old age, then the world is peopled for me—just peopled with them. . . . They're the centre of the world, and everyone else is on the periphery. It is an obsession. . . . And that's how I see things. I wrote a book about bachelors, and it seemed to me that everyone was a bachelor.

And so we find poor Gordon Lowther attempting to sustain the same relatively mundane double life as Miss Brodie, on the one hand teacher, church elder and choir-master, on the other hand Miss Brodie's secret lover. But there is no hint of the stuff of Deacon Brodie in Gordon Lowther: he does not relish his secret life, and would always have preferred to marry Miss Brodie. At last his melancholy outweighs 'her bed-fellowship and her catering' (104), and he settles for a straightforward married life with Miss

Lockhart. Retrospectively, even Mary Macgregor can be seen to have lived a double life at school: her life has been fairly intolerable throughout, but as a young adult she remembers Miss Brodie's class, and its magic for her lay in 'all those stories and opinions which had nothing to do with the ordinary world' (15): Miss Brodie herself was Mary's brief double life. And everything comes to have at least two aspects, not only Miss Brodie but the city of Edinburgh itself. This is summed up in a telling description of Sandy's different attitudes over years to images of Miss Brodie:

> Sandy felt warmly towards Miss Brodie at those times when she saw how she was misled in her idea of Rose. It was then that Miss Brodie looked beautiful and fragile, just as dark heavy Edinburgh itself could suddenly be changed into a floating city when the light was a special pearly white and fell upon one of the gracefully fashioned streets. In the same way Miss Brodie's masterful features became clear and sweet to Sandy when viewed in the curious light of the woman's folly, and she never felt more affection for her in her later years than when she thought upon Miss Brodie as silly (111).

This profound ambiguity is central to the effect of the book: no simple attitude toward Miss Brodie can last with any justice.

And no simple picture of Miss Brodie emerges from the brief novel: however briefly, she is supplied with suggested and suggestive contexts in culture, art and history, in religion, in matters particularly Scottish or typically Edinburgh, in the politics and life of her time. Perhaps the outstanding of these suggested dimensions is the one which typifies her notions of virtue and dedication and heroism and goes far to explain her devotion to Mussolini and his fascisti, her ideal of Italy throughout history, stemming from ancient Rome.

Her first appearance in the novel is when she interrupts the set, aged sixteen, talking to boys at the school gates, and informs them of 'a new plot' to force her to resign. The understanding girls, who have clearly heard such things before, react to her appearance and their notion of her character in terms she has no doubt taught them:

> She looked a mighty woman with her dark Roman profile in the sun. The Brodie set did not for a moment doubt that she would prevail. As soon expect Julius Caesar to apply for a job at a crank school as Miss Brodie. She would never resign. If the authorities wanted to get rid of her she would have to be assassinated (9).

The image is unexpected, forceful, and a shade ominous—and Caesar was betrayed by a set including his most trusted friend.

There are a few other memorable ancient Roman moments. Miss Brodie tells her class about an Italian holiday, reliving her scorn of the vulgar American tourists and her own excitement at seeing 'the Colosseum where the gladiators died and the slaves were thrown to the lions' (45). Recreating that memory, she again appears in ancient Roman guise to the girls, until she herself destroys the mood:

> Miss Brodie stood in her brown dress like a gladiator with raised arm and eyes flashing like a sword. 'Hail Caesar!' she cried again, turning radiantly to the window light, as if Caesar sat there. 'Who opened the window?' said Miss Brodie dropping her arm.
> Nobody answered.
> 'Whoever has opened the window has opened it too wide,' said Miss Brodie. 'Six inches is perfectly adequate' (46).

Here the ancient Roman Miss Brodie and the archetypally Edinburgh Miss Brodie uneasily co-exist. She has a 'fine dark Roman head': 'her dead Hugh had admired her head for its Roman appearance' (47), and there is another splendid image of Miss Brodie in Teddy Lloyd's presence: she 'seated herself nobly like Britannia with her legs apart under her loose brown skirt which came well over her knees' (49). A few pages later, as Miss Brodie encounters unpleasant colleagues, the image of patrician Roman heroine and warrior is still about her:

> 'Good mawning,' she replied, in the corridors, flattening their scorn beneath the chariot wheels of her superiority, and deviating her head towards them no more than an insulting half-inch (54).

Till the end of the set's schooldays, 'Miss Brodie as a Roman matron' remains an important image (111).

Her ardent admiration for the antique Roman past is complemented by Miss Brodie's devotion, shared by Teddy Lloyd, to Italian art through the ages. So the girls are offered Italian paintings as well as pictures of Mussolini's fascisti as holiday trove. They are made familiar with the Italian Renaissance and the Mona Lisa, and instructed that the greatest Italian painter is not Leonardo but Giotto, because he is Miss Brodie's favourite (11). For Miss Brodie, Mussolini is a natural and admirable part of her Italian ideal. She admires what he seems to stand for, dedication and discipline, efficiency, elimination of unemployment, and his charisma, and she apparently remains blissfully unaware of the bullying tactics he and his henchmen ruthlessly employed. It is easy for us, of course, with benefit of hindsight, to blame an Edinburgh school-teacher for admiring Mussolini and his followers in 1930: a great many better informed people than Jean

Brodie shared her admiration at the time. During the walk through Edinburgh we are made particularly conscious of the impact Mussolini has made on both Sandy and Miss Brodie: the event is mainly seen from Sandy's viewpoint, but we can distinguish clearly what she has been and is being taught by Miss Brodie from her new reflections on it.

We begin with Sandy's understanding of the corporate unity of teacher and girls, 'a body with Miss Brodie for the head', the girls as if created to fulfil Miss Brodie's purpose. Miss Brodie's clear dislike of Girl Guides 'with their regimented vigorous look' prompts Sandy to remember her paradoxical admiration for Mussolini's marching troops. Sandy ponders on juxtaposed set, Guides and fascisti: and she sees

that the Brodie set was Miss Brodie's fascisti, not to the naked eye, marching along, but all knit together for her need and in another way, marching along (31).

At this stage Sandy obviously understands even less than Miss Brodie what Mussolini is up to: he 'had put an end to unemployment with his fascisti and there was no litter in the streets'. The resemblance is in the discipline, the perfect way in which the troops are bent to the will of the leader. And so it *does* seem paradoxical that the marching Guides are disapproved, until Sandy begins to suspect jealousy: the Guides are 'too much of a rival fascisti, and Miss Brodie could not bear it'. On the walk Sandy experiences two early temptations to 'betray' Miss Brodie, one by being nice to Mary Macgregor and one here by joining the Brownies, but she recoils from them quickly. Her basic reason is interesting, because this is the only time it is ever put in terms as strong as love: 'Then the group-fright seized her again, and it was necessary to put the idea aside, because she loved Miss Brodie' (32).

Now her reactions are to be further tested, by the walk through the previously unvisited slums, 'Sandy's first experience of a foreign country': she is to have her first intimation of the real meaning of unemployment, as she shrinks fearfully from the 'snaky creature', the queue of unemployed. They are first glimpsed, talking, spitting and smoking, and Miss Brodie enjoins the set to pray for the Unemployed, repeating the conventional wisdom that, 'In Italy the unemployment problem has been solved' (39). It is a powerful argument, faced with Edinburgh reality. Again the men talk and spit a great deal, reinforcing negatively the famous dictum of Lord Howard of Penrith in 1923, as blinkered as Miss Brodie: 'Under Fascism, Italians no longer spit in public.' Sandy's discomfort and fear are acute here: when she betrays Miss Brodie she disclaims interest in 'world affairs', but she remains concerned about Edinburgh's poor and unemployed: 'It did not seem necessary that the world should be saved, only that the poor people in the streets and slums of Edinburgh should be relieved' (122–3). Again now she experiences the impulse to desert the set and this time she acts on it, home being the necessary warm notion to oppose to her shivering cold and fear—but she rather repents her self-exile from tea at Miss Brodie's shortly after.

It is of course possible that the reader knows a little more about Fascism than Miss Brodie and Sandy, and Spark gives oblique hints for such readers. Mussolini preached the superficially attractive idea of a corporate state, in which unions, employers and all worked and collaborated together: it is not wholly unlike Miss Brodie's benign dictatorship over her girls, and is lightly referred to here when Sandy finds 'the corporate Brodie set' insufficiently warm.

But Miss Brodie's Fascism is basically very simple-minded and straightforward. After her next summer holiday in Italy she tells the girls; 'Mussolini has performed feats of magnitude and unemployment is even farther abolished under him than it was last year' (45). Her devotion persists until she transfers it, in 1933, to Hitler:

> a prophet-figure like Thomas Carlyle, and more reliable than Mussolini; the German brownshirts, she said, were exactly the same as the Italian black, only more reliable (97).

Notice that she seems unaware of the racial persecution in Hitler's Nazism which was not inherent in Mussolini's Fascism. Hitler's methods again resemble her own, arguably, in that some historians say that his singling out and persecution of the Jews helped unite and cement the relieved majority of the Germans thereby passed over: Miss Brodie's outrageous picking on Mary Macgregor and making her a scapegoat has something of the same effect. In chapter three when the class gets sex-conscious giggles, Miss Brodie ejects Mary, one of the last to laugh, and shuts her out:

> returning as one who had solved the whole problem. As indeed she had, for the violent action sobered the girls and made them feel that, in the official sense, an unwanted ring-leader had been apprehended and they were no longer in the wrong (50).

Nazi or not, this is acutely unpleasant behaviour. Miss Brodie may be a born Fascist, as Sandy claims (125), but she is an instinctive and a relatively uncomprehending one: before the war she is sure Hitler will save the world, and afterwards she innocently admits: 'Hitler *was* rather naughty' (122), surely one of the great understatements!

The Italy that has become home to Mrs Spark attracts Jean Brodie almost totally: she is under the spell of its art, history, tradition and contemporary politics—all but the church: she rejects Roman Catholicism, and the narrator suggests that that was the one church which might have 'normalized' her (85). Miss Brodie is not averse to meeting the Pope. That was part of her Italian holiday, and her Presbyterian soul was satisfied by her bending over the Pope's ring but not kissing it (44). This was part of her visit to Rome, as her London stay was marked by a visit to A A Milne, the creator of Pooh and Piglet. But the narrator pauses on her rejection of Roman Catholicism (85). The long paragraph begins by detailing the rota of different denominations she did accept and patronise, indicating at the least an indifference to sectarian strictness. Her rejection of Roman Catholicism is arguably as simple-minded and ignorant as her approval of Mussolini: it is a middle-class Edinburgh belief that the Church of Rome was a church of superstition, 'and that only people who did not want to think for themselves were Roman Catholics'. The narrator suggests that only the Roman Catholic Church truly suited her temperament: 'Possibly it could have embraced, even while it disciplined, her soaring and diving spirit, it might even have normalized her.' The implication seems to be that the Roman Church provides norms, provides in its rituals and regularities, doctrines and hierarchies a stable framework for the extreme individual to respond to: Calvinist ideas, in part born from a reaction against the notion of a priesthood coming between the individual and God, can help the extremist toward her extremity.

MacColla's critique of Calvinism, we recall, concentrated on the doctrine of the total depravity of man and human society, and his belief in the life-denying consequences of such a doctrine. Spark in contrast concentrates on the doctrine of election and subsequent dangers of antinomianism, as Hogg did in the *Justified Sinner*, and Burns in *Holy Willie's Prayer*. The problem about predestination to grace, about election, is that, as the Justified Sinner found, it is difficult to be sure one *is* of the Elect. The temptation, as he also found, is that once convinced of his or her election to salvation, the individual can see him- or herself as above the law thereafter, bound for Heaven irrespective of behaviour in this world. This is antinomianism (i.e. flouting the principle of law,—*anti* plus Greek *nomos*, law). We seem to recognise this syndrome, for example, when Miss Brodie sees Rose as Venus incarnate, and above the moral laws (38).

Here we are told that Miss Brodie persists in her non-Roman rota of church visits with a sublime confidence in her own status:

> She was not in any doubt, she let everyone know she was in no doubt, that God was on her side whatever her course, and so she experienced no difficulty or sense of hypocrisy in worship while at the same time she went to bed with the singing master.

Not only that, but she assumes the election of all her girls also:

> The side-effects of this condition were exhilarating to her special girls in that they
> in some way partook of the general absolution she had assumed to herself.... All
> the time they were under her influence she and her actions were outside the
> context of right and wrong (85–6).

From the beginning she has promised to make her girls members of 'life's
élite, or, as one might say, the crème de la crème' (23). And as time goes on
by her special attentions and confidences she makes them 'feel chosen' (79).
So Miss Brodie elects herself and her girls—as Sandy at last perceives, she
has a God-complex:

> She thinks she is Providence, thought Sandy, she thinks she is the God of Calvin,
> she sees the beginning and the end (120).

It is all of course a million miles away from orthodox Calvinism, where the
election is from God, and the part of the individual is to wait humbly and
fearfully. Mrs Spark is criticising the effects of Calvinism, but by no means
suggesting that Miss Brodie is a representative Calvinist. She does not
know God through the Scriptures as the Reformers insisted, but by the
wrong and dangerous means of unassisted reason and private revelation.

Miss Brodie's religion is not in the end Christian at all. It is in the end
personal and perverse, a monstrosity of egotism. Early on she applies
Calvinist ideas to artists and outstanding personages: Florence
Nightingale, Cleopatra, Helen of Troy, Sybil Thorndyke the great actress,
Pavlova—these are above the despised 'team spirit', which is only for lesser
mortals: effectively, they are above the law. So Miss Brodie takes all the
furniture of Calvinism, so to speak, all the formulations and habits of mind,
and applies it to her blurred perception of reality and fantasy. She never
shows any sign of seriously believing that God exists or that she herself
could be so lowly a thing as a creature. Is she 'quite an innocent in her way',
as Sandy later on suggests (127), or is this outlandish pride, the sin whereby
the angels fell?

Italy, Fascism, the Christian churches; these are perhaps the main
contexts outside the school in which Miss Brodie is presented, but there are
others. There are the women she most admires, those just listed, plus the
Queen of England, Joan of Arc and Britannia. There is her favourite
reading, and the authors she quotes without acknowledgement: they show
no bias toward religion, unless a religion of art, including chiefly Keats,

Tennyson, Pater, Rossetti, Swinburne, the early Yeats and Charlotte Brontë. There is her contempt for contemporary British politics, whether of right or left, in comparison with Mussolini. Miss Mackay admires Stanley Baldwin, the Conservative Prime Minister who presided over the General Strike of 1926, and was premier of a coalition government when the Brodie set was in the Junior school, but Miss Brodie does not—and posterity admits that Baldwin was no match for the ruthless challenge of Fascist dictatorships abroad. Miss Brodie also prefers Mussolini to the Scottish Labour politician Ramsay MacDonald, who formed a National Government with mainly Conservative support in opposition to most of his own party in 1931, when the girls were eleven.

What we get is a real flavour of the 'thirties, the more effective in that we are repeatedly reminded that it is the period between two wars, with reference to the 'felled fiancé' and 'war-bereaved spinsters', and flashes forward to the aftermath of the Second World War. And we see Miss Brodie in the context of her fellow spinsters (42–3), and of the fads and trivia of the time, and of her own idiosyncrasies. We (and the Brodie set) hear of the Buchmanites, followers of an American evangelist, and we hear of Marie Stopes, the great pioneer of birth control. Marie Stopes was another remarkable woman: at thirty-eight, virgin and with a divorce behind her, she wrote her classic manual *Married Love* from books—and like Miss Brodie, she was Edinburgh-born.

The endearing nature of Miss Brodie's Edinburgh-based mentality is seen when her notion of the near-unrefusable proposer of marriage is 'the Lord Lyon King-of-Arms' (23): the Lord Lyon King-of-Arms is king in a Scottish context only, and in the most limited of ways: he is chief heraldic royal officer-of-arms, *for ceremonial purposes*. This can seen as a harmless little limitation, linking Miss Brodie back to her Edinburgh context. There are several other instances of this: Eunice may not do cart-wheels at Sunday tea-parties, 'for in many ways Miss Brodie was an Edinburgh spinster of the deepest dye' (26), and we have quoted above (p. 108) her anticlimactic interruption of her gladiatorial fantasy to complain that the window has been opened to a 'vulgar' extent. Another such instance interrupts even the affecting story of the felled fiancé; and the comic effect is considerable:

> . . . he fell on Flanders' Field,' said Miss Brodie. 'Are you thinking, Sandy, of doing a day's washing?'
> 'No, Miss Brodie.'
> 'Because you have got your sleeves rolled up. I won't have to do with girls who roll up the sleeves of their blouses, however fine the weather. Roll them down at once, we are civilized beings. He fell the week before Armistice . . . (12).

The city of Edinburgh is also very important in the novel, and the old churches and the castle are omnipresent. And this is in no way surprising: Mrs Spark admits to a more pervasive influence:

> But Edinburgh where I was born and my father was born has had an effect on my mind, my prose style and my ways of thought.[1]

So, unobtrusively, Mrs Spark supplies a vivid context of the time and the character of her main protagonist. The novel may centre on the influence of one spinster schoolteacher on six little girls, in a middle-class, all-female school in a city some have suggested is hardly part of Scotland at all, but the subject matter turns out to be wide-ranging, and the issues universal.

But the school is also and always credible, and with great economy as ever the narrator informs us right at the start about the general knowledge of the Brodie set when it moved up into the Senior school (5). The headmistress describes them as 'vastly informed on a lot of subjects irrelevant to the authorized curriculum, and useless to the school as a school'. The list includes elements of very different importance, world affairs, skin care and puberty, as well as Einstein and 'the arguments of those who consider the Bible to be untrue'. It is implied what Miss Mackay would rather have them know, and the authorised curriculum sounds on the dull side: 'They knew the rudiments of astrology but not the date of the Battle of Flodden or the capital of Finland' (6).

We get several glimpses of Miss Brodie teaching, and by no means all are in the classroom: if she is not settled under the elm tree with the English grammars open as a cover, making the little girls weep at the sad fate of her war-slain Hugh, she is likely to be taking them to the theatre, or an art gallery, or on that most significant landmark in Sandy's education, the walk through the old Edinburgh of the castle, the cathedral and the slums. Her teaching is certainly unorthodox, and the girls are unaware how unusual the relaxed atmosphere of her class is until her disappearance with Mr Lowther for a fortnight precipitates them into the untender mercies of Miss Gaunt. Miss Brodie's class is remarkable for absolutes and large understandings which most of us may not associate with school at all, as when Miss Brodie declares: 'Art is greater than science. Art comes first, and then science' (25). She turns back to the geography map, but turns again to the girls to amplify: 'Art and religion first; then philosophy; lastly science. That is the order of the great subjects of life, that's their order of importance.' And in spite of her dictatorial ways, the class is at ease:

[1] Quoted by Alan Bold in *Modern Scottish Literature*, 1983.

'We do a lot of what we like in Miss Brodie's class,' Jenny said. 'My mummy says Miss Brodie gives us too much freedom.'
'She's not supposed to give us freedom, she's supposed to give us lessons,' said Sandy (25).

Our last set-piece of Miss Brodie's teaching is on her return from an Italian holiday in 1931, when she brings them a Cimabue and a new picture of Mussolini's fascisti, and details of all her summer experiences and a reiteration of her famous belief in education as a leading out, 'from *e*, out and *duco*, I lead' (45): nonetheless, she immediately continues: 'Qualifying examination or no qualifying examination, you will have the benefit of my experiences in Italy.' She gets carried away as a gladiator, and returned to Edinburgh spinsterhood by an unduly open window, and back to the romantic subject of Rossetti and Swinburne: no wonder the two new girls stand up 'with wide eyes' (47)!

Is there any harm in all this? One is tempted to say no, or to argue that any harm is well compensated for by the interest and liveliness of it all: Eunice later describes Miss Brodie as 'an Edinburgh Festival all on her own' (27). The girls *do* scrape through the momentous qualifying examination, with a great deal of extra knowledge, some very bizarre, and an inevitably blurred notion of where truth ends and Miss Brodie's opinion begins. They are enthralled by her personality: in term time she seems the centre of their lives. Being a member of Miss Brodie's set seems the most entertaining possibility by a long way, in the Junior school at Marcia Blaine. Arguably, no harm would have come to the girls if Miss Brodie had let them go when they moved up to Senior school, but her hanging on to the girls, keeping and building on her influence with them—this was where the whole thing began to be out of hand. The evidence of the book indicates that all the Brodie set except Sandy shook off her influence in the end without much trouble: but the example of Joyce Emily Hammond shows in a very dramatic way how dangerous that influence could be.

So we come at last to consider the most enigmatic character in the book, Sandy Stranger, the girl who loved Miss Brodie, fantasised about her, wrote of her love life, and deduced its real life character; who was Miss Brodie's confidante, her proxy lover of Teddy Lloyd and her betrayer, who became a Roman Catholic to Miss Brodie's bafflement and a nun to her hurt despair. Although we see a great deal of her thought processes, Sandy remains for us ultimately, as her name suggests, a stranger. We do not see *all* of her thought processes, and as she grows up we seldom learn of her emotional state, and so her character is very much open to different interpretation by the individual reader—so that Maurice Lindsay in his *History of Scottish Literature* can describe her betrayal of Miss Brodie as motivated by 'bitchy jealousy', while Peter Kemp attributes it to 'a strong moral sense'. In part it depends what emotional life the reader supplies for Sandy. 'She loved Miss Brodie' during the walk in chapter two, when this love is sufficient to quash temptations to join the Brownies or be nice to Mary—but it is a ten-year-old's understanding of love, which we can hardly rely on completely. Much later we see her bored and afflicted by the betrayed Miss Brodie, nostalgically remembering 'the first and un-betrayable Miss Brodie' (60), and one general passage indicates warmth and affection toward Miss Brodie whenever she was seen as fallible (111). But it is not a lot to go on. In general, we are unclear as to her feelings for Miss Brodie, and her feelings for Teddy Lloyd, and her feelings about her conversion to Roman Catholicism and her vocation to the convent: all we have is that repeated image of her hands clutching at the grille: the enigma persists.

Sandy's conversion is something we sense as crucially important to the book, but we are told very little about it, and what we know is cerebral or psychological; that she was interested in Teddy Lloyd's mind because he was so obsessed with the ridiculous Miss Brodie, that when she lost interest in him as a man, she retained interest in the mind, and eventually extracted his faith (123). But this submerged conversion matters, as does Caroline's conversion in *The Comforters* (1957), or the bizarre conversion and eventual martyrdom of Nicholas Farringdon in *The Girls of Slender Means* (1963), the novel after *The Prime of Miss Jean Brodie*. Sandy's situation is after all a little like what we know of Spark's: both were born and raised in Edinburgh but not entirely of it, within a couple of years of each other, and both had an English mother. Spark's father was Jewish, which helped separate her from a conventional middle-class Edinburgh situation: we hear nothing about Sandy's father, but home is a very warm and comforting notion (40). Both were educated in the same Presbyterian school, and neither exactly had Scottish Calvinism sternly presented to her, to react against: instead, Sandy had Miss Brodie. Both eventually became converts to Roman Catholicism. All sorts of intriguing questions about Sandy's young adulthood and conversion remain tantalisingly unanswerable—how important was Miss Brodie's adamant opposition to Catholicism to Sandy's eventual acceptance of it? How important was the notion of rivalry with Miss Brodie in her love affair with Teddy Lloyd? Or was it important, mainly, just to frustrate Miss Brodie's plans and roles for Rose and Sandy, to thwart her?

Sandy emerges as a central consciousness in chapter two, with her birthday party *à deux* with Jenny and her insights during the walk. But from the beginning her too-often-insisted-on tiny eyes are on Miss Brodie, scrutinising her chest and noting its different appearances (11). The collaborative writings with Jenny inevitably centre on Miss Brodie, and they mirror very accurately the changes in the set generally indicated by the narrator. In the first year with Miss Brodie they are essentially little girls, with only the beginnings of the following year's sexual obsession, so *The Mountain Eyrie*, the continuing story of Miss Brodie and Hugh, rings hollow with melodramatic romance. But in the 'sexual year' (44) the set senses the onset of sexual awareness between Miss Brodie and Teddy Lloyd and Gordon Lowther before any of the teachers do (48), and when Miss Brodie and Gordon Lowther disappear from school for the same fortnight, it is Sandy who casually suggests an affair, 'merely in order to break up the sexless gloom that surrounded them' (59), and then she suspects that the affair exists in fact. She is of course only eleven, and subject to the onset of adolescence like any other little girl, so it would be dangerous to make too much of her ambiguous attitude towards sexuality at this time. While in fantasy with Sergeant Anne Grey she was dedicated to eliminate sex from Edinburgh and environs, she was very excited and interested in Monica Douglas's story that she has witnessed a kiss between Miss Brodie and Teddy Lloyd (51–2), 'excited and desperately trying to prove the report true by eliminating the doubts'. Sandy is only typical of the set in her interest in Miss Brodie's changed appearance, and fantasies about the possibility of her engaging in sexual activity, and she is still sharing them with Jenny, but her thoughts gradually become more private. It is Sandy alone who looks at Miss Brodie as she looks at Rose 'in a special way' when Teddy Lloyd has remarked on her profile (80), though she and Jenny continue to speculate on whether Miss Brodie can be desirable to men (86). And it is Sandy alone who attempts to detect 'any element of surrender about her' in the affair with Gordon Lowther, although Sandy and Jenny collaborate on the outspoken and highly comic fictional correspondence.

Sandy was only eighteen when she finally betrayed Miss Brodie, but the seeds were sown long before. In a sense they were sown by Miss Brodie herself, in her constant raising of the possibility—or impossibility: 'I do not think ever to be betrayed' (39). But it is when the girls are fifteen that Sandy begins to feel that 'the Brodie set, not to mention Miss Brodie herself, was getting out of hand' (102). She has discovered the weird phenomenon of Teddy Lloyd's paintings, that all portraits of Brodie girls come to resemble Miss Brodie herself. It is when her little eyes meet his 'with the near-blackmailing insolence of her knowledge' (102) that he kisses her, an important moment, balancing the solitary kiss Monica Douglas witnessed between Lloyd and Miss Brodie. Not surprisingly this, and Lloyd's cruel comment that Sandy is 'just about the ugliest little thing I've ever seen in my life', leave her in some confusion. At about this time, Miss Brodie has begun to look for a confidante: she was in fact now on the look-out for a girl amongst her set in whom she could confide entirely, whose curiosity was greater than her desire to make a sensation outside, and who, in the need to gain further confidences from Miss Brodie, would never betray what had been gained. . . . Almost shrewdly, Miss Brodie fixed on Sandy, . . . (105).

A round of golf full of bunkers and power images (105–8) is the setting for the first confidences, and they seem harmless enough, reasons why Miss Brodie has no great ambitions for the set, except Sandy and Rose. Obliquely and then directly, Sandy begins to understand:

> It was plain that Miss Brodie wanted Rose with her instinct to start preparing to be Teddy Lloyd's lover, and Sandy with her insight to act as informant on the affair. It was to this end that Rose and Sandy had been chosen as the crème de la crème. There was a whiff of sulphur about the idea which fascinated Sandy in her present mind. After all, it was only an idea (109).

The Sandy who feels deprived of Calvinism, 'something definite to reject', is tempted by the whiff of sulphur here, and 'for over a year Sandy entered into the spirit of this plan' (110). She enjoys the long temptation shared. But Sandy was always more a realist than Miss Brodie, could always more clearly discriminate between fantasy and reality. So one day in her sixth year Sandy fully realises the extent and nature of Miss Brodie's manipulative plan:

> All at once Sandy realised that this was not all theory and a kind of Brodie game. . . . But this was not theory; Miss Brodie meant it. Sandy looked at her, and perceived that the woman was obsessed by the need for Rose to sleep with the man she herself was in love with; there was nothing new in the idea, it was the reality that was new (119).

Miss Brodie's plan is serious, and Sandy has connived at it, feeding her unreality: 'She had told Miss Brodie how peculiarly all his portraits reflected her. She had said so time and again, for Miss Brodie loved to hear it.'

That summer Sandy leaves school, and while Miss Brodie is in Germany and Austria and Deirdre Lloyd and the children are in the country, Sandy seduces Teddy Lloyd by a repetition of her 'insolent blackmailing stare' and her knowledge of Lloyd's obsession with Miss Brodie. We have little detail, but both Sandy and Teddy Lloyd seem more interested in Miss Brodie than in each other. That curiosity which Miss Brodie required in a confidante is Sandy's main spur: 'The more she discovered him to be still in love with Jean Brodie, the more she was curious about the mind that loved the woman' (123). And when she loses interest in Lloyd in due course she retains her fascination with his religion: 'She left the man and took his religion and became a nun in the course of time.' Arguably, Sandy has already twice betrayed Miss Brodie, in embracing the art master, contrary to the terms of the plan, and in embracing his religion, which Miss Brodie so despises. But it is doubtful if she would ever have betrayed her to Miss Mackay had it not been for Miss Brodie's utterly casual throwaway remark about Joyce Emily.

The much expelled Joyce Emily has been present from chapter one, anxious to join the sixteen-year-old Brodie set, who are too preoccupied to bother with her. So, perhaps a little through their faults, Joyce Emily is taken up by Miss Brodie. For the most part the reader, like the set, knows little about Joyce Emily and cares less. We do know that she has a brother fighting in the Spanish Civil War and wants to go too: we know that she is anti-Franco. We learn that she ran away to Spain and was killed in an accident. And in Miss Brodie's throwaway remark we learn a little more:

> sometimes I regretted urging young Joyce Emily to go to Spain to fight for Franco, she would have done admirably . . . (124).

Sandy checks that Joyce Emily went to fight for the Fascist Franco, and Miss Brodie agrees: 'I made her see sense.' It is difficult to know which outrages our expectations of a schoolteacher more, talking the girl into changing sides in the war, or 'urging' her to go and fight at all. Both betray a terrifying unconscious egotism which sees Joyce Emily as a pawn rather than a human being, fulfilling a minor ambition of Miss Brodie's, as Rose was intended to fulfil a major one. The juxtaposition of this conversation with Sandy's betrayal clearly indicates that this discovery about Joyce Emily finally triggered the betrayal, Sandy's determination to 'put a stop to Miss Brodie' (125).

The betrayal itself was a sordid affair which Sandy clearly did not enjoy. Miss Mackay was ready with questions about Miss Brodie's sex life (94). It is a nice irony that Sandy impeaches Miss Brodie for teaching Fascism although it is 'a side interest': it *was* a side interest in Sandy's experience of Miss Brodie, but a very central and final one for Joyce Emily.

It is easy to understand why Sandy felt is necessary to 'put a stop to Miss Brodie', and the narrator adds an implication of the 'strong moral sense' pointed to by Peter Kemp: 'She was more fuming, now, with Christian morals, than John Knox' (125). The question that is never directly answered is whether Sandy continued to feel justified in the betrayal. References to her later life in the convent and visits from various members of the set are sprinkled through the novel, and the conversations always centre on Miss Brodie and the betrayal. We would suggest that Sandy attains some wisdom, some detachment in the years in the convent when she writes her psychological treatise on 'The Transfiguration of the Commonplace'—although how much *that* owed to Miss Brodie it is impossible to say. There is no evidence that she regretted the betrayal, ever felt it had been unnecessary, though the cumulative evidence suggests that retrospectively she began to revalue Miss Brodie's positive side. She has accumulated a lot of information. Monica visits Sandy in the late 1950s, and asserts that she really did witness the Brodie/Lloyd kiss; and we learn that Sandy knew this 'even before Miss Brodie had told her so one day after the end of the war' (55): presumably Sandy had been confided in by Teddy Lloyd as well.

These convent interviews years after Miss Brodie's death show us also the continuing naïveté of the other members of the set. It is of all people Rose who innocently asks 'Why did she get the push? Was it sex?' And it is Monica who asks Sandy if Rose ever *did* sleep with Teddy Lloyd, and who ruminates that if Miss Brodie and Teddy Lloyd were in love, 'it was a real renunciation in a way' (121)—although in the past they saw the renunciation claims as comic. Eunice recalls Miss Brodie as marvellous fun, and Jenny wishes she could tell Miss Brodie about her sudden falling in love: 'Miss Brodie would have liked to know about it, sinner as she was' (127). And that is the point at which Sandy famously replies: 'Oh, she was quite an innocent in her way.' Perhaps the best way to understand this is that Sandy has become able to separate the evil Miss Brodie was undoubtedly doing in the 'extremities' of her late prime (43) from her inability to realise this evil or to will it as such. But it is also another of her enigmatic utterances, for 'an innocent' can mean many things, from 'an innocent or guiltless person' through 'a young child' and 'a guileless, simple or unsuspecting person' to 'one wanting in ordinary knowledge or intelligence; a simpleton, a silly fellow'.

At her worst, Miss Brodie *is* simple-minded: if she can see no harm in changing Joyce Emily's politics and packing her off to war, to fulfil by proxy her own aim of dedication, she is seriously lacking in the insight on which she prides herself. Her ambitions for her girls were always alarming, if one took them seriously, because her imagination fed her ideal of dedication with a highly coloured extremism—so, when Eunice had a religious phase Miss Brodie 'tried to inspire Eunice to become at least a pioneer missionary in some deadly and dangerous zone of the earth' rather than a Girl Guide leader in the respectable Edinburgh suburb of Corstorphine (62). The only moment at which Miss Brodie has enough insight to suspect Sandy is when she is angry at the news that Sandy has entered the convent. She has hardly learned from the betrayal if a few weeks before she dies she can respond to such news thus:

> What a waste. That is not the sort of dedication I meant. Do you think she has done this to annoy me? I begin to wonder if it was not Sandy who betrayed me (63).

Any woman who can seriously think another may have entered a convent to 'annoy' her has perhaps a lopsided view of the universe: perhaps Sandy was right: 'She thinks she is Providence. She thinks she is the God of Calvin' (120).

The book ends with Sandy in the convent, now for at least a dozen years Sister Helena of the Transfiguration. The Roman Empress Dowager Helena, mother of Constantine, was reputedly British—said indeed to be the daughter of 'Old King Cole'. She transformed a conventional life by departing for the Holy Land in her old age to search for and find the True Cross on which Christ was crucified. The 'Transfiguration' element in Sandy's convent name recalls the occasion when Jesus was transfigured, appeared in his full glory, to a few of the disciples: it recalls of course as well the title of Sandy's treatise, and perhaps records a debt to the woman who first indicated to Sandy the possibility of transfiguring the commonplace.

Sandy is described as 'in her middle age, when she was at last allowed all those visitors to the convent' (33): in fact she is approaching forty, the age at which Miss Brodie entered her prime. Sandy will not have a prime. The visitors are 'a special dispensation . . . enforced on Sandy': dispensations are usually granted, not enforced, and she does not seem very happy in her interviews, but very evidently ill at ease:

> She clutched the bars of the grille as if she wanted to escape from the dim parlour beyond, for she was not composed like the other nuns who sat, when they received their rare visitors, well back in the darkness with folded hands. But Sandy always leaned forward and peered, clutching the bars with both hands (35).

That is our lasting image of the unquiet nun.

FURTHER READING

Our page references are to the Penguin edition of 1965.

Muriel Spark was born in Edinburgh in 1918, and educated at James Gillespie's Girls' School. She spent some years in Central Africa, returning to Britain during

the war and working in the Political Intelligence Department of the Foreign Office.
She went on to edit two poetry magazines, and produced critical biographies of nineteenth-century figures and editions of nineteenth-century letters. She became a Roman Catholic in 1954. For some time now she has lived in Italy.

She has produced distinguished poems and short stories, as well as a play, *Doctors of Philosophy* (1962), and many novels. Readers who have enjoyed *The Prime of Miss Jean Brodie* should find all of these interesting, especially perhaps *The Comforters* (1957), *Memento Mori* (1959), *The Bachelors* (1960), *The Girls of Slender Means* (1963), *The Mandelbaum Gate* (1965), *The Hothouse by the East River* (1973), *The Abbess of Crewe* (1974), *Territorial Rights* (1979), and *Loitering with Intent* (1981).

Her work has attracted many interesting critics, including the following.

Francis Russell Hart, *The Scottish Novel: A Critical Survey* (1978)

Peter Kemp, *Muriel Spark*. Novelists and Their World Series (1974)

Frank Kermode, an interview with Muriel Spark in 'The House of Fiction': reprinted in Malcolm Bradbury's *The Novel Today* (1977), 131–5

David Lodge, *The Novelist at the Crossroads* (1971)

Allan Massie, *Muriel Spark* (1979)

Muriel Spark, 'My Conversion', *Twentieth Century*, CLXX (Autumn 1961), 58–63

Muriel Spark, 'What Images Return', in Karl Miller (ed), *Memoirs of a Modern Scotland* (1970), 151–3

Ruth Whittaker, ' "Angels Dining at the Ritz": The Faith and Fiction of Muriel Spark', in *The Contemporary English Novel* (eds M Bradbury and D Palmer), Stratford-Upon-Avon Studies 18 (1979), 157–79

CHAPTER SEVEN

Gordon Williams:
From Scenes Like These

In *From Scenes Like These* young Duncan Logan staggers towards an obvious dead end before he even reaches the legal drinking age. Dunky starts as a lad o' pairts, duly recognised as such by a sympathetic if jaundiced teacher. Dunky loathes the life of respectable Scotland as he envisages it, prim, proper and emptied of adventure. Objectively, school is his clearest means of escape from the decaying industrial environment and the housing scheme which between them have circumscribed his life. Nonetheless he chooses to leave school at fifteen and heads for his first job on, of all things, a farm.

By this neat ploy Williams yokes urban and rural Scotland together. The one is, as it turns out, as derelict and charmless as the other. Skilfully playing on Dunky's naïveté, Williams gives us a precisely drawn, anti-romantic, anti-pastoral picture of life down on the farm in which the principal crop turns out to be Dunky's own self-doubts and disillusionment. Having given up on Scottish education at fifteen, he abandons at sixteen the even more potent dream of being a football star. On the slopes of Ibrox, Dunky merges into a raving mass of people, abandoning his very identity as an individual.

Dunky is doomed to a dead end, and Williams makes sure we are all too aware of it. Is the novel then one of social criticism, with a clear message about the faults of society, class or education system, something that can be changed, however daunting the prospect? No: that account would be too simple. The novel seems less social criticism than social description: there is no authorial voice coming in with judgement or analysis, and apart from the unlikely mouthpiece of Willie Craig's friend the Tink, there is no character who can conceivably be carrying an authorial message or point of view. The character with the biggest say in giving us the 'evidence' is a sparsely educated fifteen-year-old boy—so if there is to be a cogent social analysis the reader has at least to collaborate in the making of it. On the face of it, all Williams is prepared to say is—this is how it is—or indeed was, in the early nineteen fifties, when Gordon Williams and Dunky Logan both came to manhood in an impoverished area of Scotland's central belt.

Dunky is doomed to a dead end, we say: is this then a tragic novel? The question is possibly more interesting than the answer. Of course tragedy is not a common genre in our time, or in the novel, and any modern tragedy will necessarily be very different from the outline we derive from such as Shakespeare, where a great and noble character possesses a tragic flaw, and is brought down, partly through his own fault. Twentieth-century tragedy is not like that: twentieth-century tragic characters will not be of high degree, but in some measure ordinary or representative characters, like Arthur Miller's Willie Loman in *Death of a Salesman*. At the centre of that play, Willie's wife asserts that Willie is a human being, and suffering, and that attention must be paid:

> He's not the finest character that ever lived. But he's a human being, and a terrible thing is happening to him. So attention must be paid.

Less obtrusively, Williams demands our attention for Dunky Logan. Maybe he thinks the basic plight of a modern urban working-class Scots lad is desperate, but it would be unlike him to use a time-honoured label like 'tragic': he avoids such terms and spurns the long literary tradition that sanctions them. We *do*, however, get one of the traditional tragic effects here, that of waste. Dunky's wasted potential strikes the reader strongly and directly.

So on the whole social criticism and tragedy look like labels that do not easily or immediately fit. Another descriptive term which may be more useful is documentary—'aiming at presentation of reality', and when it is used as a noun, 'a motion picture presenting an activity or professional occupation of real life without fictional colouring or professional actors'. For all the obvious inaccuracy of this definition when applied to the novel, it remains a reasonably useful term. There is an important documentary level in *From Scenes Like These*, and the work of the farm is presented with relentless realism, however much it is interspersed with, for example, Dunky's daft thoughts or other men's preoccupations with sexual rivalry. Work is so solidly important that it is almost like a dimension in the novel. This becomes the more clear if we look back to a novel like *Sunset Song*. Gibbon presented the work of the croft with anti-kailyard vividness and realism for his time, and was not afraid to underline the hardness of the life or the smells of the farmyard, but there is no scene in *Sunset Song* that is preoccupied with work and the hardness of physical labour to anything like the degree of the first or the twelfth chapter of this novel.We recall a reviewer writing of Gibbon: 'He is for ever calling a spade a spade, when there is no need whatever to refer to the implement at all'. If Gibbon calls a spade a spade, Williams does more to tell us how to use it, and how much sweat, pain and effort it can cost.

Williams tries and succeeds at two different, difficult and inter-related tasks. He presents Dunky Logan as representative of many thousands of lads in similar situations, presenting a documentary-type realistic view of a society in which such lads have few prospects for the future. But Dunky Logan is also a very individual youngster in whose personality, life and thoughts we develop an ongoing interest. We will look first at some of the ways in which Williams draws a *general* picture, and then at some of the ways in which Dunky is special and individual and presented as such.

The book gives a grim but highly convincing picture of a class, a locality, a time—and all these only too well known to Williams. He came from Paisley, his family was aspiring working class, they even lived in one of the older Council houses that were obscurely regarded as better than the new scheme around them. He admits that he and Dunky have more than a little in common:

> Yes, that's the basic information that's programmed into the computer. The interesting bit of the fusion of the facts and the fiction. Sometimes I can't remember which is which myself. Dunky in *From Scenes Like These* plays football. So did I. He works on a farm. So did I. But that's where it ends.

We have described the novel as anti-romantic and anti-pastoral. One way in which Williams *does* betray attitudes is in his title. Here he takes on Burns, the Scottish bard himself, and his celebratory pastoral poem, 'The Cottar's Saturday Night', a poem which Dunky Logan could well have read with stupefied disbelief at school. 'The Cottar's Saturday Night', published in 1786, is a poem about unreal virtue, piety and happiness down on the farm, and many people before Williams have found it unconvincing. The blame for this does not belong entirely to Burns: the poem is written in a lofty, moralising, pious, pastoral mode popular among English poets in his day: he was only following the fashion. But some writers complained bitterly about the mode at the time, in the name of realism. Thus Crabbe in 'The Village', about two years before Burns wrote his pastoral, declared defiantly:

> I paint the cot
> As Truth will paint it, and as Bards will not.

Following the tradition, Burns does not simply describe: in 'The Cottar's Saturday Night', he imposes attitudes, thoughts and beliefs on his characters. Williams in contrast eschews authorial comment and gives us the impression of direct evidence—what his characters think about themselves and their lives. Burns' descriptions are inextricably intertwined

with pious and moralising commentary, and by choosing his title as he does
Williams is deliberately setting out to oppose Burns' idealised Kailyard.
He goes so far as to print the last three stanzas of the poem at the beginning
of the book. The contrast between the pictures these writers paint and the
commentaries they do or do not make is one of the clearest possible indices
of what Williams' main concerns are in his novel. Looking briefly at the rest
of Burns' poem helps us to measure Williams' general picture.

Burns' main concern is as his title suggests, the cottar's one holiday, his
night off, so he doesn't pay the attention Williams does to work, its nature,
its hardness, its back-breaking monotony. This forms what we might call
the documentary aspect of *From Scenes Like These*, described with real
authority—unsurprisingly, since Williams has done this kind of work
himself. The cottar is poor, but he seems in no danger of unemployment,
and the security of his but and ben is hardly in question. No doubt if Burns
in this vein were describing the Cottar's Monday morning, he would praise
the bond between employer and employee, mutual loyalty and security.
Not in *From Scenes Like These*: here there seems no such loyalty: Auld
Craig will obviously sack Coll as soon as Dunky is strong and experienced
enough to do the same work for less money. Similarly Mary O'Donnell gets
a job on the farm as housekeeper, but Auld Craig immediately takes
advantage of her being crippled to reduce the offered wages by twenty per
cent. The Craigs exploit all their workers as far as they can, employing the
poorest and least independent, women and schoolchildren, and not even
supplying hot soup for the children on the excuse that they are between
housekeepers. Burns simply presents the weary cottar going home for his
well-earned rest.

In the next few stanzas, he describes the cottar's home and family. We
read of 'His wee bit ingle, blinkan bonnilie' and 'His clean hearthstane', in
conjunction with his 'thrifty wifie'. Burns' home and family and all their
relationships are perfect. What about the homes in *From Scenes Like
These*? An old, inconvenient farmhouse, dirty and dog-polluted, with a
half-starved, man-eating dog on guard—two crowded rooms in an old
tenement where Dunky Logan lives with his family, all crowded on top of
each other—no ideal homes here! Most of all because families are what
make homes, and unlike Burns', Williams' families are not ideal.

Happy families? We get a vague impression from his senile ramblings
that Auld Craig's marriage to his Jessie was happy—but that is all. Mary
O'Donnell never thinks about her family, except to get further away from
them. Elsa's family life is so disastrous that she is an Undesirable—because
of her father's anti-social behaviour: he is known as 'Noble the wife-
beater'. Because of this, the family lives in a special part of the scheme,
righteously looked down on by everyone else. She and Dunky want to

escape from their families. His parents' marriage has clearly been disastrous more or less from the beginning, and the concept of family life is a mockery here. Telfer's father left long ago, and his relationship with his mother is tainted by their consciousness of an occasion of drunken incest. The traditional family has splintered apart, and twentieth-century attitudes to sexuality transform the idealised world that Burns painted out of all recognition. There is *no* equivalent in *From Scenes Like These* to the four fulsome stanzas in which Burns describes the cottar met by 'The expectant wee-things' with 'Flichterin' noise and glee', and the 'lisping infant' that makes the cottar 'quite forget his labour and his toil'.

In the poem, the older children arrive, eager to spend Saturday night at home, ready to help their parents out with their hard-won earnings—no ambitions to get away to Canada here! And brothers and sisters meet on Saturday 'with joy unfeigned'. Brothers and sisters in the novel never communicate at all. In Burns, mother is a great manager of their slender resources, and father is full of good advice about obeying their employers and saying their prayers. To take one example only from Williams, Dunky's mother is a joyless, class-obsessed, frigid and undemonstrative woman, and his father a bitter cripple who was only once in living memory nice to his son: Dunky remembers him at Hogmanay, drunk but nice, once.

Burns introduces an admirer for the eldest daughter, whose intentions are, of course, strictly honourable: is anything else conceivable?

> Is there in human form, that bears a heart,
> A wretch, a villain! lost to love and truth!
> That can, with studied sly, ensnaring art,
> Betray sweet Jenny's unsuspecting youth?

In stark contrast, there is a great deal of sexuality in *From Scenes Like These*. It is stressed throughout, and becomes almost a metaphor for the failure or unreality of all human communication. Essentially, and generally, characters in the novel do not see members of the opposite sex as human beings, but as sex objects. We must perceive this through the consciousness of the characters, and so here is one reason why the narrative is fractured as it is.

The narrative at first is entirely through Dunky's eyes: we get the impression that this is *his* story, and we are to be concerned with *his* attitudes. But for the general picture this needs filling out: first we see into the thought-processes of Mary O'Donnell and gradually and sporadically into most of the other characters. This is crucially important on the topic of sexuality, because for most of the book Dunky experiences a conflict between his physical desires and needs and his high ideals of real love and communication: what an insight into the other characters shows us is that Dunky is the odd man out in this respect.

Almost at the beginning of the first chapter we meet McPhail the knee padder, the voyeur: sexual activity at a fairly low level by any standard! 'Crawling about on his knees in bushes to watch courting couples on the job' (11). In chapter 4, having Mary in the house has put Willie Craig 'in the notion', and the heat of the Tink's brazier keeps him that way, so he pays the world's least glamorous sexual visit to Morag Coll, with her woollen knickers on the kitchen floor (69). Interestingly, Morag is sorry for Willie, and accepts his sexual exploitation: 'She always thought of him living in that dirty old house, all alone, a man of his age, poor Willie, it was the least a woman could do'. She is recognisably human, but what of Willie? He goes to Morag because he has been thinking about Mary; he thinks about Mary while in the act, and afterwards he thinks:

> And now there was a young hole under his own roof he might not need to stravaig about the countryside on dark nights looking for an old hag who'd lift her skirt on the kitchen floor (70).

Sex then is generally seen as squalid and sordid. The men seem most excited by rivalry: Telfer and Willie compete at different times for the attention of Mary and of Elsa, each excited by the idea of getting something the other wanted. Telfer also experiences sex as part of the class war, as we see, for example, in his early relationship with Agnes:

> At first it had been enough to give him a hard-on walking down the street, just thinking of him, a scheme fella, a midden-scraper, riding Agnes from Barcraigie, the floor manager's daughter, enough just to get into their toffs' living room on a Sunday night, when the pan-loaf McFarlanes had gone to bed, to get him steaming, enough to know they thought he was a scruff (60).

And when Mary is eventually married to Willie and unfaithful with Telfer, he wins the class war again: 'Look at me now, Willie Craig, who's the man and who's the common tyke?' (165). Telfer also seems typical in being most interested in girls who are hard to get. He tires of Agnes because she is so available: he fights her off in the cinema because he is more interested in Burt Lancaster, and realises he will not care if it is too cold or too wet to end the evening with the by now routine sexual encounter (59). It is interesting that eventually Telfer finds himself marrying Elsa, the only girl who will not yield to him beforehand: there seems little hope of permanence in this alliance.

For the most part in the novel we get the male view of sex. But an interesting contribution is made by the character and personality of Mary O'Donnell. She is the only woman who seems fully to understand the nature of the sex war around her, and to take on the men on their own terms and win. Just after her arrival at the Craigs' she discovers she is pregnant by her previous employer, and singlemindedly sets about finding the most suitable man to marry, to give the baby home and father. She is quite unsentimental about this; it is a question of wealth. She is more attracted to Donald Telfer, much, but Willie Craig is the only appropriate husband, however physically repulsive she may find him. She can always have an affair with Telfer later—and she does.

Arguably chapter 6 is the one in which Williams most directly takes on Burns. It is a long chapter (101–36), and has more contrasted voices than any other. And it is about Saturday. We get at least glimpses of the thought processes of Willie, Mary, McCann, Telfer, Dunky, Auld Craig and Magda, some of them many times, and we at least seem to get a more realistic and honest picture than Burns' lofty description.

Willie is weighing the pros and cons of marriage to Mary. Do him justice, it is not just a question of sexual attraction! He appreciates the improvements she has made to the farm, but worries whether she'd keep it up, once married: 'You could throw a leg over any women alive but you didn't marry them for that' (102). Perhaps he doesn't know enough about her: she 'might even have a couple of wee bastards hidden away somewhere'. The irony is fairly crude, but the reader is likely to enjoy seeing Willie outsmarted. He even sees an advantage in her crippled leg: 'Mind you, a cripple woman wouldn't be wanting to be running away to the town all the time, she'd count herself lucky to get a place of her own' (103). Mary meantime wants to be as hard as the men are: she fights her attraction to Telfer.

Willie begins to feel that tonight would be a good night, and his thoughts are both coarse and impersonal—after all, it is nearly a week since his encounter with Morag Coll! He has become more certain about it all:

Something else had been keeping him back. Other men might laugh at him, for wedding a cripple, an Irish Pape at that. But the moment he'd realised that Telfer was after her as well he knew he wanted her, married if it had to be that (120).

Mary meantime reads his mind and is more than a match for him:

It being Saturday he'd be thinking he wanted a bit of fun and games tonight. All right, you smelly brute, I'm ready for you. Once you've enjoyed yourself you're as good as its father. She would do it, because it was the best way to get what she needed (121).

This part of the chapter ends up with Willie's proposition, which has to turn into a proposal, and Willie and Mary go unceremoniously to bed. We might say 'not a good pair spoiled'. Williams makes no overt comment: if the reader is more shocked, say, by Mary's calculations than by Willie's behaviour, it is a question of the reader's preconceptions. If the reader is a betting man, his money will already be on Mary. Indeed as the relationship progresses there is a scene where Willie beats up and virtually rapes his clearly pregnant wife, but Mary wins that battle, as she looks like winning the war.

The other main focus of interest in this Saturday chapter is Dunky himself. He works in the morning, and his Saturday afternoon is of course dominated by football, but the climax, almost the purpose of the whole thing, is Saturday night at the dancing. There is a marvellous description of what it is like to be an insecure boy at the dancing; here Dunky is very much being used as representative of his peers, rather than marked out from them. The long description (126–9) serves to conflate a number of Saturdays, and wonderfully conveys the various phases of depression, shyness and embarrassment:

> You stood with all the other blokes at one side of the hall, looking across the empty floor at the dames. You looked for girls you knew, because you weren't so embarrassed at the start if you got a dance with a girl you knew from school or from some other dance. You discussed the talent with your mate, trying to make it sound as though you were a couple of bigtime guys who'd been to bigtime places and thought this was smalltime jigging for kids. You felt you'd never have the nerve to walk across the floor, all the way across, and ask a girl to dance with you.

Dunky's annotation of his own behaviour is wholly convincing, whether he is agonising or lying about his sexual exploits: 'You knew you were lying so you took it for granted he was lying.' There is the horrific possibility that a girl would refuse to dance: 'Everybody would see you getting the brush-off, that was the worst thing of all.' This teenage preoccupation with what everyone will see is one of Dunky's most constant concerns: even when his world is pleasantly shattered by his encounter with Elsa and they arrange a date, telling people he hopes to impress seems almost more important than keeping the date: 'He'd still not been able to tell anybody about Elsa Noble, and he was gasping to hear what Telfer would say' (107). The next paragraph, about the horrors of a ladies' preference dance, is again obsessed with how it will all look to other males, not the ladies at all. It's always possible to avoid the whole ordeal, to 'nip out to the lavvy', but the boy reflects, 'you could get tired of going to the lavatory' (128).

The most important problem is looking for a lumber, 'a girl who'd let you take her home'. Again, we get the impression that this is all Saturdays, any Saturday, not just this particular February Saturday in Dunky's sixteenth year. Elated though he is about his date with Elsa, Dunky looks for a lumber, and at his audience, self-conscious as usual: 'It wasn't so much what you thought of her that mattered but what the other guys would think of you for going out with her.' The decision is made for Dunky on this occasion: threats of violence, and the danger of a fight alarm him to a degree of panic, and this in part causes him to see Magda home. The chapter climaxes (134–5) in another sad, squalid and detailed scene of unsatisfactory sexual activity, from which Dunky walks home disgusted with himself and some aspects of sexual activity. From scenes like these old Scotia's grandeur springs. Indeed.

Williams' world has increasingly less and less in common with Burns' pastoral idyll. The poem climaxes in seven stanzas about family prayers and family Bible-reading, led by one man, 'The Saint, the father and the husband'. Religion is conspicuous in *From Scenes Like These* only by its absence. The hiring of the scheme boy Rafferty, a Catholic, towards the end of the novel, does give room for some of Dunky's not-so-daft thoughts about religious prejudice and bigotry, as he questions the anti-Catholic myths of his Protestant upbringing (187–8). We see no serious believers in the novel, and essentially religion in Kilcaddie is reduced to residual bigotry and an automatic selection of football teams to support.

Williams prints the last three stanzas of Burns' poem as an epigraph to his text. They are resoundingly highflown and patriotic: the poet never feels the need to defend the notion of 'old Scotia's grandeur'. He ends with a prayer to the God who inspired Wallace, still to supply patriots, and patriot poets for Scotland: Gordon Williams was perhaps not the sort he had in mind, but we might defend Williams as patriot on the grounds of truth, remembering what George Douglas Brown said about his angry novel *The House With The Green Shutters*, that it was 'more complimentary to Scotland, I think, than the sentimental slop of Barrie, and Crockett, and Maclaren'. Burns' finale claims that as far as virtue is concerned, 'The cottage leaves the palace far behind.' He even prays for his noble poor to be protected from Luxury, and so remain a 'virtuous populace'.

Some of the general characteristics of Kilcaddie that Williams seems most concerned to illustrate do not occur at all in Burns. There is the extraordinary system of class distinction even inside the Council housing: the Logans' old house in Shuttle Place is somehow superior to the rest of the scheme, and there is a poor end of the scheme, and at the extreme the Undesirables. Furthermore, as we have seen when discussing sex, class seems a basic factor in most people's consciousness. Education again is an issue in the novel. It is the one obvious chance for a boy like Dunky to escape the wage-slavery of his class, but Dunky never sees it as a sane alternative:

> Education was something you went in for if you weren't good at anything else—guys who played football well never bothered with school much, guys who could get off with women easily never came top of the class. Who did? The swots—and everybody knew that swots were always hopeless with women or football, or anything but their lessons. It wasn't quite the same with girls, in his class the four or five smashers all got good marks at exams. But it was different for girls—education suited them, they'd nothing else to do with themselves anyway (90–1).

Education is a topic which is carefully aired in the novel. We are encouraged to wonder why Dunky leaves school at the first possible moment. If we don't wonder ourselves, the schoolteacher Ian Nicol is there to pose the question. Here is another advantage of the fractured narrative method: Nicol's regrets for Dunky, his worries about his own performance of his own job, and even the ways in which he envies Dunky are all conveyed, and it is inevitably suggested why school has little to offer Dunky and his like. Nicol goes home after meeting Dunky and Alec at the Communist Party meeting. He expresses his rage and frustration to his wife: Dunky had seemed really talented, but now:

> You should've seen him, like a Hollywood gangster, hard as nails, I didn't know whether to laugh or cry, you know, brown shirt and lots of Brylcreem (92).

He comes out with a fairly honest statement of envy compounded by frustration with his own job, indicating that Dunky grieves him because he was one of the few who might have done better, not that he has any idea how to change the system usefully:

> 'I pity Logan and envy him at the same time,' he said. 'I know his life's being wasted but he doesn't, he'll just sail along, sex, booze and football, thinking he's having a great time. Next year or the year after it'll be the pub. . . . And in ten years time I'll be just like our beloved headmaster, dry as dust . . . and the one or two who might have a spark of something different see the whole thing as a fraud' (94).

Again, it is typical of the novel that the analysis is as honest as possible, but there are no solutions offered. Nicol is right about Dunky and the pub, but he is in the last resort an uncomprehending part of a bizarre system, as are most of the characters in the book.

Dunky and Elsa encounter Nicol again in chapter 7 (149–55), and Nicol invites them to coffee. But the kailyard picture of the wise and kindly dominie helping the lad o' pairts will not come right. Nicol tries to make Dunky consider his career, but the conversation tells *us* a lot more than it tells Nicol. There is Dunky's immediate typical reaction:

Dunky could see that Nicol was working up to some serious gab. When it came he put on his classroom face, eyes on the teacher, mouth neither yawning nor smiling, head shaking slightly to let him know you were still listening, mind wandering through football matches, rabbit hutches, necking sessions, looking up his wife's legs, grown-ups talking at, at, at you, from a different life, boring, going on and on and on ... (155).

Nicol's attempt at contact is real, but fated. The more he asks why the boy left school, the more silent Dunky becomes. Here again the answer is that of Everyboy, and it is not articulated, just desperately thought by Dunky:

Because I felt silly. Because I hated it. Because I got the belt from Miss Colquhoun and Miss Peacock and Mister Sinclair and Mister Everybastard. Because I hated exams. Exams and more exams. Because I hated being treated like a wee boy. Because you got an hour's homework every night and two hours after the third year. Because it was *official*. ...
    I didn't want to get like you, I mean, snobbish, peely-wally, pan-loaf, stiff-collar, useless hands.

Nicol's attempted offer of hope with the possibility of night-classes rings terribly hollow: it is impossible to imagine Dunky finding a reason to continue his education like this. Williams then seems to introduce Nicol mainly to raise questions about education that Dunky would not be bothered with, to give us more evidence about the state of society and its attitudes, in this case, to education. He also turns out to be quite an effective character, the disappointed teacher consciously in the process of losing faith and interest in his job.

Another character is introduced to give us a more detached view of society—Willie Craig's friend the Tink. In so far as Dunky Logan is representative, he has an ideal of Scots macho man: he wants to be a man—and a hard man. It is world of social and sexual rivalry, a world where undeclared war seems the truth of every situation, from parenthood to football, and a world where no one seems to have any friends. Except Willie's friend the Tink.

The most important encounter with the Tink (63–8) goes back to the wartime conversation when the two became acquainted. The Tink tells Willie how he was in training for the ministry when the Great War broke out, but that war destroyed his faith in God. He also came to see it as an English war, irrelevant to the Scots suffering and dying in the trenches.

> I said to myself, if you ever get out of this, Archie Stewart, you're never going to have any more to do with them and their civilisation. I think it was all these wee men from Glasgow, men I wouldn't have hardly spoken to before, wee bowly legs from rickets and whatnot, hunger on their faces, even boys of eighteen. I kept asking in my prayers, what the hell has the King of England ever done for these wee men? Ship them out to France to feed a lot of rats? No, I came home and I left my family and I wandered the countryside till I found this place, the mines were spent by then, and I just built my wee house and here I'll stay (65).

His revolt is essentially political, and based on his perception of social inequality: 'I'll maybe believe in their civilisation the day I hear of God and the King of England sharing a two-apartment corporation house.' But the Tink does not organise, or take any form of political action: 'One day Scotland will wake up to itself, but I doubt it'll be after my time.' When he is casually smashed up by 'the neds', he is both understanding and prophetic:

> 'No, no, it's my fault,' he'd said. 'They know I'm free and they aren't, it's only natural they resent me, I know how they feel. But someday, Willie, they'll wake up to the truth and then they can look out, they'll be kicking down the walls of Buckingham Palace.'

But no more than Gordon Williams himself does the Tink offer a recipe for action or social change: he is content to remain apart, a spectator and not a combatant.

So far we have been deliberately trying to see the community Williams is intent on depicting, with Dunky Logan only as a representative young member of it—and it is a very different community from those of *A Scots Quair*, or *The Silver Darlings*, for example, with very little to nourish young roots. We have seen why Williams is concerned to listen to a range of characters in the community, to show their different consciousnesses, without presenting an omniscient authorial overview. Now let us look at Dunky himself, as an individual, no longer as merely representative of his plight. He is of course very young. He is naïve: he has opinions, lots of them, often contradictory: he is swayed by adolescent exhilaration and despair. His thoughts are fluid and stimulating for the reader, whether about when and why people talk Scots and English (22–3), or how people talk in well-worn cliches all the time (221). He worries above all about his 'daft notions'.

This subject is crucial, and comes up as soon as the harsh reality of the farm has been established in the first chapter. The boy has apparently only left school in the nick of time: his daft notions are encouraged by his literary experience:

> He didn't consider himself a scheme kid and yet he lived in the town, so he wasn't one or the other. Like young Jim Hawkins, able to talk to both Long John Silver and Squire Trelawney, was one of his dafter notions. It was just as bloody well nobody knew how many daft notions he actually had. Sometimes he thought he might be a bit soft in the head. Ever since he could remember he'd had these funny ideas running about his brain, sort of play-acting . . . he'd noticed that the more he stayed at the silly school the dafter these notions had become. He'd wanted to get a job, be a hard case, a real working man, not a silly schoolboy whose brain was affected by too many pictures (12).

But the thoughts do not disappear on the farm: in the very next chapter (34–5) we see Dunky pondering the violence of Blackie McCann, and his own attitudes to violence and fighting and football. It is characteristic of Dunky that this long meditation is inconclusive, full of questions rather than coming to any answers.

Dunky's main ambition is to become a man—a hard man, a man like Telfer. The book covers almost a year, starting in the January with him fifteen and newly left school. Most of the book's action takes place from January to the end of harvest, and the final chapter describes Dunky's adventures the following New Year. As far as Dunky is concerned, the boy becomes a man. The book seems more concerned with Dunky's puzzling over his experiences and his reactions than with experience itself: certainly there is no tight plot such as we are accustomed to in fiction, and no strong sense of time and development. It is just that some things happen, in a fairly realistic way, in the course of the year. It is Dunky's first year at work; it is the year his father decides to go to hospital. Dunky falls in love with Elsa— and then they split up. The nearest thing we have to a plot follows from this: because Telfer inherits Elsa, Dunky feels obliged to fight him, terrified though he is at the prospect. When Telfer meets the offered fight with laughter, Dunky has a desperate need to prove he is not a coward. As a result he goes out on the football pitch and behaves like an animal, breaking his nose, and losing his teeth, and causing greater damage to his opponent. As a result of *that*, we learn in the final chapter, he becomes afraid to play, or at least to tackle; he starts drinking for dutch courage, and finally and inevitably he gives up playing football and takes up serious drinking.

Dunky is an intensely insecure adolescent, a bundle of secret fears. In the first chapter he is afraid of McCann and the fight he senses coming, he is afraid of the horse Big Dick, and afraid of people knowing he is afraid. He is afraid of fighting Telfer—and perhaps most of all he is afraid of ridicule. One of his strongest, angriest memories is of the occasion when Uncle Charlie finds, reads, and reads out his diary, with helpless laughter and mockery (221–2):

> ... Dances I have Attended ... Cafe's Visited ('Oh Beth, your boy's a rerr terr so he is, listen to this, The Rainbow, Ayr, food no bad, service grim, dames rotten, oh Dunky, my sides'll burst from laughing') ... and worst of all he could have *died*, when Uncle Charlie came to the last page where he kept a list of all the girls he'd dated or lumbered, with comments on them in French! And his mother wondered why he never went near Aunt Bessie or Uncle Charlie!

Dunky dimly realises that the effect of the incident is more far-reaching than putting him off Uncle Charlie: if he is going to be mocked for using words like appertaining, he will not: 'He'd show them he could win the Scottish Cup for ignorance.' When Dunky resolves: 'He'd grow up into a real moronic working-man and balls to them', we may be witnessing, retrospectively, an incident crucial to his whole attitude to education.

So we can look again at some of the major subjects we have considered in general terms, and see Dunky's very individual reactions to work, home and family, sexuality, class, education, football and drink.

Work is important to Dunky for most of the book. To stop being a boy and start being a man, Dunky's main ambition, you have to leave school and prove yourself at work, 'a real working man, not a silly schoolboy'. He goes through agonies to prove himself strong enough to hold down a man's job: his concentrated descriptions of physical effort are a recurrent and convincing element in the novel. It is only in the last chapter, when Dunky seems to have lost most of his positive ideals, that he thinks of work as merely a cash bargain:

> *It was for money you worked, not to show you were decent and steady, nobody thanked you for working till you almost dropped, they laughed at you* (241).

What of home and family in Dunky's experience? Well, again his attitudes fluctuate: it is worth looking at two passages from chapters 5 and 7. On pages 71–84 Dunky comes home from work. He looks up at the windows of his home with hatred:

> If only he never had to go up there again. Lights behind curtains, coal fires, windows closed, cramped and hot, no room to move, no place you could hide away on your own, away from *him*. His father and mother and Senga in the bedroom, Senga's bed behind the curtain, his bed in the kitchen, no room to move.

The simple repetition of 'no room to move' convinces us of Dunky's claustrophobia. It is tempting to see the old pigeon loft where he keeps his rabbits as more truly his home: 'This was his place, his and his only ... he was the boss. Only he knew what went on here.' This is a refuge even from soft Alec, who thinks of rabbits as 'only silly pets for wee boys'. Dunky's tenderness to the rabbits, and his practicality about mating or killing them are important to his development and his individuality.

But when he goes into the house tenderness is not in evidence. He is afraid of his mother and very anxious to have no physical contact with her. He 'didn't know why they hated him so much', and he tries not to care, resolving to leave home at the earliest possible moment. The reader sees more sides to the family misery than Dunky does: we learn his mother's class-ridden history and the tale of her joyless sex life, and get a glimpse of the bitterness and frustration of the crippled father. But the focus is on Dunky and his unhappy reaction to his parents: 'Did everybody hate their own father?' (82). If the crippled housekeeper at the farm had been his mother, she'd have known 'that working men shouldn't be nagged at all the time like wee boys' (81). Dunky sadly remembers 'the one time when his father had really seemed to like him', the Ne'erday match at Ibrox with father and Uncle Roddie both drunk. He remembers that one instance of drunken affection with adolescent rebellion:

> His father had smiled at him.
> But his eyes were funny from drinking whisky, he remembered that all right. Pity the bastard hadn't got drunk more often. Jesus Christ, why in the name of hell did *he* have to have a father who lay on his back, paralysed, and looked at *him* and made him feel *he'd* done something wrong? (84).

A parallel home scene occurs on pages 159–62, when Dunky's father announces his decision to go into hospital. Again, Dunky's feelings are very confused:

> He didn't know what to say.
> 'I think it's terrible you going away from your own home,' his mother said. She seemed to be talking to *him*.
> 'What, can they do anything about your back?' Dunky asked. That would mean more room in the house, God strike you down for thinking evil thoughts (160).

In this atmosphere of reproach and emotional manipulation, he lashes out at his father: Dunky's adolescent self-centredness protects him from realising what it must be like to be crippled. The whole of this scene re-pays careful consideration, betraying as it does Dunky's characteristic emotional conflicts. He feels to blame for all the unhappiness, then deprived of affection, cursed, horribly unlikeable, and anxious to please:

> If only he could say something nice to them. His own father was going away, maybe for good, and he was such a thrawn, unnatural person he couldn't think of anything nice to say. God had given him bad blood. He felt like being sick, anything to get out of the bedroom (162).

Dunky's home life seems to illustrate Thoreau's dictum that 'the mass of men lead lives of quiet desperation.'

Sexuality is of course a big topic for Dunky, and one on which many conflicts depend. On the one hand, he wants, like his peers, to be a hard man with lots of bigtime women, many lumbers to boast of: on the other, he secretly cherishes ideals about real love, about having a steady girlfriend, someone he will respect as well as love. His feeling for Elsa is not simply sexual, and as far as we can see he is atypical of his society in this. He wants a relationship; he respects her physically, and most important, he talks to her and trusts her as he has never trusted anyone else. Some of the daft thoughts can at last be shared. So it is very precious. The reader, of course, can see that it is all impossible—they are too young, they *cannot* escape to Canada, or even get engaged—a split is probably inevitable, and sooner rather than later. So the reader is conscious of a sad and mocking irony as Elsa sobs in Dunky's arms, afraid of the future:

> '... you don't know what it's like, I don't want to get pregnant and be married like that, you get old and fat, they're always fighting and shouting at each other, I don't want to be like that, will I be like that, Dunky, tell me I won't' (146).

He reassures her with impossible visions of a future where they will save money and have a home of their own, enjoy themselves before they have babies, and never call each other Mum and Dad:

> 'And I won't get my legs burned from sitting in front of the fire, will I?'
> 'No, if I catch you sitting in front of the fire with your legs splayed out I'll smack your bum for you.' ...

Only at the end of the comic but affecting scene does he come out with his terrible secret, which Elsa forgives, but time cannot:

> 'Elsa, there's something I lied to you about.' ...
> 'I'm not seventeen yet, I just told you that in case you thought I was too young for you.'
> 'How old *are* you?'
> 'Eh, sixteen—just about. My birthday's in May. I left the school early' (146).

When the relationship is over, Dunky misses Elsa terribly, but his greatest fear is betrayal—will Elsa tell Telfer *his* secret thoughts?

Class is something that Dunky often wonders about. His mother desperately clings to a claim to middle-class status, but Dunky wants to be just like other working men. He remembers his initiation into class consciousness at the age of four or five, when he wanted to play football with slum boys and they called him a toff: he threw his cap away to prove he hated it—and did they let him play? 'Maybe he'd invented that part' (33).

Class is an important problem in his education too: at his mother's insistence, Dunky was sent to the Academy, the toff school, where he felt forever out of place. Given that, as we have seen, Dunky shares the general attitudes of his peers to education, perhaps Uncle Charlie's laughter over the diary and his angry memory of early days at the Academy are the basic personal reasons for hating school quite so much. He remembers Billy Aird refusing to go for the football he kicked away. Dunky went instead and was punished. So he attacked Billy Aird, betraying all the characteristics of a 'scheme scruff'. He was dramatically punished, first by the senior school headmaster and then by his father, an embarrassing and shameful memory. His final punishment was being shunned at school by the others, who inexplicably sided with Billy Aird. Now, lying awake, he ponders it:

> Was it silly to remember things like that? When Nicol asked him why he didn't like the school he would have felt like a big gawkit schoolgirl telling him *that*. But it was the start, no doubt about it (170).

He remembers every name with unforgiving bitterness, recalling them like a litany: 'If he lived till he was ninety and he met any of them in Kilcaddie High Street he'd still want to kick the ballocks off them' (171). No wonder then that Dunky left school. No wonder either, that he can never explain it to Nicol.

We are left with football, and drink. Williams once said in an interview in *Scottish International*: 'I'd rather have played once for St Mirren reserves than written *War and Peace*.' And he sees football as the main undercurrent in *From Scenes Like These*: 'Football is the one practical possibility the boy has for achieving some of the magic that life appears to offer when you're young.' Football is the only way in which Dunky understands or can express patriotism: 'That was the greatest thing he could imagine in the whole world, being picked against England—he'd *die* for Scotland' (35).

So we can chart his progress by his attitudes to football. We see three games, all through Dunky's eyes. First there is the match in the 'Saturday' chapter (113–20). It most clearly expresses his confusions: how does a man play football, as opposed to a silly schoolboy? Dunky never fully solves this question: if school believes in fair play and sportsmanship, is the right answer simply foul play? He tries it, but with no happy results. In this first match he is characteristically tense and nervous. He is afraid of the spectators, desperately afraid of Baldy Campbell because his longing to get into the first team is so great—come to that, his dreams about being 'discovered' and signed up by a professional team are so urgent; and yet the bad possibilities are always there too—each game is a tightrope, and falling off is a real and appalling possibility.

All Dunky's 'narrative' is in effect a pondering on and questioning of experience, but occasionally a crucial thought or memory is emphasised in italics, as was that worst school memory (168–70). Here Dunky becomes aware of 'two parts of his brain': one instructs the other, in italics, to go in hard:

> *Hard as nails. Don't care about being hurt. Only get hurt if you go in half-hearted. Do or die* (115).

But Dunky soon gets caught 'in two minds', and gives away a goal. All Baldy says at half-time is that he mustn't be scared to take his man. Dunky interprets this as something stronger than Baldy's actual words: he thinks Baldy believes in '*REAL football, not a lot of namby-pamby schools stuff*', and spends the rest of the game encouraging himself to 'go in—hard as nails', first risking and receiving a nasty kick in a hard tackle, and then deliberately and repeatedly fouling, without much reaction from the referee. Baldy approves afterwards, 'We'll mibbe see about trying you out in the first team.'

In the match in chapter 12 (228–34), Dunky gets his chance to play for the first team. The 'bigtime' nature of the game, proper dressing-room, real football stadium, exhilarates him. This is his big chance to impress, and he begins with a hard tackle. He goes on to fouls, and threats; his team goes three goals up and half-time is wonderful. Baldy's very presence 'made you feel you were somebody' (230). The second half becomes very dirty. Dunky's team identifies the opposing inside-left as the danger man, and they gang up on him. When the referee fails to award a foul, Dunky thinks exultantly, 'He was weak!' Dunky sees playing a violent game as the one way to justify himself, in all departments of his life:

> So they wanted a kicking match? Right. Let's get tore in properly. Next time he'd tramp on the bastard's hands. All the people who watched him thought he was a coward. They all remembered him being frightened of the horses, of Blackie McCann, of guys at the dancing, of Telfer. There was only one way to show them.
> It was the only way to play. To hate the other team. To want to destroy them (231–2).

It is hate, then, that motivates his final foul, a quite unnecessary tackle from which he only wakes up in hospital. And still Dunky has not found answers as to how to play. He is still deeply involved; almost his first question is 'Did we win?' But again his moods vary. He first blames himself: 'He'd behaved like an animal and he'd got what he deserved.' For a moment he is repentant, even anxious about the opponent he has injured, but the two minds from the first match persist:

> No, that was soft, to think like that. . . . If you were going to put the mockers on another player you had to do it the canny way. Learn to get away with murder, that was the motto. . . . Know better the next time.

What Dunky is definitely left with is fear: 'Thinking about the next time made his stomach rise' (234).

His football career is now virtually over. The next match is Dunky's last as a player. After drinking for dutch courage, Dunky plays a great first half: 'He ran quicker than anybody else and tackled harder than anyone else' (242). But the drink does not help his fitness, and its fear-reducing power wears off:

> whenever he went for the ball he felt himself wincing, ready to cover his face with his arms in case he got a knock on the nose. . . . If you had to screw up your courage before each tackle you might as well not bother. . . . By the end of the game he was too winded to chase butterflies. . . . It was only a bloody game. It wasn't worth the effort. Drinking was better (242–3).

He is left with drinking, and his new mates who neither believe nor care about his fears on the football pitch, but help him to 'drink his rabbits' without compunction.

The last chapter happens some five or six months after the football game that landed Dunky in hospital, and it makes depressing reading. Most of the things that individuated Dunky, the rabbits, his love for Elsa, his football ambitions, are long gone. He attempts to supply their lack with repetitive claims about what men are and how he is one, now: 'Whisky was for men. . . . Fags were for men. . . . Men knew about whisky. . . . It was like a man to have mates like them. . . . It was like a man to stand at the bar. . . .' He seems to be trying to convince himself: and hardly succeeds at that better than at convincing the reader that he is now free, adult and happy. His new mates are wonderful—but they are not interested in his worries, or each other: Shanky unconcernedly leaves Jakie, drunk, in the middle of the road, and tells Dunky a story the moral of which is that you should look after number one, and only number one.

Happiness is a New Year party? Dunky mixes his drinks, beer and sweet
VP wine and whisky, and becomes stupidly drunk:

> Holding the glasses above his head he tried to show them the sword dance. The
> rug slipped and he sat down on his spine. He lay on his back and laughed, the beer
> and wine pouring on his chest. A girl said something nasty about him (254).

Later he wakes to his first real hangover. Next day at Shanky's insistence,
they travel to the traditional Rangers–Celtic game at Ibrox. Williams ends
the novel there, with Dunky momentarily happy, part of a drunken, united
crowd: 'He held his hands high above his head and roared and roared until
his throat was sore.' But unfortunately for Dunky, he cannot remain in that
state. He has reached a dead end, and is trying to be happy there. But the
daft thoughts have not left him, and show no sign of doing so. Even in the
pub, he had misgivings:

> Great. So why did he suddenly feel peculiar? Alone and not really part of it (249).

The last insight we get is between the hangover and the match, and all the
old questions are still troubling him: Dunky cannot be happy in his dead
end unless he can strangle these questions, and they show no sign of going
away:

> What did it all mean? What were men, anyway? Why wasn't he a man himself? He
> was a nothing, a collection of poses. Easily led, his mother called it. Nobody knew
> anything about you. You didn't know anything about anybody else. . . .
> . . . You wanted to be like other people but they did the dirty on you, one way or
> the other. You started off trying to be different, trying not to turn out like all the
> others. You ended up worse than them. You ended up knowing you were a
> disgrace, full of all the things you hated in other people (254–5).

You need your mind to be much deader than Dunky's to be happy in a
dead end.

FURTHER READING

Our page references are to the Allison and Busby edition of 1980.

Gordon Williams was born in Paisley in 1934, and grew up there, working briefly on
a farm like his hero Dunky Logan. He did his National Service in the RAF and
became a newspaper reporter before becoming a fulltime writer. He lives in
London. He has produced a prodigious amount of work, by no means all under his

own name—there are the books about the wise-cracking private eye Hazell, for example, written jointly with football manager Terry Venables under the pseudonym of P B Yuill. Some of his novels have been bestsellers, such as *The Siege of Trencher's Farm* (1969), which became the film *Straw Dogs*: others of his novels have been avowed potboilers.

His best and most serious novels share a common theme, the struggle of a central character to make something of his life after, in each case, an unpromising upbringing in post-war Scotland: their seriousness never precludes comedy. Apart from *From Scenes Like These*, which was runner up for the Booker Prize in 1968, they are *The Camp* (1966), *The Upper Pleasure Garden* (1970), *Walk Don't Walk* (1972) and *Big Morning Blues* (1974).

Williams is deeply suspicious of and hostile to anything self-consciously literary, let alone academic criticism, and not surprisingly there is to date very little critical work about him. These are all brief treatments.

Alan Bold, *Modern Scottish Literature* (1983)

Francis Russell Hart, *The Scottish Novel: A Critical Survey* (1978)

John Lloyd, 'A Novelist in the Mirror', an interview with Gordon Williams in *Scottish International* (August 1971), 22–8

Bob Tait, 'A Profile of Gordon Williams' in *Leopard Magazine* 85 (Dec/Jan 1982/83), 28–9

— 'Scots Apart: The Novels of James Kennaway and Gordon Williams' in *Cencrastus* 5 (Summer 1981), 20–22

CHAPTER EIGHT

George Mackay Brown:
Greenvoe

Miss Margaret Inverary is a schoolteacher from Edinburgh with romantic notions, a very pale shadow of Jean Brodie, teaching at a village school on an Orkney island which is portrayed with realism, affection and comedy:

> A singing lesson was proceeding in the school. Miss Inverary thumped the piano. A score of faces had lost all human expression and were caught up in one cold seraphic trance. The mouths opened and shut.
>
>> *Speed, bonny boat, like a bird on the wing*
>> *'Onward,' the sailors cry.*
>> *'Carry the lad that's born to be king*
>> *Over the sea to Skye.'*
>
> 'That was *nice*,' said Miss Inverary. 'Ernie Kerston, take your finger out of your nose. Now I'm going to write the next verse on the blackboard. Those who can write, copy it down in your exercise books, neatly. Now tell me, who has a boat like the boat in the song? Think hard. Hands up.'
>
> My dad,' said Ernie Kerston, and drew a long pale worm out of his left nostril with the nail of his right forefinger (11).

Greenvoe is no Eden, and as we see it contains at least one serpent. The people of Greenvoe are rendered, characteristically, with unsentimental realism and wry comedy, and this is a major part of the book's impact.

But George Mackay Brown first became known as a poet with a clear new voice from Orkney, with volumes such as *Loaves and Fishes* (1959) and *The Year of the Whale* (1965). Later he was recognised as one of the most gifted and original living short story writers, with *A Calendar of Love* (1967) and *A Time to Keep* (1972). Only after this did he attempt his first novel, *Greenvoe* (1972). He remains a very fine poet, and this is what we want to start from, a poet's perception of a divine cosmos, of a natural harmony. He is very conscious that the Orkney of which he devotedly writes, either of the past or of the present, is *not* Eden: it is a very imperfect place because of the imperfections of man—although Mackay Brown is not on the whole judgemental or disapproving, but accepting and apparently tacitly forgiving.

His imagination is possessed by natural and supernatural rhythms, the rhythm of the seasons, of man's life from birth to death, of ploughing, sowing, reaping and harvest, and a less tangible rhythm of divine protection and care, often expressed in the language of the rituals and ceremonies of the Roman Catholic church, which Mackay Brown joined as a mature adult in 1961.

Mackay Brown is by no means unique in his large, symbolic view of the world, time and eternity: most obviously his poetic master Edwin Muir had similar perceptions and preoccupations, evinced, for example, when he called the first version of his autobiography *The Story and the Fable*: he was most concerned with the fable, which lay at a deeper level than the surface story. And the author of *The Silver Darlings* had a similar bent, as we have suggested. It was of Gunn that Kurt Wittig wrote: 'He is not interested in chance happenings; he is looking for the pattern of life, the underlying ritual, the myth.' Mackay Brown is in some ways like these two; if possible more so, because of the richness and resonance of all his central images, which in his best work are often simple, prosaic and descriptive and yet deeply symbolic at the same time.

So in his story 'The Tarn and the Rosary' (*Hawkfall*, 1974, 168–200) the hero is asked to explain his conversion to Roman Catholicism to a free-thinking old friend who feels betrayed by it. Unusually in Mackay Brown, Colm is fairly clearly a projection of the author: he writes to his friend:

If I *have* to argue, all I can offer is an unfolding sequence of images: stations that lead to a stone, and silence, and perhaps after that (if I'm lucky) a meaning (195).

This is true of Mackay Brown's imaginative writing: he does not argue, as MacColla argues through Fearchar: he offers a sequence of images. Notice his natural habit of mind in his expression here: 'stations ... stone ... silence.' A station is merely a stopping place on a journey, but we would suggest that Mackay Brown never uses it without some reference to the Stations of the Cross, the series of images or pictures representing fourteen successive incidents of the Passion and death of Christ which are visited in order by Roman Catholics for meditation and prayer. The stone in this context inevitably becomes the stone rolled to the mouth of Jesus' tomb (compare *An Orkney Tapestry*, 31), and the silence is self explanatory. In Christian terms, thereafter, we *are* lucky, because the silence is broken by Christ's resurrection—that indeed provides a meaning. The same situation is evoked at the end of *Greenvoe* by the Horsemen, without specific Christian reference: the Harvester appears dead, and silent: the Lord of the Harvest intones:

But what did the dust seem to say? He was looking for a word. Unless he has found the word we ourselves are locked in the stone. We belong to the kingdom of death (248).

When the word 'Resurrection' is spoken, the darkness and silence are broken by dawn, rejoicing and a common meal: the images lead to a meaning.

So we suggest that Mackay Brown's imagination is interestingly compact, and suffused with coalescing images: images from his real life Orkney experience, fishermen with ploughs, simple pastoral images of silver fish and green or golden cornstalk, and images from the New Testament where Jesus called fishermen to become 'fishers of men', performed miracles with loaves and fishes, and told parables in simple country language: 'A sower went forth to sow ...'; 'Except a corn of wheat fall into the ground and die ...'. And also images of Christ's life and death rendered through Catholic devotional tradition, the joyful, sorrowful or glorious mysteries, the Passion, and the sacraments. Mackay Brown's Christianity is essentially sacramental, his imagination moved by the water and salt of baptism, the consecration and the breaking of bread which is at the centre of the Mass, when the bread, it is believed, actually becomes the body and blood of Christ.

. It is a potent brew, in a poet's mind, although he is born into a time when all his preoccupations may seem relatively peripheral, or irrelevant to a vast majority of his potential public. We would argue that he succeeds better in his poems, stories, novels, proceeding imagistically, than in his occasional outspoken *argued* prose. To get a quick resumé of Mackay Brown's ideas it may seem useful to consult his contribution to *Memoirs of a Modern Scotland* (1970), 'The Broken Heraldry'. Here he succinctly opposes 'progress' to the ancient heraldry, the meaningful community of Orkney, and traces the destructive agent 'progress' back to the Reformation, seeing Calvinism as a 'catastrophe' for Orkney—and the rest of Scotland—and looking back to a (Catholic) community with a 'single interwoven identity':

> In earlier times the temporal and the eternal, the story and the fable, were not divorced, as they came to be after Knox: they used the same language and imagery, so that the whole of life was illuminated. Crofters and fishermen knew what Christ was talking about ... because they bore the stigmata of labour on their bodies—the net let down into the sea, the sower going forth to sow, the fields white towards harvest. ... Most marvellous of all was that their daily labours were a divine image for their strivings heavenwards, and were rewarded at last by the Bread of Heaven, the Blessed Sacrament, Christ himself dwelling in them. Here was the ultimate intermingling of the earthy and the holy (145).

But this is just a kind of code, giving us some idea of how to read the poems, stories and novels: Mackay Brown is at his best in his 'sequence of images', and the success of *Greenvoe* depends on his combination of wholly recognisable human individuals portrayed with realistic and comic detail with the intimations of other layers of meaning, in natural life and in a spiritual sense.

Much—perhaps most—of Mackay Brown's imaginative writing is concerned to celebrate the natural lives of small communities, close to nature, to natural rhythms, and to their own past. Usually, these communities are in the native Orkney he knows so well, sometimes set in the past ages of Viking longships, of Magnus Martyr, of the trials of witches or the iconoclasm of the Reformation, and often set in the present, a timeless present, suffused with continuity and awareness of history. But the scene does not have to be Orkney, or the time past or present—'The Seven Poets' (*The Sun's Net*, 1976, 257–68) is set in a post-cataclysm future, where people worldwide have returned to living a simple life, in villages of not more than 250 inhabitants. Each village has its shepherd, baker, fisherman, weaver, priest and poet: Mackay Brown values each individual, but affirms also the identity they take from their occupation. In the Preface to his poem cycle *Fishermen with Ploughs* (1974) he writes:

> the same people appear and reappear through many generations—the laird, the crofter-fisherman, the shepherd, the tinker, the beachcomber, and the women who watch the sea with stony patience.

At the beginning of *Greenvoe* our first impression is of a very similar cast of characters, the fishermen, the merchant, the beachcomber, the ferryman, the publican, the schoolteacher.

It is in this kind of community, with its 'single interwoven identity', that Mackay Brown believes men best come to the fullest understanding of the meaning of life: a long poem, 'Fisherman and Boy', from *The Year of the Whale* ends:

> Thorfinn, you will learn more in Orkney
> Than Mansie did
> Who made seven salt circles of the globe.

If Mackay Brown's major theme is this celebration, it is often shadowed by a more sombre note. Mackay Brown perceives only too well that this old hallowed life is receding, small agricultural communities are becoming depopulated, the old ways are dying. Frequently he points us to the beautiful green valley of Rackwick on the island of Hoy, shrunk from a thriving community to one farm only (e.g. *An Orkney Tapestry*, 25–52). He blames the nature of the modern world, the worship of material 'progress', and also the dislocation of religious and natural life that we have seen he blames on the Reformation and Calvinism. So an undercurrent in Mackay Brown's works about modern Orkney is always one of lamentation at modern change, which impoverishes the community, and at the gradual disappearance of the communities themselves.

Beyond this sadness is a further horror, what Mackay Brown calls 'the atom-and-planet horror at the heart of our civilisation' or 'a Black Pentecost' (*An Orkney Tapestry*, 51, 52). The possibility of nuclear war, of mankind's simultaneous self-destruction and the destruction of all creation, is a horrifying, constant threat. This gives potency to the evil image at the heart of *Greenvoe*, the Black Star. And as long as civilisation as we know it is threatened by nuclear holocaust, *Greenvoe* will have a profound effect on readers who may share few of the novelist's detailed beliefs.

Greenvoe is a fine statement of Mackay Brown's beliefs, hopes, fears, which never stridently argues a case, and which presents a picture if anything biassed against a simple acceptance of his values. For the community of Greenvoe is far from ideal, interwoven and harmonious: it is an ageing community—virtually a dying one—before the advent of Black Star. Even the sympathetic Welfare Officer admits:

> the village was moribund in any case, a place given over almost wholly to the elderly, the fatuous, the physically inept. Black Star merely accelerated the process (217).

And the imperfect, often feckless but likeable people of Greenvoe are apparently faced not with nuclear war or destruction but the faceless nature of bureaucratic man, the unspeaking guest who labels, files and disposes of them, with only hints of an atomic horror, '*utterly essential to the security of the western world*' (243). On the face of it, what happens in the novel is that a vividly created small community suffers a twentieth-century version of the Clearances; Hart calls it 'the serious novel of latter-day Clearances'. And we react to all this with the sad indignation we reserve for the cruel results of that historical phenomenon.

But the face of it is not all: behind the face is a vision as black and monstrous as that of the poet Milton in Book II of *Paradise Lost*. Milton set out to retell the central story of Christianity: he tells of the creation of the angels and their fall under Satan, the creation of man and the fall of Adam and Eve tempted by Satan, and the offer made by God the Son to restore the damage to mankind by his own sacrifice, his Incarnation as man and his crucifixion. All this Milton does powerfully, recreating the traditional story in his own voice. Christian doctrine is acutely meaningful to Milton as to many other poets: in particular the doctrine of the Trinity, three persons in one god, the Father, who begets the Son, and the Holy Ghost who is the expression of their love. One of the most powerful parts of *Paradise Lost* is the odious anti-Trinity Milton draws in Book II, largely his own creation. Instead of Father, Son and Holy Spirit we have here Satan, Sin and Death, the father and his incestuous progeny. During the conspiracy in Heaven Sin is born (a 'virgin' birth) from Satan's head: he finds her wonderfully attractive, because he sees himself in her, and he makes her pregnant. After the Fall she brings forth Death, the result of their incestuous union, both Satan's son and his grandson—who immediately rapes his mother and begets monsters on her. It is a truly Hellish picture, vividly created, a vile parody of what Milton most centrally believed in.

Part of the impact of *Greenvoe* comes from a similarly powerful and outraged vision of evil and obscenity. Mackay Brown believes ultimately in broadly the same basic doctrines as Milton: he sees the Incarnation of Christ as the ultimate and abiding fact of all history, in which history is transformed, the ultimate paradox, when God the all-powerful takes on the littleness of man and eternity breaks into the dimension of time, spreading shock waves back and forward. T S Eliot calls the Incarnation, 'the point of intersection of the timeless with time'. Christ as man accepts death, and conquers death, and in his resurrection the resurrection of all men is made possible. Mackay Brown's powerful vision here is of a different Incarnation, an evil or black one. Satan enters the world of time and Greenvoe as a Black Star, a hideous, death-dealing parody of the liberating, life-bringing Christ. The Black Star then withers, destroys, freezes, produces an apparently final negation. Of course the very word Incarnation is inappropriate here: Christ was 'made flesh', but the Evil that enters Hellya with Black Star is so anti-human that it takes the form of inanimate modern building materials, especially the concrete Mackay Brown so much deplores (245).

We all know of the star that led the three Magi to the place of Christ's birth: its message adds dimensions to the natural associations of stars, brightness, shining, whiteness, beauty. *Greenvoe* is full of stars, from fleeting comparisons to underground constructions: what could be more opposite to the high bright stars we are accustomed to than the laborious underground construction we find at the end of the novel? But Black Star has a precedent, which we learn of in The Skarf's first part of his history of the island. He describes the first-comers to Hellya as 'children of darkness . . . the grave was their kingdom' (24). What did they leave behind?

a chamber, a long barrow corbelled with some skill that opened out into minor chambers on each side, a dozen of them, radiating from the central barrow like rays of a dark sun (24–5).

And the whole construction was filled with bones.

When at last we gather something of the physical nature of Black Star by report, it may well remind us of that chamber of death, and indicate that this kind of visitation can be recurrent in history:

it seemed, from things the labourers said in drink, that a system of tunnels was being dug into the heart of the island, five of them in all (said Jock MacIntosh the foreman from Glasgow) radiating out from one central underground chamber. So it was indeed a kind of black star that was being burned and blasted under the roots of Korsfea and Ernefea and The Knap. What it was for, of course none of the navvies could say. . . . It could be some kind of atomic work, they could not say (216).

All kinds of stars recur in *Greenvoe*. Timmy Folster takes great pleasure from a bright starfish he finds which 'blazed from the floor' (134): Simon McKee's first failed attempt at preaching makes him look 'awful as if a white star of shock had burst upon his face' (172): the face of dead Ben Budge is 'remote as a star' (200), and when Johnny meets the guest at the hotel he concludes: 'This creature and I, indeed we live on different stars' (86). Only once before the end is there a black star, and that is when the children bully gentle, simple-minded Gino Manson: 'They kicked mud at him. A black star filthied his cheek' (48).

But by far the most important star is the terrible, parodic Black Star which takes over the island in the final section. It seems quite clear that this demonic parody is deliberate and self-conscious: earlier Mackay Brown has even the atheist Skarf voicing anti-Calvinist prejudice (as Johnny is quick to point out), when he describes the palace of the wicked earl Robert Stewart:

The earl's palace stood there like a kind of blasphemous parody of the divine cosmos, with shrieks and fire underground, and banqueting and love on top, and in between the hosts of servants, the milk-maids, sty-keepers, cooks, brewers, who bore unquestioningly the burden of humanity. There was no sign of a Christian chapel in all these ordered exquisite harmonious damned stones (77).

We are told in the final section that Greenvoe 'shrivelled slowly in the radiance of Black Star' (217). Mackay Brown extends his parody:

The black star exploded slowly under the hills and at last drew the whole of Hellya into its mystery and passion (240).

Even after the abandonment of the project, the labourers leave 'disturbed dust . . . on a seedless island', while: 'Deep in the heart of Hellya the Black Star froze' (245).

At the centre of Christianity is God the Word, a powerful concept for Mackay Brown, connected with poetry, humane values, images, beauty. Black Star is described on the contrary by its devotees as 'a pure rite of science' (242). This contrast harks back to the perceptions of Indian Johnny about the guest, the bureaucrat, 'Western Man arrived at a foreseen inevitable end', ruling the world with a card index file (86). Non-Christian Johnny reflects:

> I have known for some time that the mysterious omnipotent life-giving word has grown very old. . . . For our worship is erected now, all over the world, in place of the Word, the Number (86).

Miss Brodie insisted that Art comes before science: a world where number, uniformity, science and card indexes replace humane values is for Mackay Brown a foretaste of Hell.

The opposition of Black Star, meaning death, and its contrary, is clear to the end. The word that the Horsemen seek, as we have seen, is 'Resurrection': before it is discovered the other word rules—black star, like 'a piece of magic, a very secret codeword' (215). So the island is abandoned after the construction of the substantial concrete and barbed wire perimeter, which makes it strangely reminiscent of the 'anthrax island' of Gruinard which was declared perpetually forbidden after chemical warfare experiments in the Second World War. There is no prospect of the people being allowed to return. Surely this is the victory of Evil, the depopulation reflecting both the end of Eden and the most savage Clearances: a despairing vision of final negation.

Mackay Brown counters this not with a Christian or specifically Catholic message of hope, but with an affirmation of man and his relationship to nature, man and his determination in time. He has made us aware at the end of every section of an ancient association of agricultural men, and this is what returns to a ritual ceremony on the island ten years after it has been fenced off: this is what leaves the message of hope. This 'Ancient Mystery of The Horsemen' (29) is neither a simple invention nor a true record of fact. What Mackay Brown does is to adapt and launder a very old phenomenon, the society of the 'Horseman's Word'. This society, apparently deriving from an earlier cult, kept its secrets very carefully, and still is not fully known. Ernest Marwick writes: 'Its avowed object was to initiate the young ploughman into the mysteries of horsemanship': it spread to Orkney from mainland' Scotland. Mackay Brown has adapted many known features, meetings at dead of night, the bread and whisky, the flails, some of the ritual questions, and the importance of the secret word. He has removed old suggestions of Devil-worship, and power for womanising, and presents the Horsemen with dignity and power: each section of the novel ends with a 'station', and as always we are reminded of the Stations of the Cross. So we are given a ritual of man-and-nature, mysterious but affirmative, and often parallel to Christian ideas, just as in Mackay Brown's basic thinking ploughing, sowing, reaping and harvest can be seen as emblematic of Christ's birth, death and resurrection.

The Horsemen are presented briefly and objectively each time, but on the first and last occasion we get some realistic detail about the seven participants, and their names. The Lord of the Harvest in both cases is Mansie Anderson, the old man who for so long refused to leave The Bu, the oldest farm on the island, built by Thorkeld Harvest-Happy in 1006. The other personnel change, for this is an initiation rite for the young. At the first station they are all farmers or sons of farmers, characters non-central to the story, which centres on the village: by the end, there are characters we recognise, including one of Bert Kerston's sons, young Skarf, Alice Voar's son, and his elder brother Sidney Fortin-Bell, and the simple-minded Gino Manson. Our recognition of these characters adds to the message of hope they bring, with sunrise, and shared meal, and earth smells and Mansie's affirmation:

> We have brought light and blessing to the kingdom of winter, however long it endures, that kingdom, a night or a season or a thousand ages. The word has been found. Now we will eat and drink together and be glad (249).

Why did Mackay Brown choose this means of conveying his message of hope? Was the notion of horses at the back of his mind already? He has written two works about the 'atom-and-planet horror', *Greenvoe* and *Fishermen with Ploughs*. *Fishermen with Ploughs* is a poem cycle about an attempt to re-establish an agricultural community after the devastation of a nuclear war, with very limited success—and a less optimistic conclusion than *Greenvoe*. It seems quite possible that the horses or Horsemen in both works are a hint from Edwin Muir and his famous poem 'The Horses'. Mackay Brown has desribed Muir as 'the poet who speaks for all of us' (*An Orkney Tapestry*, 18), and arguably both *Fishermen with Ploughs* and *Greenvoe* can be read as complex and individual variations on that poem.

Muir's poem is narrated by a survivor of 'the seven days war that put the world to sleep'—an ironic balance of the seven days of creation described in Genesis, when God worked for six days and rested on the seventh. The six sections of Greenvoe seem to mirror this same pattern: in a way they are six

'days', one fine, one rainy, one narrated by Johnny, etc., but in the course of
them Mackay Brown evokes the whole life of the island and its history, so
that his six 'days' are more like the symbolic days of creation than Muir's
terse six days of war. Muir's survivors have turned away from all that led to
war, rejecting 'progress', machinery, 'That bad old world that swallowed its
children quick / At one great gulp.' They have gone back to hard, ancient
methods of cultivation, letting tractors uselessly rust, ploughing with oxen,
determined but implicitly joyless. Then, like a gift, 'the strange horses'
appear, to offer 'free servitude':

> as if they had been sent
> By an old command to find our whereabouts
> And that long-lost archaic companionship.

This gift marks a new beginning in hope, as it were a renewal of the
relationship established between man and beasts in Genesis. At the end of
Greenvoe it is still possibly a far off hope, but it also seems a promise of an
eventual new beginning.

The technique Mackay Brown chooses for this, his first novel, is
experimental, and he performs like a virtuoso. He builds on his established
strengths as a short story writer, and builds up his picture of the community
like a patchwork, fitting together large and small scenes, representative and
very individual characters. Sometimes he uses the same type of technique in
miniature, within scenes, deliberately varying style, language or viewpoint
to achieve ironic detachment or wry amusement in the reader. We should
not look in the book for amazing, strong or very individual characters:
Mackay Brown's attempt is clearly to render a community, a more difficult
task. But his characters do gradually have different kinds of importance,
are less or more developed. Some are very simple: when we have met the
Evies in the first section we can predict their non-development as characters
and their final Kirkwall prosperity, and Alice Voar will surely remain
gentle, and generous, with inevitably a larger family. Other characters
develop to varying extents, the most extreme case being that of Mrs McKee
and her son Simon, whose story it has been suggested overbalances the
novel in its concentration and detail.

We will offer another reading. So we will look at the short first section,
where Mackay Brown sows the seeds of his various characters, then
comment on the further development of a few of them, and finally we will
look in detail at a few scenes of fine 'patchwork', where styles are used to
great effect, to ends very different from any conventional realism.

Like all of the first five sections, the first begins with dawn and finishes
with the village asleep again, only the Horsemen awake and active. This

section sets the pattern. Our introduction to the village is appropriately to three fishermen's cottages where the lights are on early. These three and their inhabitants begin to form a neat pattern. The first character we meet is Bert Kerston, setting off to fish in his boat the *Ellen*, which we rightly suppose to be named after his wife. Bert is the ordinary, fleshly fisherman. In contrast is the 'mild chant' from next door, where the religious fisherman Samuel Whaness reads of the power of the sea monster leviathan from Job. Samuel and Rachel are earnest, grave, Hebraic: their extreme Protestant piety is emphasised as Samuel sets off in his boat, *Siloam*, named after the pool of miraculous healing. The third fisherman completes the pattern: The Skarf decides not to fish, but to write: he does so much writing and so little fishing that it is not until much later (78) that we discover the significant name of his boat, the *Engels*. (The Skarf describes himself as a Marxist-Leninist-Maoist (229).)

The short initial section ends with the Budges, Bella outside feeding her chickens, including the incongruously named Kitty, and Ben the much travelled, coarse-tongued old seaman. Their characters will not exactly develop, but Ben's death, the only one in the first five sections, represents the dying community, and Bella's timid love for him is one of the book's under-stated positives: 'she had liked him, if that was possible, better than herself' (149). Ben was an unbeliever, but Simon McKee comforts Bella appropriately: when she laments Ben is in the dark, Simon replies: 'He's sailing into the sunrise, old Ben' (154): Simon is no simple dead loss. All these characters have been introduced in less than two pages: all will be developed or at the least further established by repeated appearances.

The next 'patch' takes us to the general merchant's store, the centre of much village life, and again deftly introduces the Evies, some customers and their characters. Mr Evie sees himself as an important figure, 'postmaster, merchant, county councillor, justice of the peace', but our first impression of his little shop is of some distaste at the bluebottles feasting on fruit and sweets. But Mrs Evie is the centre here: 'her eyes took in the wakening village in one caustic probe' (8). For the first of many times we see her probing, enquiring nature, the source of considerable comedy in the book. We will soon see that the correct Mr Evie always ignores her questions: here also Ivan Westray the ferryman evades her interest in the ferry's early start—'Who's crossing over today?' He replies: 'President Nixon and Mao Tse-Tung.' But Mrs Evie works it out, like her literary ancestor the old kailyard woman Jess in *A Window in Thrums*—it must be the laird's granddaughter. After probing Bella Budge and warning her of the 'death hunger' in Ben, Mrs Evie in three short sentences condemns Alice Voar and her illegitimate family, Scorradale the publican for his late hours and The Skarf for socialism and atheism. This is useful information, an entertaining exposition for the new reader, economically also indicating her character: Mr Evie's reply is tersely typical: 'It is a lovely morning, Mrs Evie.' As we leave the shop we learn that there is something very queer about the minister's mother, and that the new schoolteacher is man-hungry.

The 'patches' are often neatly linked. The first two are linked by Ben's call for breakfast and Bella's visit to the shop, while the second, third and fourth are linked by Mrs Evie's aspersions on Alice Voar and the schoolteacher: Alice appears in the third and the schoolteacher in both: this kind of neat linkage is often noticeable throughout. Alice Voar is glimpsed 'herding' her children to school, their mouths crammed with 'bread and jam and dry cornflakes'. The details are few and well-chosen: we never see Alice failing to care for her children, but we cannot imagine her as a good cook, and it seems typical fecklessness in her to have no milk for the cornflakes. Enter Skarf for a ballpoint and other shopping, and again we usefully learn from Mrs Evie that Skarf has determinedly refused the role of lad o' pairts: he *could* have gone to university, chose instead to help his uncle with the lobsters: he is also officially unemployed, like Timmy Folster drawing state benefit.

Timmy is soon introduced, in his unrepaired, burnt-out cottage. His amiable conversation with himself, 'Timmy's a good boy', etc., confirms for us that he is rather simple-minded, and it is evident from his conversation with Mr Evie that he is in the habit of drinking methylated spirits. It is wholly characteristic of Mackay Brown that virtually no condemnation of these characters is offered, although it is interesting to see later what the wise and humane young Indian makes of them all in the third section.

But occasional Mackay Brown prejudices surface, often endearingly. We have mentioned his dislike of 'progress' and modern machinery, and he repeatedly admits to it: here he prejudices us against the laird and his family with the breach of the peace in the village which occurs every time the laird's old car enters it, shaking, coughing, rattling. The relationship of gentry and islanders is finely illuminated by the way, the islanders amazed at the 'heroic voices' of the gentry, especially Miss Fortin-Bell, who 'spoke as if she were shouting into a gale'. Economically again we glimpse the incipient relationship of Inga Fortin-Bell and Ivan Westray, the girl clutching a copy of *Women in Love* and apparently ready for an encounter with a handsome peasant; the complacency of the gentry and the wonder of the children; and before the two-page 'patch' is complete the complication of the ferryman's love life is again suggested. The children have already detected Miss Inverary's weakness for Ivan Westray: now as she buys apples in the store, apples that will acquire increasing sexual connotations,

Mrs Evie apparently inconsequentially begins talking about hereditary oddness in the Westrays.

Possibly the novel could become tedious and predictable if such brief and economical patching were to continue indefinitely: certainly, each section has interruptions in it, of varying length, the most regular of these being close-ups on Mrs McKee and The Skarf's public performances of his writings. In the first section of *Greenvoe* Mrs McKee hardly undergoes the kind of mental assize we find later, but we are introduced to her mental state to a quite different degree from the other characters: we learn of the regularity of her trials, four times a year, with a hint that her assizes coincide with Simon's drinking bouts—but we do not specifically know of these yet, we just have a mention of 'his own little private cross' (15). Here, longer narrative comment than we have been used to establishes that Mrs McKee paradoxically enjoys the pain of these trials, even looks forward to them. Only one charge is made here, by a phantom advocate, that Mrs McKee possesses a tea-pot which is the rightful property of her sister Flora, deceased. The triviality of the charge may give us a clue as to how to read later, apparently much more serious charges: Mrs McKee's extraordinary and convoluted sense of guilt will finally convince her that Black Star itself is her fault: '*This is happening because I live here.*' Mrs Evie was surely right when she said: 'There's something very queer about that woman, more queer even than ever I thought' (10).

Mrs Evie's village gossip is now filled out by Ben Budge's, as he writes to his absent nephew Tom, offering help, support and local news. He reinforces our suspicion of a blossoming relationship between the schoolteacher and Ivan Westray, and tells us Ellen Kerston is expecting her sixth child by her drunken Bert, thus preparing us for the 'immense woman' who is about to visit the shop. There she has to apologise for her husband's drunken insults—to the pious Whanesses, that they were whited sepulchres, and to Alice Voar that she was a whore: we do not imagine this is Ellen's first or last such apology. Our picture of the regular, ongoing life of the village is filled out even by the contents of the postbag and the periodicals ordered by different characters.

The day wears on. After a lively account of the play of the children newly out of school, we have a terse encounter between the schoolteacher Miss Inverary and Ivan Westray. He has waited seven weeks for her, and suggests he may wait no longer. His previous conquests have taught him no grace: 'I want to know, what you are going to do about it?' (21), and he instructs her again about signalling when she is ready to capitulate.

The only important part of the village we have not yet seen is the hotel, and Mr Scorradale its landlord, 'like a toby jug come to life', reflecting 'a lifetime of grease and unction' (22). Like Mr Evie, we can safely predict Mr

Scorradale will do well out of the destruction of Greenvoe. The two fishermen of the first page are briefly contrasted again, as Ellen Kerston catches Bert about to enter the hotel to sell a lobster and buy drink, while Samuel Whaness returns home with a basket of fish and Rachel visits Timmy and Alice with gifts of fish. Now The Skarf comes to the pub to read the first instalment of his history of the island. To Mackay Brown this is important: he writes in *An Orkney Tapestry*: 'Contemporary Orkney, cut off from the story of its past, is meaningless' (19), and of his object in that book he writes:

> I will attempt to get back to the roots and sources of the community, from which it draws its continuing life, from which it cuts itself off at its peril (23).

The method here is possibly over-ingenious, over-economical: Skarf supplies not only an imaginative history, but one which at different times illuminates not only his atheism and socialism but also, for example, Mackay Brown's prejudices against the Reformation and its ill effects. This has to be acknowledged, finally, in the Black Star files, where The Skarf is a self-described Marxist-Leninist-Maoist—'but', the card continues, 'his ideas much tinged with mysticism' (229). To see the extent to which Skarf's ideas in this section parallel Mackay Brown's, it may be interesting to compare it with the similarly imaginative history given in *An Orkney Tapestry* (chapters 1 and 2): the resemblance is fairly close.

At the close of Skarf's reading, Bill Scorradale attempts half-heartedly and unsuccessfully to close the bar in observance of the law, and announces that he expects a guest the next day: this is our first intimation of the faceless, featureless, type-writing bureaucrat who is to pass judgement on the people of Greenvoe and the future of the island: the best description of him perhaps occurs when the laird's car calls for him:

> A hat and coat and scarf and brief-case—one thrusting fluent articulation—went from hotel to car and relaxed into the seat beside the laird (137).

Although drinking goes on till midnight, the workers go to bed fairly early: at half past eleven Timmy Folster's meths-inspired singing gets short shrift from Bert Kerston, preparing to be at the creels before long. The whole village is silent and asleep, when the Horsemen assemble in the stable of The Bu for their first solemn initiation rite, which ends the first day.

The characters which most invite further comment seem to be Samuel Whaness, The Skarf and Mrs McKee. All three of these characters in some way voice or live by opinions Mackay Brown holds to be importantly right or wrong, and if he is making criticisms in religious terms it is here, but all three are presented at best with a fine mixture of gravity and comedy. Take Samuel Whaness, for example. His case is not complicated, but the moods of the narrative are varied. His lot as fisherman is hard and dangerous, and after a close call when the *Siloam* is almost wrecked at the Red Head (45–7) he develops a fear and dislike of the sea—and his misgivings are secretly shared by Rachel. His experiences at sea are always vividly and realistically depicted, and his basic character is respected and taken seriously; as we see when he confronts Bert Kerston who has clearly poached in Samuel's creels, but finally blames himself more for loss of control: there is no mockery here (111–13). Eventually another hazardous day's fishing in fog seems to prove fatal (154–6): it is the more effective and suspenseful in that it repeats the first near-wreck in tiny detail like the proximity of the sea-pinks. He 'dies' in faith and with joy at last, and we assume he is dead for some thirty-four pages.

The genuine piety of the Whanesses is never doubted, and so it is appropriate that his 'post-death' experiences are rendered heavily under the influence of the Vanity Fair episode from his favourite book, *The Pilgrim's Progress*, where Christian and Faithful had to go through the Fair to reach the Celestial City. This longest passage relating to Samuel (190–9) convinces us of his true love for his childless wife Rachel, and indicates his (never stated) opinions of his neighbours, from the publican Bill Scorradale and the drunken Bert Kerston to crafty Mr Evie and the inadequate shepherd Simon McKee and his monster-making, monster-ridden mother. Samuel's journey, always in Bunyanesque prose, is serious and convincing, as are his final doubts about his Election, his worthiness, and his clinging to faith, and his difficult climb back to the boat, apparently to save Bert Kerston, and his eventual coming to, in Kerston's boat, with a new eye for life and beauty.

So essentially Samuel is a good man, treated with respect. Only two real jokes are made at his expense—one is the repeated assertion that the Whanesses keep money between the leaves of *The Pilgrim's Progress* (135, 219), with some kind of implication of a correlation between 'gifts and grace', and the other is the extremity of the pair's anti-Catholic prejudice. Rachel gives Johnny of all people a tract called *The Scarlet Woman—The Menace of Popery* (73): Johnny seems to be Hindu. And Samuel's final appearance in Hellya is in an undignified dead-of-night departure when he discovers that the hall he is now tending is to be used for a Mass. But, seriously again, there is nowhere for Samuel to go bar the sea, and at the end the two are living with Rachel's brother and Samuel has a new boat, renamed *Sion*, standing for God's chosen Israel and his church, and Samuel resumes the sea.

Perhaps the least successful character in the novel is The Skarf. He performs his main function, feeding in instalments of an imaginative history of Hellya, but we are given almost no sense of him as a character, and the roles he has to play are rather at odds: he hardly convinces in the sum of them, as artist, drinker, historian, Marxist and mystic. He makes routine gestures towards Marxism, with a clenched fist salute to the 'dead worker', Ben Budge (153), and contemptuous reference to the minister: 'Incursions from the realm of superstition and obscurantism' (56). But his history is both entertaining and puzzling: the predictable gentle anti-Catholic satire is fun, when he recounts the disputed opinions in the time of Thorkeld Harvest-Happy as to whether or not a whale was a fish and could properly therefore be eaten in Lent. Sometimes, as in his account of Mansie Hellyaman in his quest for light (141–4), he does seem an atheist and leftwing intellectual, but at others he is oddly of the Mackay Brown persuasion, managing to incorporate an anti-Calvinist message rather over-regularly: Johnny twice in his detachment remarks on his 'arrogant slanted rigmarole' (96).

It is very briefly hinted (209) that The Skarf believes firmly in progress and the future, but the end is still shocking, partly in an unsuccessful way, because it is simply insufficiently prepared for. In a few pages (228–31) he gets a job with Black Star, allying himself happily with 'industrial man, bureaucratic man', and then his card is found in the file. We get information late on that could have rounded out his portrait, such as his incipient multiple sclerosis. But his sudden suicide when he loses his job is quite unexpected and indeed unexplained, although his weakness and clumsiness in accomplishing it is both moving and grim. Essentially the character is underdeveloped and has too many functions to fulfil.

The other problem case is Mrs McKee, and her character is far from under-developed: we have to answer the suggestion that her story distorts the balance of the novel to a serious extent. Even on a simple count of words or pages devoted to her, Mrs McKee is outstanding in the novel. A minor character like Alice Voar, whom we feel we know well by the end, accumulates tiny passages, rarely appearing for as much as a page at a time, and approximately five pages of the novel concern her. As we have seen, Samuel Whaness is considerably more developed: and his total is twenty pages. But out of the 242 pages of the Penguin edition, Mrs McKee occupies 64, more than a quarter. And it is not only quantity but quality of attention that makes her outstanding: we are introduced into her injured psyche and powerfully re-live with her events of her life for which she holds herself obscurely responsible.

The episodes build up in extent, seriousness and power. In the second section it is a kiss of which she is accused: five weeks after her engagement to

Alan, three weeks after his departure to fight in France, Liz Alder goes to
Millicent's twenty-first birthday party, one of the wonderful and memorable nights of her life, with Millicent a powerful rendition of the coming
phenomenon, the Bright Young Thing—and at the end of the evening Liz
Alder kisses the man who drives her home, himself on leave from France:
'the charge was serious enough, in all conscience' (38)! Later Mrs McKee
sees it as 'being unfaithful' to Alan (82).

In the third section, Mrs McKee is partly aided by Johnny to resist the
assize. The charge here is that Mrs McKee was responsible for Millicent's
death years later, by persuading her to go up Arthur's Seat on Mayday to
wash her face in the dew when she still had a cold. It is clearly as
preposterous as the other charges. But Johnny takes her situation very
seriously, and not just as fabrications of her imagination. He sees her as 'a
gentleness' and a 'gentle frightened old lady', and divines that she was once
'a most beautiful girl'. He feels the presence of her tormentors: 'Never have
I felt the pressure of so many earth-bound preying ungenerous spirits' (81),
and he declares a need for exorcism:

> What is needed is some pure blessed deliberate ritual to rid this old woman of her
> ghosts. They feast on her flesh. They drink her blood, obscenely, like black bats.
> What can one Indian boy do in ten minutes? I am not a holy man.

Johnny lightens the room with talk of flowers, and the beauties of his pack:
'It is like springtime in that Victorian room. The mingled laughter, the
spread of scarlet, the promise of flowers' (84). He tries to persuade her to get
rid of the shadows, that they are unreal. He articulates his own essentially
religious view. Mackay Brown has the impressive precedent of
T S Eliot for introducing a spiritual message in Hindu terms:

> —Dear lady, I say, unfortunately to be lost in these shadows is not to die. It is to
> be, for a space, a burdened ghost. One has not found silence, peace, the song of
> Krishna. The wheel turns. You must suffer it all over again—birth, desire,
> hunger, remorse, death.
> —So, she says sadly.
> —Until at last one escapes. Perhaps only after many turnings of the wheel. At last
> the soul, loving both God and man, will be free. It is lost then in light and silence
> (84–5).

This advice is the only outside view we have of Mrs McKee's trials, and
Johnny seems always a reliable observer, so perhaps he is a reasonable
gauge here of the author's attitude.

Two 'trial' sessions remain, both lengthy ones. There is the story of
young Winifred's visit to the McKees as a girl, their holiday in Edinburgh

and on the West coast, Winifred's story-telling capacity—and the shower of rain from which Mrs McKee pulled her into a doorway. It was the door of a Roman Catholic church, and Mrs McKee is blamed for her later conversion to Roman Catholicism. The prosecutor has begun by indicating that Satan is still trying to return the Church of Scotland to the gauds of Popery, and regretting that supposedly clever, artistic and cultured people convert to Rome every year. Winnie is to be one of them—and somehow her entire subsequent career, lass o' pairts, novelist, unmarried mother, is part of Mrs McKee's disgrace:

> 'Become a Catholic,' said Aunt Flora. 'What's good about that? If you ask me, it's worse than the illegitimate child. Poor Wattie. Poor Phillis.'
> I have finished. With these last words of Miss Flora Alder I come to a close. For hers is, thank God, the authentic affirming voice of religious Scotland (132).

Clearly Mackay Brown is satirising the voice of religious Scotland here, but we cannot help taking Mrs McKee's tormented conscience seriously.

The final session is of course the worst. Alcoholism is a great traditional Scottish affliction, more prevalent in Scotland than in most parts of Northern Europe, and apparently much connected to stern social or religious disapproval of any consumption of alcohol at all: statistics indicate that the children of alcoholics and the children of total abstainers are more liable to alcoholism than others. The prosecutor here smugly boasts that 'since the evangelical and temperance movements of the nineteenth century it is almost unheard of for a Presbyterian minister to touch alcohol' (184). We have no chance of getting an objective view of Simon's condition and its causes. From his history we see that an important initial cause of his indulgence is fear of public speaking (173f); and we suspect his indulgence before his mother and aunt, because of his increased loquacity after every ordeal successfully passed. We are offered the possibility by Aunt Flora that Simon's problem may be hereditary; that Simon may take after his great-grandfather, the taboo John Dunbar:

> A taint like that could be inherited. It might skip a generation or two, then inexplicably in this member of the family or that the fatal pattern might re-establish itself (170).

The book does not adjudicate, but there seems some truth in this, too.

This prosecutor's accusation stays, unlike the others, in the prosecutor's voice throughout, not underlining Mrs McKee's happiness in memory as elsewhere. The only softer note comes from the words of Simon's minister Dr Fordyce, who takes a much less bleak and judgemental view than the prosecutor's. He says to Mrs McKee:

You see, dear woman, I have known for some time that Simon is an alcoholic. And it grieves me to the heart, for I love the boy (179).

And he goes on implicitly to reject simple notions of sin or blame when he sees the whole thing as 'a matter of the utmost delicacy, between a sick man and his God' (182). Certainly no one but Mrs McKee begins to date it all from the moment she gave her barely convalescent son a glass of tonic wine.

In the final section Mrs McKee is ill, clearly deranged, as Simon consults the visiting Winnie about her and she sees herself responsible for all the unhappiness she has ever witnessed:

> *I have brought ruin to everything I have touched and known. Millicent. Alan. Simon. Now I am bringing ruin to this whole island. This is happening because I live here* (223).

She cannot listen to Winnie's conversation, arguably because she is now so involved in this half-pleasant guilt that anything irrelevant to it is merely distracting. Her confusion and loss of touch with reality become greater: 'her communion with the shadows was almost perfect now.'

At last she wakes back in Edinburgh, in hospital, and regains a feeling of youth and joy, a loving recognition of the visiting Simon. Hopefully Johnny's prophecy is fulfilled, and her soul is becoming free, to be lost 'in light and silence'.

But what do we make of all this as part of *Greenvoe*? There are all kinds of minor explanations or justifications we could suggest: the picture of Hellya is confirmed and complemented by evocations of a different place, particularly the vividly rendered Edinburgh. The complex but unobtrusive timescale of Hellya, incorporating a timeless present *and* an ancient historic past of which we are made conscious, is interestingly complemented by a different timescale, one individual's modern consciousness of a continuity in time from 1916 to the present. This helps us to understand the continuity of the island in time, and reminds us that for most readers it is the island life that is long ago and far away.

But more basically we find a great, a crucial difference between the values of Hellya and the traumas of Mrs McKee. As we have suggested, the values of island life are not rendered in a specifically religious context in this novel, but by implication by the Horsemen and their acceptance of natural and agricultural rhythms and life, expressed in ritual, and so impersonally. In contrast we have Mrs McKee's very personal traumas, inextricably involved with Calvinistic guilt, obsession and self-blame. Mackay Brown does not embark on a theoretical or argued critique of Calvinism; he sticks to his 'sequence of images': but this juxtaposition of natural, healthy harmonious life with a highly disturbed, distorted and yet gentle sensibility may invite the reader to some such consideration.

Psychologist and social analyst Erich Fromm has indicated some aspects of Reformation thought that could be harmful to the individual:

> its emphasis on the wickedness of human nature, the insignificance and powerlessness of the individual, and the necessity for the individual to subordinate himself to a power outside himself (*The Fear of Freedom*, 1960 edition, 31).

The insistence on the total depravity of man may result not only in the naysaying MacColla so much resented, but in a terrible sense of guilt. So Mrs McKee tries to postpone one trial session, but then thinks:

> You are just postponing the inevitable; what had been predestined before you were born; for which all the same you must answer. You are simply putting it off (107).

Fromm talks about the psychological mechanisms of self-accusation and self-humiliation, and seems to point to the possibility of cases like Mrs McKee's:

> But while hostility against others is often conscious and can be expressed overtly, hostility against oneself is usually (except in pathological cases) unconscious, and finds expression in indirect and rationalized forms. One is a person's active emphasis on his own wickedness and insignificance, ... another appears under the guise of conscience or duty (*Fear of Freedom*, 83).

Mackay Brown's picture if anything goes further, because he accepts the basically religious view that Fromm is detached about. Samuel, we remember, in his Vanity Fair experience, saw Mrs McKee *making* monsters as well as ridden by them. And the last section shows Mrs McKee in an apparently final retreat from life into a solipsistic circle, with no room for God or anyone else not contained in her past, apparently fulfilling Johnny's prediction about being 'a burdened ghost', and 'suffering it all over again' (84) before a final escape.

So it is possible to argue that as much as our other two Catholic converts, MacColla and Spark, Mackay Brown does have an implicit critique of Calvinism and its effects at the centre of his novel. Product of city, not country, of industrial not agricultural Scotland, of the Reformation, this essentially good and well-meaning woman is plagued by monsters that attack no other inhabitant of Hellya—except Simon, to a lesser extent.

Back now, briefly, to Mackay Brown's virtuoso technique, and a few examples of the different anti-realistic effects he interestingly employs in different patches. There are two scenes at the shop which begin realistically but gradually develop into something very different. In the first (102–5), Mrs Evie is frankly bullying the women of Greenvoe. She takes her knitting outside in the morning before there are any customers, but then allows four to congregate, saying she must turn the heel of the sock she is knitting. Her character is implicit in the image: 'The needles clacked in her lap like the beak of an angry bird.'

Ellen Kerston comes to do a lot of shopping and has to abide insults about poor payers: we gather there are times when she has to ask for credit, so she cannot afford to take too much offence at the talk of bad debts, although she is ready to pay cash today. Alice and Rachel arrive, and they stand 'silently' in the sun. Mackay Brown describes what is happening:

> Thoughts rose in them and faded, unspoken. Sometimes one frowned, another smiled, another uttered a few trite syllables. They had nothing much to say to one another. They kept mute stances about Mrs Olive Evie until she had turned the heel of the stocking she was knitting. They were stone women, statues.

There follow two rounds of 'speeches'', in which what each woman 'says' is her internal preoccupation: they 'speak' in turn, and reinforce our perception of their (essentially simple) characters. Alice is occupied with her brief affair with Johnny: 'His kiss was like eating purple plums', and 'It was like taking the sun into a winter bed'. Rachel is anxious about Samuel and the sea, and regretful about her own barrenness. Mrs Evie is characteristically curious about the guest at the hotel, suggesting he has come 'to clean up this island'—wish fulfilment here! Ellen Kerston rehearses her perpetual conflict, fighting Bert—and making peace with him again. All action is suspended for this ritual until Mrs Evie stops knitting: 'The wool-bird stopped whetting its beak at the centre of the silent meditative ring of women.'

The vignette is neat and patterned beyond any accepted notion of realism: it ends again with Mrs Evie's veiled insults about money, and poor Ellen repeating: 'I have my purse.'

Not long after, we return to the shop and a similar scene is even more simply accomplished, building on the one just described. Again the women are at the shop (134–6), this time in the early evening; again they communicate not with each other or out loud: 'Mostly they existed within a huge horizon of silence; there, while the stone withers, souls with angels dark and bright negotiate.' Again Mrs Evie is bossy and self-important, this time about the approach of closing-time and the importance of Mr Evie's tea.

Each woman says one phrase to Mrs Evie, the rest in silence. Ellen Kerston parrots from last time: 'A tin of syrup, and I have my purse.' She exults in her Bert, proud and happy at his successful haul of lobsters, and of course unaware that many of them were stolen from Samuel Whaness. Alice is still preoccupied with Johnny, and her delighted conviction that she has conceived. Rachel is still concerned about Samuel and the black cloud that troubles his spirit. Everything is fairly timeless, representative, non-urgent, non-specific: we only have a wry smile in this pastoral community that Mrs Evie cannot supply New Zealand butter, just Danish—no sign of Scottish, let alone Orcadian! But this scene ends with Bella Budge, in to buy two yards of grey flannel, and her silent thoughts tell us that the doctor has despaired of Ben, and she will have to sit up all night sewing his shroud: this in contrast is a very specific and urgent intrusion into the timeless world of Greenvoe.

Another interestingly mannered scene which would bear detailed investigation is the one where Miss Fortin-Bell—'old Horse Face'—comes to distribute the welfare clothes (186–90): 'the parley of beasts on the heraldic shield of Greenvoe.' Mackay Brown gives a different and appropriate animal name to each of her customers, so that vastly pregnant Ellen Kerston and Miss Fortin-Bell have the (brief) 'dialogue of whale and horse'. Miss Fortin-Bell, a ridiculous figure in her kilt, her hair 'a bed of seed-pearls', gets what she deserves all through this scene, especially when she imperiously pushes into the Budges' and encounters Ben's corpse— 'colloquy of horse and hen and skull', and when she encourages Alice Voar to talk about herself in the 'dialogue of pigeon and horse'. Alice's gentle account of her children's fathers culminates in the matter-of-fact announcement that Sidney is the laird's son: Miss Fortin-Bell retreats in haste, giving Alice a bounty of clothes, much as Johnny makes a killing out of surprising Bill Scorradale at his nefarious whisky-bottling.

We will point to one last virtuoso 'patch', which is prepared for throughout the book *and* given a wry retrospective touch later, and which will repay any reader's detailed attention, and that is the sexual encounter of Ivan Westray and Inga Fortin-Bell on the way back from the lighthouse (201–7). Much deft and unobtrusive preparation has gone into this: the careful reader has become aware in the very first section that the schoolteacher and the ferryman are engaged in an unresolved conflict of sexuality, and that the schoolgirl Inga Fortin-Bell, with her copy of *Women in Love*, may have unrealistic expectations when she exchanges looks with the ferryman (14). Westray is more interested in conquering the reluctant schoolteacher, and only finally rapes Inga as part of that campaign. He is an unpleasant but intriguing character from the first, with his two bed-time books, *The Orkneyinga Saga* and a volume of seventeenth-century sermons, *On Love Carnal and Divine* (33).

Inga is smitten with Ivan: Johnny sees her at his mercy, apparently 'pleading with him', while he is 'sullen' and 'contemptuous' and 'half turned away' (95). When Inga goes bathing she definitely yearns for a Lawrentian encounter, 'mindless peasant' and 'golden-skinned woman'. But Ivan Westray 'did not behave like a D H Lawrence peasant at all' (110). The wry restrospect of Ivan's card in the Black Star files not only confirms the suspicion of his mental instability, his hereditary tendency to the local 'morbus orcadensis', but dispels any notion of mindless peasants: he turns out to be another lad o' pairts, who was a medical student in Aberdeen before a disagreement with the authorities caused him to leave (220).

The rendition of his virtual rape of Inga is both weird and abrupt. In the earlier part of the trip to the lighthouse we have become aware of the endless foghorn, 'like a bull in passion', and always in this section we are aware of the enveloping fog. This scene is rendered in three interleaved voices, a prosaic twentieth-century one, suited to Ivan's down to earth behaviour, a traditional saga voice, as it might be out of *The Orkneyinga Saga*, and a counterpointing voice, perhaps from *Love Carnal and Divine*, which is rich in the vocabulary of Shakespeare, Herbert, Donne and Milton, and even back to Malory, putting forward a view of love diametrically at odds with anything here. The main impact of the scene is in the juxtaposition of these three voices.

The encounter is less than satisfactory, and the seducer's farewell is brutal: 'I don't fancy you at all. You're too thin. You're too full of bullshit out of books' etc.: nothing we learn later about 'morbus orcadensis' is going to make us warm to him. But the relish of the scene is in the ironic interplay of the three voices, seventeenth-century, twentieth-century and saga:

And moreover who knoweth where the one jewel of love is to be found? . . . Yet on a day set apart and hallowed it may chance, . . . that a knight cometh to a certain place, and . . . there abideth his heart's desire, the one pearl that all his life he hath sought.

Ivan Westray put the kettle on the gas-ring and cut slices of bread and stabbed a tin of corned beef with an opener.

Inga watched in silence.

The granddaughter of the chief man in Hellya asked a certain boatman to take her to the sea tower. There was much fog on the way back. The boatman whose name was Ivan forced Inga to lie with him in the cabin of the boat called *Skua*. Inga said he had done her a great wrong that day and that he would suffer for it. Ivan laughed. He said they would see about that (207).

FURTHER READING

Our page references are to the Penguin edition of 1976.

George Mackay Brown was born in Stromness, Orkney in 1921, although a beguiling note in *Scottish Short Stories 1983* asserts that he 'has *always* lived in Orkney', certainly an impression it is possible to get from his books! He studied under Edwin Muir at Newbattle Abbey, and read English at Edinburgh University, graduating in 1960: he also did postgraduate work there, on Gerard Manley Hopkins. Otherwise he has lived in Stromness.

His reputation as a poet was ensured by *Loaves and Fishes* (1959) and *The Year of the Whale* (1965): several other fine collections followed, including the poem cycle *Fisherman with Ploughs* (1974) and *Winterfold* (1976). His short story collections include *A Calendar of Love* (1967), *A Time to Keep* (1972), *Hawkfall* (1974), *The Sun's Net* (1976) and *Andrina* (1983): he has published one play, *A Spell for Green Corn* (1970). Apart from *Greenvoe* (1972), he has as yet published only one other novel, *Magnus* (1973). Most of his creative work is concerned with Orkney, and any admirer will find good reading in his miscellany *An Orkney Tapestry* (1969), quoted here in the Quartet Books edition of 1973. We have also quoted from his contribution to *Memoirs of a Modern Scotland* edited by Karl Miller (1970): that piece is called 'The Broken Heraldry', and appears on pages 136–50.

Very little beyond reviews has been written about George Mackay Brown's fiction, but the following may be of interest.

Alan Bold, *George Mackay Brown* (1978)
Francis Russell Hart, *The Scottish Novel: A Critical Survey* (1978)
J Graeme Roberts, 'Tradition and Pattern in the Short Stories of George Mackay Brown' in David Hewitt and Michael Spiller (eds), *Literature of the North* (1983)

For more about the 'Horseman's Word', see Ernest W Marwick, *The Folklore of Orkney and Shetland* (1975)

CHAPTER NINE

William McIlvanney:
Docherty

When the reader of *From Scenes Like These* turns to William McIlvanney's *Docherty*, he will find that the novels have a lot in common, in terms of the surroundings and social pressures which impinge on the characters. But the first sense is of contrast, not similarity. For while in *From Scenes Like These* harsh surroundings are generally echoed in the bleak, loveless consciousness of the characters, a major component of *Docherty* is its celebration of aspects of humanity. McIlvanney seems to indicate more belief in human beings than we find in the Williams novel: if the characters in both are caged, or everywhere in chains, it is possible for McIlvanney's characters to 'sing in (their) chains like the sea'. While dog ate dog—or man— consistently in *From Scenes Like These*, in *Docherty* there is insistence on love, on real relationships, the affirmation of a real community.

But McIlvanney is certainly no less critical of the social situation his characters are trapped in, and he sees the trap as just as effective. Is there a way out? In both novels, poor teachers have themselves seized on education as a way out: in both, education is seen as a possible escape for intelligent boys, lads o' pairts. Nicol cannot understand why education does not seem a sane option to Dunky: Tam Docherty is totally earnest in his desire to give Conn an education which the boy does not want. The analytical voice of the narrator explains how Conn sees school as a rejection of home and all it stands for—and also that Tam's wish was only ever a wistful dream: the Dochertys could never have afforded to keep Conn at school.

Other escapes tantalise: Dunky might have 'made it' at football. In *Docherty*, echoing Dunky's rabbits, we find a series of possible activities discussed to sweeten captivity—poaching, keeping dogs or pigeons. Although we are very much aware of the harshly matured Mick observing and making political points in the latter part of *Docherty*, in neither novel is any political solution seriously entertained or promulgated.

The books are also very differently written. Williams concentrates on his characters' thoughts, and limits himself to what they can verbalise, virtually enacting some of the constrictions of their lives by his narrative method. McIlvanney renders his characters' thoughts also, but outside direct dialogue we often find the unobtrusive intervention of a much more sophisticated, articulate authorial voice, analysing and interpreting the material—and doing so on occasion with hindsight. So for example in Book II chapter 17 we get an over-view of how Jenny retrospectively and over years came to know that Tam had faced defeat and secretly admitted it, something impossible to realise at the time, so imperceptible were the changes.

This indicates another difference: while Williams chooses a hero of his own generation, and presents just one year of his life in the span of the novel, McIlvanney is writing what amounts to a historical novel, beginning seventy-two years before the time of publication, and covering quarter of a century. In some ways this undertaking could more appropriately be compared to Gibbon's *Quair*; and the unending debate between the non-aligned Conn and Communist Mick at the end of the novel arguably to some extent echoes the stances of Chris and Ewan at the end of *Grey Granite*.

Docherty is a strange and interesting book, not least because it is possible to read it with such different emphases: there are at least two views here of Tam Docherty. In what seems to be a characteristic first reading, the novel strikes the reader as warm, celebratory, witty and uniquely affirmative of the value of Tam Docherty and people like him. This is a fair reading, but can dissolve in memory into a suspicion of cosiness, softness, a touch of the kailyard. We would argue that these suspicions will hardly survive re-reading.

Indeed, re-reading may sooner or later precipitate the reader to a very different view of the novel, seeing it as essentially gloomy and pessimistic. In this view, the most the novel can possibly be said to 'celebrate' is a very brief momentary stay against confusion: fate or inevitability is briefly defied by the will of Tam Docherty, but his faith is always undermined, always seen by the reader to be precarious and doomed. Tam Docherty will be defeated: this is inevitable, and we know it from the start.

The main thrust of this chapter, then, is an attempt to survey the book from beginning to end, with our main attention always on Tam and the way the author/narrator adjusts our focus on him, and uses the focus on Tam to gauge other characters. Inevitably also we will consider other members of the family and their developing and varying importance, and the slightly wider social span of High Street with its dependence on the Dochertys. At times, important but subordinated themes may insist on our notice— Conn's introduction to class consciousness in Book I chapter 1, when his father offers to fight an accidentally patronising stranger; Conn's traumatic discovery at school about the difference between Scots and English (Book I chapter 15); Angus's rejection of Tam's morality when he refuses to marry his pregnant ex-girlfriend (Book III, chapter 5), or when he flouts Tam's political faith by contracting to dig his own coal (Book III, chapter 2).

A central theme of the novel, inseparable from the portrait of Tam himself, is his search for a faith, for an alternative to the religion that has failed to be relevant to his experience. Tam is in many ways a naturally religious man, and he is a man who lives by faith more markedly and more admirably than any of the Christian characters in the novel. Tam's finest years are sustained by faith, faith in an amalgam of the ideal of Keir Hardie and the community of his class, and above all in the ideal of family: he sees families in terms of little fortresses, held together by love and solidarity, in an essentially unjust if legal world of conflict. It is the most blatant demonstration that the family fortress is no protection, the mutilation of Mick in the Great War, that cracks open the creed that Tam has lived by. In a startling development of the recurring metaphor, McIlvanney describes Tam now:

> He was like a gunfighter, practised to perfection, unafraid, heroically hard, and pitted against germ warfare (211).

Tam can find no replacement for the faith, or illusion, that he has lost: he simply has to live with his failure. The crippling of Mick is for him only the underlining of his failure, his misguided faith. A few chapters earlier, Conn's start down the pit ends the futile dream of his escape by education: the family provision of all the appropriate gear is to Tam like giving him 'a suicide-kit for Christmas' (191). Now he has only to live out his natural span in the knowledge that his failure was inevitable and his faith always illusory. It is possible to consider Tam's heroic and self-sacrificial death as a happy release for him.

The search for faith is echoed in other members of the family. Jenny's faith in Tam and her family was always more practical and immediate and down to earth, less a matter of willed idealism than Tam's and so it survives time, if saddened. Andra Crawford finds in Tam's determination to give a home to old Conn in the face of the unwillingness of the 'religious' daughters, a triumph of humanity:

> Andra sensed quite simply that Tam was not defeated. And if Tam wasn't, neither was he (101).

Angus develops a faith based largely on his own physical strength and an embattled attitude towards the world as a whole: refusing to be bound by family or class loyalties or traditional moral ideas, he embraces an ethic of success: 'Frem noo on, it's just Annie an' me. An' we're gonny make oot' (291). Mick's wartime experience is devastating: all he is left with, at the Front, is the ordinariness of his fellows: 'They became what Mick had in place of a religion' (194). His postwar reflections and reading lead him to an act of faith when he joins the Communist Party, while young Conn has reached no conclusions as yet. All the sons find Tam's beliefs to some extent redundant to their present, but Conn resists the logical clarity of Mick's faith:

> Ah don't want tae smash folk. Ah jist want them tae see hoo guid men like ma feyther were. Tae gi'e us room tae leeve. . . . Ah canny hate folk the wey you dae, Mick (321).

It is significant and appropriate that Conn is left in two minds at the end. He has always been less than a fully formed or highly individualised character. McIlvanney uses him throughout as a sensitive human recording mechanism which is more involved in reacting to or simply registering things and people, and above all Tam, than in initiating ideas or opinions. This is the crucial aspect of Conn, from the first chapter of Book I. He is realistically presented, of course, and his development is fully credible, but often related on the side. Odd chapters fill in his adolescence, his secret happiness in the Bringan, his school experiences, his obsession with sex, but often these are only loosely connected to the main thrust of the book. In essential respects he is a responder, and almost a representative character, not a million miles away from Dunky Logan: what Dunky might have been, brought up in Docherty warmth instead of Kilcaddie bleakness?

In a mere thirteen pages, the Prologue to *Docherty* establishes a number of facts and indicates central themes and a complex world picture in the context of which we are to read the book. It is done with marvellous economy.

The very first paragraph looks at the absurdities of world news in 1903 with apparent gravity, but effective irony. Events of wildly different status and importance are juxtaposed as the newspapers would have juxtaposed them, as John Dos Passos did in his 'Newsreel' sections in *USA*. Most of these items will be forever unknown to the characters in the novel, who only become interested or involved in world affairs when their rulers require them for wars: the drunken singing of Josey Mackay, and his 'garbled mutterings' about the Boer War, as Tam and Buff wait helplessly for news of the birth, form an unpleasantly ominous indication of the relation of the 'great world' to High Street.

Perhaps surprisingly, we are introduced to High Street, and Tam Docherty in particular, through the genteel consciousness of Miss Gilfillan: appropriately enough, we come to realise, she introduces the reader to this working-class ghetto, with all the puzzlements and conflicts of her middle-class upbringing. McIlvanney signals clearly enough that she does not understand all that she sees; he says that her vision of the lives of her neighbours was 'as stylised and unsubtle as an opera' (14), and blurred with self pity. Nonetheless, this inturned, prejudiced, lonely old lady has formed a very striking impression of Tam Docherty, which is both memorable and just, a foundation for the book to build on.

So we have a physical description with implied character traits:

> She knew him coming home from the pit, small even among his mates, one of a secret brotherhood of black savages, somebody hawking a gob of coaldust onto the cobbles. Cleaned up, dressed in a bulky jacket and white silk scarf, a bonnet on his black hair, he looked almost frail, his face frighteningly colourless, as if pale from a permanent anger. Yet shirtsleeved in summer, his torso belied the rest of him. The shoulders were heroic . . . (14).

From behind her curtain, Miss Gilfillan has seen him totally involved in his children, and has sensed the reaction of his peers, liking tinged with respect, almost fear. The very first submerged image of Tam as heroic gunfighter is established by her observation: 'It was a strange, uncertain feeling, as if wherever he stood he established a territory' (15). Tam Docherty is not simply to be a fine man, he is to be an unpredictable and occasionally frightened one. Other images build up this aspect of him later—'It was like being friends with Mount Etna,' thinks young Conn when Tam has faced down the priest (63), and Andra Crawford comes to see him as a dangerous caged animal (101).

Miss Gilfillan's observations crystallise into the word 'independence':

> She felt it was a ridiculous word in this place. For what claim could anyone who lived here have to independence? (15).

Arguably, the whole theme and dilemma of the book is clearly and economically stated here. The paragraph goes on to investigate the question, coming to another recurrent, submerged metaphor which repeatedly echoes Rousseau's famous assertion, 'Man is born free, and everywhere he is in chains.' The inhabitants of High Street, Graithnock, a slightly fictionalised Kilmarnock, are all slaves, to pit, factory and family, to drink and to poverty. All the contradictions of Tam Docherty are implied in her reflection:

> Poverty was what had brought herself to this room. It defined the area of their lives like a fence. Still, in that area Mr. Docherty moved as if he were there by choice, like someone unaware of the shackles he wore and who hadn't noticed that he was bleeding (15).

The rest of the Prologue moves between the observing Miss Gilfillan as Jenny Docherty's labour is protracted, Miss Gilfillan's own childhood memories of class and injustice, and the time of Jenny's labour as experienced by Tam, Buff Thompson and the rest. The two ways of reading the book are implicit in the two attitudes to the baby's birth. For Tam and Jenny and their neighbours, it is a wonderful and transforming event which makes Agnes Thompson temporarily girlish, and makes them all happy and content; and for the doctor there is an insight into 'a tacit but deeply held sense of triumph in which all these people shared ... this unsmirched new beginning' (25). He wishes them a fulfilment he cannot for a moment believe in—and we are back with Miss Gilfillan and the 'ooze of hopelessness': 'None of them here had any chance' (26).

We see Tam more directly in his reaction to the baby's birth. His pride in wife and baby makes him very human and likable, and the short conversation about the baby again establishes a number of central facts. The first question is, what is his name to be. Tam's answer is more significant on a second reading, when the reader knows that the name Cornelius is Tam's father's name. Although he is at odds with his parents and sisters over religion, and will refuse to bring young Conn up a Catholic, Tam's family feeling remains strong, and he honours his father in naming his son. The new reader now learns that there are already two religions in Tam's house; what will Tam make young Conn? And Tam's answer is not conventionally religious: 'He's a' Ah wid want tae make 'im as he is. A perfect wee human bein'' (24). The final point is about the new baby's future career: the doctor realistically takes 'the pit' for granted, but Tam is determined otherwise, and jovial with the happiness of the occasion:

'He'll never be ready fur the pits. No' this wan. He'll howk wi' his heid. Fur ideas.' He winked at the baby. 'Eh, Conn? Ah'm pittin' his name doon fur Prime Minister. First thing in the moarnin'' (25).

All these matters will be developed in the novel as a whole.

Book I opens with Conn old enough to play, under supervision, at the entry-door (perhaps 1906?), and closes in March 1914. Its eighteen short chapters do not form a conventional plot. The Book quietly celebrates the great days of Tam Docherty, and chronicles family matters and characters' thoughts. The novel generally concentrates not on actions but on reactions. And detailed traditional chronology is frequently flouted—a chapter can relate a specific memorable incident, and the next may chart a child's exploration of his environment over years, and the third centre on a confrontation of father and son which sums up the internal struggles of years: the linear progression of 'what happens next' is rarely important.

Plot in any major form would be inappropriate to the central understanding of the book, the fact that the characters are relatively helpless, to initiate action or to change their situations: what *is* chronicled here, lovingly, is the happiness they can give each other by love and warmth and loyalty and solidarity. Conn's boyhood is lapped in all of these, and his consequent security and his observing eye are very important in this Book.

The division is into short chapters, and the narrative method quickly becomes clear. We are to see into the minds and emotions of some characters, mainly but by no means exclusively Conn and Tam. So far, it parallels *From Scenes Like These*. But McIlvanney rejects the limits Williams accepts for his novel—that we only learn what the characters think, and in the words they would readily use. McIlvanney chooses to intrude, in as unobtrusive a way as possible, to ponder, analyse and explain his characters' attitudes beyond what they can fully understand or articulate.

Inevitably, Book I is much concerned with description, evocation of the place and the people. This is often usefully accomplished through Conn, as in Chapter 2, which is mainly concerned with High Street as home for a child in pre-school years, but it amounts also to an authorial essay on the situation and the codes people have evolved to cope with dignity with the restraints of prison life—for that is how it is presented. That half-submerged image of chains, of prison, is present throughout: 'It was a penal colony for those who had committed poverty, a vice which was usually hereditary' (31). The richness of texture means any chapter is worthy of comment, but we shall concentrate on those which concentrate on Tam.

As in the Prologue, his readiness to fight, his anger, are registered almost at once: in chapter 1 a peaceful scene of relaxation at the entry-door on a summer evening is interrupted, not so much by the well-to-do family, out for a walk, looking at the tenements, as by Tam's enraged response: 'Why don't ye bring fuckin' cookies wi' ye? An' then ye could throw them tae us!' (31). Prison, zoo, Tam knows where he lives and has no notion of meek acceptance. His attitudes are elaborately analysed in chapters 3, 4 and 5. In 3 we are introduced unequivocally to Tam's occasional and recurrent experience of despair. The inevitability of its persistence, and indeed of its growth and potentially fatal consequences, is rendered in an image of disease, of cancerous growth:

a kind of malignancy, a small hard growth of bitterness which lay dormant most of the time but would spasmodically be activated by an accumulation of imperceptible irritations. When that irreducible nub of frustration discharged its pus, it created in him an allergy to his own life (39–40).

It is on such an occasion that Tam takes a modest drink, and has a confrontation with his father over young Conn's attending the Protestant school. They range over old Conn's past and Tam's refusal to see the (better) present as in any way satisfactory. The scene foreshadows later confrontations Tam will have with his *own* sons, especially in Book III chapter 2. As Tam angrily denounces the Catholic teaching that he believes has robbed old Conn of brains and independence, so Mick will angrily denounce the inadequacy of Tam's views in their turn:

> ootside this room, the rules are different. . . . An' whit Ah learned is that we're a joke. . . . Naebudy is about tae set us free, feyther. . . . Whit offends you aboot Angus is he's no' goin' tae shove his heid in the same halter as you. You are pathetic (259).

Succeeding generations reject the faiths of their fathers: they offer at best only ways of living in prison with dignity: Mick wants to burn down the prison.

Tam is described here in chapter 2 as despairing in his blood. Apart from the 'oasis' of his family, there is only unfulfilling work, insecurity, inarticulacy. Facing his father here, he accepts their alienation and his inability to accept the answers that satisfy his father. In the next two chapters he seeks for an alternative. He comes to terms with the notion that he must be himself, and 'might not be a Catholic' (46): 'he had to meet life without protection.' After this, instinctively, he goes to the street corner where the men habitually meet together. In one sense he knows part of the answer already—Tam's belief in his fellows always helps sustain him, and these men provide history, order and context for each other.

But chapter 5 is concerned with his lack of faith and his search for one, and he is not alone in his desperation: he stands at the corner with Buff Thompson and Gibby Molloy, and 'Their silence was the infinity where three parallel despairs converged' (49). Gibby, periodical drinker and breaker down of toilet doors, has already been compared to Tam (40): his 'dark neurosis' is accepted by his fellows. Buff was the neighbour Tam waited with while Conn was being born, and a very basic relationship was insisted on:

> He was at sixty much of what Tam, in his early thirties, would become. And as Buff was Tam's future, so Tam was his past. The mere presence of one enlarged the other (21).

The sad description of Buff in this chapter, then, implies another forecast for Tam. Buff's nature has contracted—he is 'clenched round a frail sense of purpose that was diminishing to nothing' (49). When Buff's death is casually recorded later in the gossip of Jenny and her mother, there is another pointer to the equivalence of the two men, which would even imply that Tam's early death was a merciful one: 'It was sad to watch when their spirit went before them. Crying like a bairn' (72).

One of the things that makes a book concerned with such desperations bearable is the vitality of the characters and the plentiful comedy of the narrative, and so here this desperate trio is no sooner established than it is interrupted and transformed by a poaching expedition. This is a liberating experience, described with as much lyricism as any such expedition in Gunn, and Tam momentarily envies Dougie's relationship with his own life, 'his separate peace' (53). But he rejects it, with an instinctively political stance:

> Being a man wasn't a hobby. That was what they would like you to do: work your shift and take up pigeons, or greyhounds, or poaching, and hand your balls in at the paydesk (54).

Tam's conclusions in this chapter are the best, the most fulfilling, he ever comes to. He goes home to Jenny and loves her, and he remembers and builds on his boyhood experience of the strike meeting where the name on everyone's lips was Keir Hardie. This is Tam's religious experience, and the language is appropriate: 'The thought of it struck him with the force of a conversion as if he had just realised he had once been present at a miracle' (55). The very name of Keir Hardie is 'like a benediction', means hope. He would go on working, and 'Keir Hardie would do his talking for him' (56). The Lanarkshire and Ayrshire miner turned politician who founded the Scottish Labour Party in 1882 and the Independent Labour Party in 1893 and became the first Labour MP in 1892 is a natural inspiration for Tam, sitting in Westminster as Tam undergoes his crisis of faith. This adds up to a pathetically fragile and unformulated faith, but one more commensurate with Tam's own experience than his father's acquiescent Catholicism.

His new faith does not enable him to make a separate peace, or even always to control himself, as we see from his wild violence in punishing Miss Gilfillan's Peeping Tom, which shocks and disturbs him. But the crucial test for Tam in this Book is surely his mother's death and its aftermath, and his belief in family sees him through. It is when his mother is dying that this is spelt out:

> He saw families as little fortresses of loyalty and sanity and mutual concern, set defiantly in a landscape of legalised looting and social injustice (93).

The testing of Tam and his sisters is not conveyed to us through any of their consciousnesses, but through that of the accidentally eavesdropping Andra Crawford. He is haunted by painful and meaningless memories of his own before voices interrupt his 'foundering thoughts' (99). Lizzie, Mary and their husbands agree that there is no alternative to the Home for old Conn, but Tam's response is characteristically angry and dogmatic: it is not a question of sense:

> If ye want tae be sensible, take yer weans up tae the market oan Friday an' sell them. Because that's what we are. Fuckin' cattle. Unless we can prove different. ... It's feenished. He steys wi' me (101).

The reaction of the uncomfortably overhearing Andra underlines for us the importance of the scene. He begins to understand why he likes Tam so much, and his understanding again uses images of zoo or imprisonment, and becomes a matter of faith and solidarity:

> He was more than anything in his life showed him to be, and he knew it. The effect on Andra was as if he had come across some powerful animal in a cage, kept fit on its own frustration, endlessly restless, knowing instinctively that the bars are an invention, nothing final, and feeling contempt for its keepers. Andra sensed quite simply that Tam was not defeated. And if Tam wasn't, neither was he (101).

This is perhaps the moment of most positive affirmation in the novel. Most of the time the reader is alerted to shackles and prison bars of which the characters are usually less conscious, but here, momentarily, is the suggestion that the bars are 'nothing final' and that the spirit of the imprisoned can transcend the cage.

Tam dwarfs the other characters, and 'his' chapters have a greater insistence on the reader's attention on the whole than the boys reading the papers to their grandparents, or Miss Gilfillan's comic efforts to improve Conn, or Kathleen bringing Jack home for the first time. But one chapter of Conn's experience here must at least be pointed to. In chapter 15 he undergoes a crisis at school which crystallises for him a lot of perceptions about education, home and school, and different kinds of speech. It is a powerful and also a comic scene, rich in irony. Mr Pirie rejects Conn's account of his skinned nose, 'Ah fell an' bumped ma heid in the sheuch, sur' (109). When Conn repeats it, Mr Pirie replies with an unwise blow and an extraordinary request: 'You will translate, please, into the mother-tongue.' The irony of *that* is further underlined when we learn that Mr Pirie, who once thought Conn deserving of advancement through education, has himself working-class origins. He has not only left them; he despises them:

'He isn't afraid to admit what his father was—a pig walking upright' etc. (110).

But Conn's experience is a crucial, determining one, 'significant beyond itself'. He had earlier been puzzled by Mick and Angus hating school, and had himself been happy there. Now he begins to understand his brothers, to envy Angus for being at work, 'real life'. Against his awareness of his father's reverence for education is Conn's sense 'of the irrelevance of school, its denial of the worth of his father and his family, the falsity of its judgements, the rarified atmosphere of its terminology' (112). He will come to clearer conclusions about all of this (Book II, chapter 7): for now, he contents himself with a very practical demonstration of his dilemma, his list of Scots words and phrases and their unsatisfactory translations into 'the mother-tongue'.

Book I draws to a close with a spring meeting of the men at the corner, a time of new life and new hope and high spirits. Gibby Molloy has become a new man, by sheer persistence an unbeatable fighter; Tadger has regretfully accepted that fourteen children is enough; Josey Mackay continues to re-fight the Boer War, and 'Tam Docherty felt inexplicably that things were going to be all right, as if hope came to him in the air, like pollen' (123). But it is March 1914: again the men forget or are unaware of their status as prisoners or pawns: again we are reminded.

The nineteen chapters of Book II cover the period from the outbreak of the Great War to the celebration of New Year, 1920. For Tam Docherty and his family, as for the larger world, this is a time of stress and trauma. McIlvanney continues his unobtrusively unconventional narrative, switching between the perspectives of individual characters and an analytical and by implication omniscient narrator: but while in Book I the main characters illumined from within *and* without were Tam and Conn, Mick is now importantly added, and is central to eight chapters. Up until now, Mick has not had a lot of attention in the novel. We have seen him often through Conn's eyes, a gentle elder brother; at the end of Book I chapter 2, the sustained description of Conn's early boyhood, Mick is outstandingly reliable: 'Only his mother and Mick were always themselves. . . . Mick was patience on legs' (37), and his characteristic response is laughter. In Book I he is particularly apolitical, 'naturally an accepter of the way things were. . . . he didn't share his father's fervour for change' (105). The War is to change him profoundly, and by no means simply by mutilating his body.

Even without the disruption of the War, a certain growing apart in the family is inevitable at this stage, because of the ages and situations of the characters. Kathleen, married, is more peripheral to the family now, although as time goes on and her relationship with Jack sours she returns more and more to her family with her own babies: her silence about her private miseries keeps her to some extent apart. Angus has begun to assert himself, and chapter 5 here is devoted to a predominantly sympathetic account of his development and his increasing need to compete with his father. When he is fifteen and his strength saves Tadger from a nasty and possibly fatal accident in the pit, Tadger's gratitude and the others' admiration become fuel to his image of himself, and Tam is alerted to the boy's egotistical, competitive bent. In passing, McIlvanney alerts *us* to future problems for Angus and his family: 'He was cavalier about accepted principles of behaviour in the family' (151). Jenny has a fairly steady presence in the Graithnock scenes, and is central to chapter 9, where she is cleaning out the house of her newly dead parents. She is uncharacteristically bitter here, about her parents' deaths, about her own lost youth and attractiveness, above all about the War.

Book II starts like the Prologue, with a momentary glimpse of the larger scene, figures on balconies in London and Berlin, then it focuses down to the High Street corner where the men habitually meet. The War to come is unimaginable: nothing can prepare them for it. Andra, unlike Josey Mackay a clearsighted veteran of the Boer War, says: 'It'll be like nothin' that's been afore' (133), and the author comments: 'Their pasts lay like obsolete maps.' It is late in this Book that Tam will be compared to an heroic gunfighter facing germ warfare. But the War becomes particularly threatening to the Dochertys with Mick's abrupt announcement, 'Ah'm gonny jine up' (135). It is now some months later: some boys from the High Street have already been killed: Tam and Tadger, while believing in Keir Hardie's opposition to the war as irrelevant to the working classes of Europe, have already secretly taken and failed medical tests. It is impossible for the characters to react rationally or appropriately to the calamity of the War: all their reactions, including Mick's determination to be a soldier, are described as 'naïve and arbitrary reactions in the face of an ungraspable complexity' (139). And naïveté is at issue again a few lines later, when Tam is forced to an awareness he does not wish for, about his faith in continuity, evolution, improvement: 'The intrusion of the war showed the naïveté of his beliefs, the triviality of any contribution he could make to his own life' (139–40).

There follows a tender interlude in which Mick for the first time is seen in a relationship outside his family. The solemnity of the scene with May, in which they both take up what they believe to be appropriate attitudes, dissolves, thankfully, into the laughter and teasing of playacting in the ruined house. But there is no suggestion that their feelings are really deep or permanent: Mick will be going to war unawakened, unsuspecting.

Mick and Danny Hawkins are the objects of general grief and sadness in chapter 6. Good advice mingles with sentimental leavetakings and a limited measure of alcohol. Family solidarity is underlined, with Jenny's parents Jean and Mairtin and old Conn important as well as Mick's immediate family: to all, he is 'an awful provocation to sentiment' (155), like a boy dressed up for Hallowe'en but bound for a very real War. The situation of Mary Hawkins, widowed mother of an only son, increases the pain and the pathos. And the abrupt departure of the train leaves bewildered shock behind.

The centre of the Book remains in Graithnock, and no more than Grassic Gibbon in *Sunset Song* does McIlvanney intend to write a novel of the trenches. Arguably, however, the economical sketching of the developments of Mick and Danny gives a more effective impression of the experience of war in the trenches than the story of Ewan Tavendale as re-told by Chae Strachan. Danny's dismal shrinkage as a human being in the terror of the trenches carries more conviction than the extraordinary transformation of Ewan after only a few weeks in training. Chapter 8 touches briefly on a brief respite from the trenches. Danny is diminished by his terror into simple sexual obsession: Jake calls him 'a porter fur his prick' (168). Jake himself claims to be a devoutly religious man, and his religion, fear: the irony, even the comedy, of his speech fails to veil his sincerity. Mick juggles with his fear, and re-reads a letter from home, still affecting him like 'a transfusion' (171): although re-reading it now does not much move him, the letter remains 'proof that he could still feel things'. There has been virtually nothing directly about the War in this chapter.

We return to Mick for a very brief chapter 11, and a letter is central here too, but this time one that Mick cannot manage to write. In chapter 8 he had written necessary lies home, and that had helped him to cope: now a Mick intensely conscious of every sensory surrounding finds letter-writing an impossible test, the distance too great. He wants to tell one truth and one lie: 'Danny Hawkins was killed yesterday. He died very brave' (186). But the facts he is trying to disguise or deny come at him in a shower of images. Danny, we gather, was as obsessed with fear of syphilis as Lieutenant Rinaldi in *A Farewell to Arms*: he ran deliberately into the bomb, Mick is convinced. In chapter 8 the letter had been Mick's proof that he could still feel things, but now he hardly feels anything, even the flame, and his attempted letter is burned and destroyed.

The only actual description of war is in chapter 13, and again it is minimal: the author is primarily concerned to chart war's effects on Mick's psyche. So amid images of fighting, fear and a comic search for lice, we are warned of Mick's 'postponed anger' (193) and images recorded by his mind 'like undeveloped negatives' (196). It is in the context of all this that Mick finds his faith, in his very ordinary fellows:

The men were the only identity he had left. . . . The others were the only sanity each of them had. . . . They became what Mick had in place of a religion (193–4).

This chapter deserves examination in more detail, to underline the harsh difficulty of this faith, how opposite it is from easy sympathy or altruistic caring. *A Farewell to Arms* seems echoed pervasively here. Mick's hostility to newspapers trumpeting on the subject of war, using words like 'honour' and 'self-sacrifice' and 'indifference to personal danger' (195) inevitably recalls Hemingway's Lieutenant Henry:

> I was always embarrassed by the words sacred, glorious and sacrifice and the expression in vain. We had heard them . . . and I had seen nothing sacred, and the things that were glorious had no glory and the sacrifices were like the stockyards at Chicago if nothing was done with the meat except to bury it (chapter 27).

Mick has learned from his fellow 'specialists in being human' (196): but the positives are very carefully undermined, and we are warned: 'Survival could only be partial.' This is clearly enunciated *before* the shell explodes, ensuring that Mick's physical survival also can only be partial.

The Mick of chapter 15 is in hospital, badly wounded, and the physical wounds seem the least of it. There is an effective account of his attempts to concentrate on and to build up physical reality. Painfully and slowly he begins to re-inhabit his own head, and to come to terms with his body and its wounds: 'He was simply going to be blind in one eye and minus an arm' (205). He remains in a terrible state of impersonality, one of the 'new elect' initiated into 'the new Nirvana' by suffering, until Tam's arrival at his bedside which produces unconscious tears but no conscious emotion.

Mick's return home in chapter 18 requires prodigies of adjustment. Old friends fail totally to comprehend the War, and Mick can experience no contact with his family: 'He was among strangers. When they thought they were touching him, he could feel no contact' (221). Only with Mary Hawkins does he experience any contact: 'She wasn't able to hide from the reality Mick was experiencing, as even his own family appeared to him to do' (222). So he remains uneasy at home and aimless outside, 'living in limbo', until Tam's characteristic outburst when Mick expresses impatience with Jenny. 'Against Mick's will, the intensity of his father impinged on him'. (224). Under Tam's tirade, Mick looks at Jenny's lowered head, and 'for the first time for a long time he touched the quick of himself. He was feeling shame' (224). And so he begins to feel again, to see his parents honestly. And he distantly approaches some means of survival:

There had to be a way to connect the truth he felt he had glimpsed to their own lives, a way that would protect them from their own simplicity, a way that would give purpose to the desecration of folk like Danny (225).

And so Mick does begin to participate again, but as 'a kind of recluse among them . . . the most of him, that deep fifth-column which was examining their lives very critically'. He sees possible hope for Angus in his fitful rebelliousness, Conn in his youth. And he goes about a painful process of self-education, overtaking his father and effectively demonstrating his limitations: 'The areas towards which his father had all his life just made desperate gestures Mick was trying to penetrate, to chart.' His reactions to peace, and to the terms of the Treaty of Versailles, are of grim expectation. This short chapter has covered a long period of time: we are not told how long Mick lived 'in limbo'; then there is the clash with Tam, a moment in time; and then a long process of adjustment and education, over years.

The 'Conn-centred' chapters in this Book also characteristically chronicle long periods of slow development as well as momentous or memorable occasions. Conn's role and life situation are continually silently juxtaposed with Mick's, and the notion thoroughly established in Book I that he like the others is a prisoner, a victim rather than a free agent, is massively confirmed by the War's intrusion into High Street and the lives of everyone. Chapter 4, which first centres on Conn, is carefully placed after the two in which Mick holds centre stage, announcing his intention to enlist, and saying his tender farewell to his sweetheart May. It is on the whole a happy chapter, and one in which it seems little has happened to alter the projections of pre-War years. More and more Conn tends 'to happen offstage' (147), with his friends. They all smoke, and have special interests, Conn's being 'fighting and girls' (148). We see the foursome banding together, conspiring in their shared confidence of youth. And what is seen to threaten them is not most immediately the War, but the world of work—and we are back with the characteristic images of warfare and victimisation:

> Yet the surrender of the streets to them was illusory. They lounged in sights that they had never known were set. The town was a carefully organised trap (150).

But two important occurrences of his boyhood remain to be recorded. The first is his helpless confrontation with Tam over education in chapter 7, and their inevitable failure to articulate and communicate their differences. Tam offers Conn the ideal of Mr Pirie, and Conn cannot express his notion of the incomparability of his father and Mr Pirie except by saying: 'Och,

feyther. Ye could easy win him.' McIlvanney's narrative freedom means
that we have a much fuller statement of the arguments against school than
Dunky Logan was able to offer, and for once, interestingly, the prison
image is turned in a different direction:

> truths he had earned for himself . . . that nothing he was taught at school took the
> slightest cognizance of who he was, that the fundamental premise underlying
> everything he was offered there was the inferiority of what he had, that the vivid
> spontaneity of his natural speech was something he was supposed to be ashamed
> of, that so many of the people who mouthed platitudes about the liberating
> effects of education were looking through bars at the time, that most teachers
> breathed hypocrisy, like tortured Christians trying to convert happy pagans, that
> the classroom wasn't a filter for but a refuge from reality (163–4).

So Tam reveres the memory of Conn's dead uncle James, the virtually self-
taught geologist, and the anthology from which he has Conn read, while
Conn impotently fails to articulate even to himself the case McIlvanney
outlines above. Only later does Conn learn the value of such evenings with
Tam, and the ironic fact that finance could never have allowed him to
pursue his education.

Conn's main attention is elsewhere. The last recorded boyhood incident
is the weekend among his parents' roots at Cronberry in chapter 10. It is an
ecstatic experience for Conn, who discovers his family anew in their
acceptance by the others. For Conn this is an initiation into a wonderful
sense of life, where he is 'bewildered with potentialities'. He returns
desperately impatient for manhood, but fed with a warmer, fuller picture of
manhood than was ever vouchsafed to Dunky Logan: 'He was going to be a
man like his father and those uncles because to be that would include all the
other ambitions' (184).

Conn's other two chapters here, 12 and 14, centre on manhood and the
proof of manhood for Conn, going down the pit. Conn's joy at the prospect
is continually contrasted with the sadness and frustration of Tam and
Jenny. Tam and Jenny mutually understand their shared vision of an
emptying future, without discussing it, but Conn's excitement carries us
through chapter 12, as he receives his pit outfit for Christmas. For Tam,
this is the full realisation of defeat over his hopes for his family: 'He had
fathered four children and all he had ever been able to give them was their
personal set of shackles' (192). At least from now on Conn feels closer to his
father, although he does not understand Tam's loss of hope. Chapter 14
vividly chronicles the first day down the pit and also, unobtrusively, implies
many succeeding days, when Conn is fulfilled by his new role. He becomes a
man, and a miner.

But as always the fullest attention and the sharpest analysis in this Book is reserved for Tam, his contradictions and struggles for faith, the paradoxes where he makes his home. And above all this Book dramatises his defeat. It is indicated repeatedly from Book I; it is frequently pointed to throughout Book II, but the process of defeat signalled all too clearly in chapter 14 when Conn is to go down the pit is underlined most painfully in chapters 16 and 17, when he has to come to terms with Mick's mutilation, and, finally, with his own helplessness.

Chapter 16, where Tam returns from his visit to Mick and has to break the news to the family, might be entitled 'The Abdication'. The faith that carried him so far is shattered, the ever-threatening despair is now accepted to be chronic. The first few pages, where Tam tries to find ways of telling them the extent of Mick's injuries, are painful and affecting, and Jenny's keening grief is right, and will not be heard again until Tam's corpse is carried into the house. But only after Jenny sends him to the pub does his conversation with Mick really begin to make sense to Tam, and to stab him. Three long paragraphs (210–11) are devoted to an authorial description of Tam's defeat here. It is described by comparison to the years when he believed himself undefeated, and simply refused to admit defeat, even in physical fight. Although we are here trying to understand the loss, it is entirely appropriate to the dual experience of reading the book that at the same time we celebrate the achievement of the past:

> Secreted so far inaccessibly inside him had been an undefeated sense of purpose, a private place where he had his dignity, that no happening could pillage, no failure violate. Through it, everything could be transformed. The unfair conditions of his work became the triumph of his physical strength. The lack of opportunity open to his children measured the remarkableness of the people they managed to be. Poverty became the defiance of itself.

But now the gunfighter is finally faced with germ warfare. Tam feels 'redundant to his own life', and the images from the last extract are calamitously enforced, to describe a cataclysmic emotional state:

> Having withstood the bruisings of despair for years, at last he began to haemorrhage. What had always been his own was invaded, broken up, trampled on, his past certainties demolished, his hopes gutted. His dreams were raped. Tam had come home.

He returns home, deliberately drunk, to make 'his abdication speech', and this is an awesome and disturbing experience for them all.

> It was the first time in the experience of any of them that he had renounced his ascendancy over the future. He was divesting himself of the image they had

always given him, and in the moment of losing it their dependence on it became clearer than ever. It seemed intolerable that he was just another bloke (212).

Left alone with Jenny, 'finally at bay', Tam cries, a thing Jenny has never seen before. All his physical strength is ironically useless in this scene of drunken indignity. When he shouts it explodes back into his throat 'like someone trying to scream under water'. His flailing arm and unsteady boot destroy the portrait of the king so long cherished by Jenny's parents, and Tam knows himself 'ridiculous, a silly man' (215).

Chapter 17 is one of those meditative and analytical chapters which stretches far into the future and can involve retrospective understandings, as the author indicates the complex process in time by which Jenny at last came to understand Tam's abdication and defeat, and her continuing fierce and undiminished love. Again it is a rich chapter, worthy of detailed scrutiny. Simply, next morning, Tam 'had become the victim of his life instead of its exponent'. There seems a submerged image of a smashed statue, perhaps of a god, certainly a most important man. Tam leans over Jenny, 'a dawn the colour of unfired clay on his shoulders': she is to discover 'broken parts' of him and piece them together, and 'reconstruct the man that he had been before they broke him and would wonder at his stature' (217). She is to gather and hoard small perceptions, possibly 'crushed like archaic pottery to powder by the clumsiness of their unearthing,' the image looking forward to his death in the pit. And again the defeat retrospectively involves the more celebration: Jenny sees in his eyes' emptiness, 'not just the defeat of what he was becoming, but the almost unbelievable victory of what he had for so long been' (218). Again the chapter quietly celebrates Jenny's devoted love, and her recording of 'the importance of a courageous living and a secret, terrible, consuming grief of failure'.

The novel would be almost unbearable to read were these moments not counterbalanced, not merely by, for example, the happy adolescent development of Conn, but by the social occasions which recur so impressively. Even just the scenes of the men talking at the corner provide the characters with sustenance and mutual strength, but a particular impact is built up through the novel in other social scenes. The wake for Tam's mother, Kathleen's wedding reception, the weekend at Cronberry are all central demonstrations of community, and at the end of a Book so bleak in its conclusions as this one, the final chapter, the New Year party for 1920, is really important. It follows a series of fairly grim chapters, and provides a happy interlude: not surprisingly, it is the longest chapter in the novel. Such chapters add indirectly to the central argument, and by their demonstration of worth and solidarity mitigate the gloomy implications of that argument. New Year begins with the crowd at the Cross, then switches to the bustling preparations of Jenny and Kathleen, and the company gradually assembles. After the men's good-humoured teasing, we are privileged to share in the secret of sixteen-year-old Conn's very private sexual encounter with Jessie. Hilarity is tempered with the arrival of Mary Hawkins and the inevitability of her breaking into tears, and in contrast to the communal comforting of Mary is the arrival of Angus and his retinue, Angus more than ready to resume the competition with his father indicated in chapter 5. The analysis is limited in extent and comparatively unobtrusive: for the most part the party is simply enacted. Two paragraphs (237) do underline the harshness of the characters' lives and the brevity of youth and even 'the illusion of freedom'. But for the most part the rendering of the party and the contests is enough. It is as if even the author is infected by the vitality of the party: when he returns to scrutinise the contests (243), he sees such acts as something more than singing in your chains:

> so many carried deep inside themselves, like a tribal precept, a wordless understanding of the powerlessness of any social structure to defeat them. Their bondage admitted them to the presence of a truth from which their masters hid, because to live with necessity is the only freedom.

This comment, echoing Hegel, is more directly persuasive in intent than usual, perhaps, but it does do something to mitigate the bleakness of Tam's desperation and defeat. McIlvanney *is* concerned to celebrate the resources of these people:

> A corner and some men was everywhere, debating-chamber, funeral-parlour, coffee-house, confessional, where they gave thoughts, hopes, laughter, words directly to the wind (244).

Only Mick here understands that they will have to be more concerned about the nature of their circumstances, says the author, but the full implications of that suggestion go beyond the confines of *Docherty* as a whole, where such subjects are not fully posed, let alone answered.

The final Book is less precise on dates, but seems to cover much less time. Before Tam's death, a long strike, or lockout, is at last defeated. McIlvanney has confirmed to the present authors that while his sources for accounts or memories of strikes or labour problems were always by preference in oral history, this particular lockout can safely be identified with the miners' strike of 1921, when the Lloyd George government 'felt strong enough to move forward to its ultimate objective: returning the mines to private ownership, ending all national agreements and in doing so opening the way to a decisive attack on wages and conditions'. Scotland is included in this comment: 'Here the aristocratic stance of the hewers crumbled badly while government tactics in the 1921 lockout did much to bring forward a new generation of often Communist local leaders.'[1] This fits not only the 'aristocratic' Tam—not a bad adjective—but the emergence of the political Mick. Tam dies an unspecified time after this, and the Book seems naturally divided in two by his death.

One of the striking changes in the early part is the increasing importance of Angus: his role and reality are greatly developed here. Tam dies in chapter 10, and Angus is central in 1, 2, 5, 6 and 8: he asserts himself as he had indicated he was determined to do in Book II, while Tam diminishes. Thus towards the end of his life Tam is newly overshadowed by Angus. The rest of the family is perhaps less prominent: Kathleen and Jack are involved in a sterile, unknown world which we do not enter; Mick conducts his 'fifth-column' investigation and judgement largely as a character we no longer see inside, and Conn is important mostly as registering consciousness rather than as an individual with a life outside his relationship to Tam and his brothers.

The new dominance of Angus is seen in the first chapter, when he goes to force Jack to behave better towards Kathleen. But it is clear to the reader that Angus is extremely naïve, and cannot begin to understand the 'desert' Jack and Kathleen live in. It is ironic that he is here self-appointedly endorsing the old morality: 'It's nae way tae treat a wumman. Ye've nae decency. It's no richt' (251). Only a few chapters later he will reject the old morality completely, when he refuses to marry the pregnant Sarah Davidson—'nae way tae treat a wumman', that too. Indeed, Angus momentarily sees that he has not come to enforce the traditional morality, but to compete again with his father:

> It occurred to him wilfully and shockingly that it wasn't so much Jack he was confronting as his father, because he knew that Tam should have been the one to do this, and by Angus's doing it he was demonstrating something about his father, putting a date on the headstone (252).

His momentary illumination does not last, any more than his momentary misgivings: 'He carried his own certainty with him like a lantern.'

A true confrontation of Tam and Angus—and Mick—occurs in chapter 2, precipitated by Angus's announcement that he is changing pits and contracting for coal. Tam and Jenny are already convinced, with others of

---

[1] See 'British Imperialism and the Labour aristocracy' by John Foster, in *The General Strike 1926* (ed Jeffrey Skelley) (1976), 35 and 37

their generation, that things are 'no' the same': the change is indeed presented as fact in this Book, although the attempts of people to modify old attitudes and beliefs or discover new ones are very uncertain and tentative. Even Mick, the family thinker, backs Angus here, but later (chapter 15) discounts Angus and is prepared to re-value Tam's life. At this point things are very simple for Tam. If Angus accepts a contract he becomes a capitalist: 'Ye don't make contracts wi' yer enemies' (257). His response is simplistic but hearfelt, and it does underline a weakness in Angus hardly spelt out now or ever, his strength giving him confidence to resign from family, class and any other loyalties and 'go it alone', without ever understanding the necessary limitations of this stance. Meanwhile Tam asserts the beliefs he has lived by, and Mick repeatedly mocks and scorns them. Tam will have no truck with Capital:

> Ah've kept somethin' alive that they've been tryin' tae kill. . . . Tae show them they can neither brek us nor buy us. Fur oor time's comin' (258).

Mick eventually shouts a reply, denunciation, a refutation:

> Oor time isny comin'. Oor time's here. An' your time's past . . . ootside this room, the rules are different. . . . Naebudy is aboot tae set us free, feyther. . . . If you want somethin', ye'd better learn tae get it fur yerself. . . . You are pathetic.

This confrontation of Mick and Tam irresistibly reminds us of Book I chapter 3, where Tam rejected *his* father and his religion in similarly passionate terms: perhaps McIlvanney's thesis lies not in one 'right' attitude for the working class, but in the inadequacy of the various philosophies of life becoming clear retrospectively to the seriously searching young. Tam spoke to old Conn *as* fiercely:

> They confiscated yer bloody brains at birth. An' stuffed their stinkin' catechism in their place. Auld man. . . . Damn yer stupidity! . . . Ye're still playin' wi' yer bloody toays! (43–4).

In this chapter Tam's defeat has become apparent to all. He comes more and more, unexpectedly, to resemble Willy Loman in Arthur Miller's *Death of a Salesman*. He avoids confronting incidents: 'Now he was more likely to take a sudden frenzy for some intense but apparently unmotivated activity' (254). This can be painting doors, going to the dog-racing, poaching: it can even have the same pathos as Willy Loman's doomed determination to make things grow in his finally overshadowed and infertile back yard. So in chapter 9 Tam comes in from the pub with a new idea:

'Gettin' a haud o' a wee plot o' grund. A gairden plot. An' growin' things.' ... The
serious consideration his mother was able to give the suggestion amazed Conn.
His father had a new idea almost every night and not one of them went beyond his
mouth. She was remarkable. Where did she find the strength and the patience to
go on suckling this man's stillborn dreams? (295).

In fact, the general resemblance of Jenny to Linda Loman is much more
striking than the brief resemblance of Tam and Willy. Like Linda, Jenny
devoted her life to the love, sustenance and reputation of her husband, and
defends him against all comers. Linda Loman admonishes her son Biff:
'Either he's your father and you pay him that respect or else you're not to
come here.' At the end of this family row in chapter 2 Jenny speaks to the
wall:

> You will respect that man, or you will not be in this house. That's the best man
> ye'll meet in a week's walk. An' you'll respect him (261).

After a chapter largely concerned to chart Conn's sexual obsessions
comes chapter 4, where the book's double stress is dramatised in Mick's
anger at the men playing together, refusing to think, contrasted with
Jenny's valuation of their goodness and the splendour of her memories. But
the confrontations resume in chapter 5, this time very much in terms of
personal rather than political morality, over the girl pregnant by Angus. It
is a case, crucially, where it is true that things are 'no' the same'. Tam's clear
morality grows from the conditions in which his people have been herded
and yet have asserted their dignity: to him, 'There's only wan thing tae be
done' (274). Angus does not trouble to argue *his* case, but Mick indicates
part of it: 'Whit dis that lassie want wi' a man that disny want her? Whit's
the *sense* in whit ye're daein'.' McIlvanney does not adjudicate in the
argument, and the modern reader's sympathy may well be with Mick's view
that marriage to Angus would only compound Sarah's misery. But Tam's
passionate assertion of solidarity and dignity also compels our sympathy.
At the end his attack on Angus seems to cover not only this personal matter
but also Angus's independence over his job:

> We're wan anither. Tae survive, we'll respect wan anither. . . . You're a fuckin'
> deserter. Ah don't harbour deserters. Ye're wi' the rest o' us or ye go elsebit (277).

With that metaphor we are back in the class war, with Tam's quasi-military
expectations of discipline and loyalty. Kathleen long ago felt an un-
comfortable intensity in her father's attitudes: 'In her family, you weren't
just a member. You had to enlist' (88). Angus willingly deserts, choosing his

own way. We learn in chapter 6 that he plans to marry, and that Annie is not pregnant. It is hard to argue today that he should marry Sarah, whom he does not love, instead—but Tam is right in all he says about respect: it is impossible to be happy about Angus's behaviour toward Sarah: he has fundamentally lacked respect, and his carelessness, even laughter, on the subject is chilling.

We see the rest of Angus's story through Conn's eyes, and Conn is sympathetic and loyal to his brother. He finds him digs and accepts his confidences. Conn has 'an unofficial coming-out party' (287) at Angus's wedding, where Angus is aware of his father's absence but able to be unconcerned. He produces his own epitaph on his father and asserts his personal ethic of individual competition, and on the way has insight into Tam's position:

> Ma feyther still believes in some kinna holiness. . . . He's no' a Catholic, all richt. An' Christ knows whit he believes. But he believes it strong. An' whit Ah did wis Ah shat in his wee church. . . . Ah'm no' playing' fur his team. An' whit Ah kens is his team's gonny lose. An' ah'm gonny win (289–90).

It is typical of Angus and his arrogant belief in his own strength that he sums it up as Tam on one side with his team, and Angus on the other, alone. Moments later, he enlarges his team: 'Frem noo on, it's just Annie an' me. An' we're gonny make oot' (291). His position and his ambitions are not taken seriously enough to be argued against in detail, but Mick refers contemptuously to them in the penultimate chapter:

> He's gave up the joab a while ago. He disny ken whit it's a' aboot. He's like a man shapin' up tae his mirror. . . . Ah like 'im fine. But don't ask me tae take 'im seriously (319).

The failure of the 1921 strike is cast up at Tam by Jack in chapter 7. And Tam accepts the failure and the way it nullifies his whole life, confessing to Kathleen his lack of hope:

> Before wis before, hen. Och, Ah'll manage. But it's no' goin' tae happen. Whit Ah thocht could happen. Funny thing. Ah'm fifty-three. An' Ah micht as weel be ninety. Fur Ah'm by (285).

Only two final family confrontations remain, if we set aside Conn's confused challenging of Angus after his failure to appear at his father's funeral. These are chapters 9 and 15. In 9, Mick baits a drunken Tam and Conn endeavours to understand what he is seeing. This, our last sight of

Tam before his death, is bleak and violent. Mick's baiting is merciless, and leads almost to a physical battle. Conn becomes 'a believer' again in his father, 'not just in what his father had been but in what he was, because he saw the frightening place where his father had learned to live' (297)—and he intuits Tam's harsh judgement of himself. In a climactically violent image he understands Tam's rage against himself:

> He had fed his children to a system that gave them back as the bread he ate every day of his life. And it wasn't until he had eaten them that he discovered what he had done. Now that it was too late, he understood.

Conn's final image of his father recalls the early descriptions—'like being friends with Mount Etna':

> his father standing making everything afraid of him, because you realised that he had learned to live where you daren't, and in his utter defeat there was an absolute power (298).

Before the last confrontation of Mick and Conn comes Tam's death, which is narrated economically and rather mysteriously. Characteristically, Tam saves another man's life with his last energy. Like all the crucial actions of the novel, it is almost passed over—what are important are the reactions. Jenny's is predictable, and moving, and on her strength the rest depend. She endorses the decision of Conn and Mick to dispense with priests, indicating that Tam's religion was family:

> If there's wan thing he loved it's his weans. His boay's'll bury 'im. An' if Goad disny want 'im like that, Ah don't want Goad (306).

At the strange burial Tadger, the staunch Catholic, gives his approval to the unorthodox procedure, and echoes Jenny's belief: 'Whaurever he's gaun'll dae me fine. Ah widny want tae be whaur he wisny' (307). And a Catholic uncle takes one of the cords of the coffin.

Conn's reaction to his father's death involves an unthought out challenge to Angus in chapter 13, and a set fight in 14. The old, telling metaphor reappears when Angus looks at Conn with 'something like admiration' and says: 'Christ. A gunfighter in the faimly' (313). But the long fight only proves something to both brothers about the passing of time and the out-of-date style of the gunfighter:

> Like the retiring champions of a way of life, they felt the pointlessness not just of their own actions but of their father's and their friends'. All they had achieved

was to pay homage to a dead ethic. What they had done had courage and dignity and even a kind of grandeur but no relevance (317).

The search for relevance is left to Conn and Mick in chapter 15. Mick enunciates his beliefs. Tam was after all right to oppose Angus going to work in the 'contract' pit. Tam, by implication, was altogether right for his time: 'Folk like ma feyther wur oor Winter Palace' (320). Tam's angry defiance made him a precursor of the revolution Mick is committed to, a necessary preparation for his new faith, the triumph of Bolshevism. Mick's morality here is radical; instead of waiting fruitlessly in queues, the workers must break into the shops. The careful mind of Conn is impressed but not convinced—Mick is ignoring so many aspects that have importance. Mick is hard, but has a programme of action: Conn is warmer, and has none. But his opinions and reactions still matter to Mick, who confides his new membership of the Communist Party. The argument points on beyond the covers of the novel:

> Because you an' me's whit's left o' ma feyther, Conn. It's between you an' me. Me wi' wan airm an' you in twa minds, eh? (322).

And that is where the novel leaves the ongoing, central question.

The last brief chapter is a coda, the end of the elegiac movement of the book after Tam's death. His epitaph is to be delivered where his life was so often defined, among the men at the corner. A year after his death there is equanimity, even humour—a quality rarely absent for long in the novel, though often hard to pin down. The epitaph is excessive, generous, hyperbolic. In passing, the author unobtrusively produces a quieter one in terms which have related Tam to his fellows since the Prologue:

> When they contemplated Tam Docherty, he helped them to define themselves (324).

FURTHER READING

Our page references are to the Mainstream edition of 1983.

William McIlvanney was born in Kilmarnock (original of the fictional Graithnock) in 1936. He went to university and training college in Glasgow, and began his very successful teaching career in Irvine in 1959, leaving Greenwood Academy, Dreghorn in 1977 to become a fulltime writer.

He has published a book of poems, *The Longships in Harbour* (1970), but his main writing consists of novels, each of which has won discriminating critical praise and prizes or awards. They are: *Remedy is None* (1966), *A Gift from Nessus* (1968), *Docherty* (1975), *Laidlaw* (1977) and *The Papers of Tony Veitch* (1983), He contributed an autobiographical essay, 'Growing Up in the West', to *Memoirs of a Modern Scotland*, edited by Karl Miller (1970, 168–78).

His work has received virtually no sustained and serious criticism to date, but a start was made by Isobel Murray in 'William McIlvanney', North East Review in *Leopard Magazine* 53 (October 1979), 26–8. F R Hart gives a brief account of the first two novels in *The Scottish Novel: A Critical Survey* (1978).

CHAPTER TEN

Robin Jenkins:
Fergus Lamont

When we come to Robin Jenkins, our most prolific living novelist, the problem of selecting just one novel for discussion becomes particularly acute. This is in part because of a bewilderment of choice: Jenkins has published so many novels since he began in 1950, so different in scope and intention, and so many of these would easily justify inclusion in this book. The choice is inappropriately complicated, however, by the shameful non-availability of so many of these: at the time of writing only two novels are available in paperback, *The Cone-Gatherers* (1955) and *Fergus Lamont* (1979).

Conventional wisdom among readers of Jenkins has a lot of time for *The Cone-Gatherers*, and rightly so. The Paul Harris edition of 1980 is now available as a King Penguin, and it is to be hoped that it will make Jenkins known to many hitherto unaware of his rich and often startling talents. It is a short, concentrated novel or fable, set in a forest during World War Two, where the local fine lady is allowing cones for eventual re-seeding to be collected before the forest is felled in the war effort. The principal characters are two brothers, Calum, a mis-shapen dwarf with a beautiful face and personality and less than adult maturity, and Neil, the older brother who anxiously cares for him: these are the cone-gatherers. Then there is the gamekeeper Duror, a figure of baleful malignancy who directs all his accumulated hatred at the deformed Calum: we are given some idea of the awful pressures on Duror over decades as his invalid wife grows fatter and sillier and his personal depression becomes worse, so that his cracking up and issuing in evil is a tragic spectacle. And there is the aristocratic Lady Runcie-Campbell, attempting in a naïve and futile way to marry her inherited class attitudes to her sincere Christianity; it is Lady Runcie-Campbell that most readers have found to be the weak link in this intensely powerful book.

So it would be possible to concentrate here on *The Cone-Gatherers*. But it might be misleading. For one thing, it *is* so concentrated, so pared down. We would argue that it is successfully so, but also that it is relatively atypical among Jenkins' best novels. *The Cone-Gatherers* followed two more extended books, of which the first was *Happy for the Child* (1953), an early treatment of a favourite Jenkins subject, the sensitive poor boy-cum-lad o' pairts at the fee-paying school where virtually everyone else is better off, with developing social awareness and conflicting themes of innocence and survival and the parallel story of a graceless unaccomplished slum boy, whose life is also full of pain. It was followed by *The Thistle and the Grail* (1954), a much more wide-ranging book, dealing with the fortunes, choices and struggles of a small town, a football team and its president, in a very Scottish world where football is the only faith remaining. So even of the early 1950s, *The Cone-Gatherers* is not typical.

Jenkins interrupted his school-teaching career in Scotland with periods in Spain, Afghanistan and the Near East, and found rich new material there, perhaps the best of the resultant novels being *Dust on the Paw* (1961), which Francis Russell Hart (before the publication of *Fergus Lamont*) called Jenkins' most ambitious achievement. Non-availability is a problem here again. But in any case, with a writer still thankfully producing very fine work there could be an impression of diminishment if we returned to the 1950s or early 1960s. Happily, in 1979 Jenkins published what we would call one of his most ambitious achievements so far, *Fergus Lamont*, a book which not only ranges wide and deep with superb comic control, but pulls together all his most characteristic and lasting concerns—a book Jenkins himself thinks of as 'one of his most important and significant books to date', a book which sheds light retrospectively on much that has gone before. We have no hesitation about choosing *Fergus Lamont* as our central novel, then, but wouldn't it be nice if *all* the novels were available and in print? A parallel could be drawn with the Bodley Head Graham Greene: Jenkins resembles Greene in many ways and many preoccupations: it would be nice to see a reissue, a collected novels of Robin Jenkins. We may refer briefly and in passing to other novels, but lack space to do more: Francis Russell Hart has a most lucid and interesting account of some of the earlier work.

So: what kind of novel is *Fergus Lamont*, and how can we usefully approach it? We would suggest that it is interesting to consider it as a peculiarly twentieth-century and peculiarly Scottish variant on Dickens' great realistic novel-cum-fairytale, *Great Expectations*. We remember that young Pip, a boy of very ordinary life and origins, is corrupted by expectations of wealth intimated to him at an early age, combined with his helpless adoration of Estella, Miss Havisham's ward, a devotion which makes him hopelessly conscious of the 'common' nature of himself and his family. This combination turns him into a selfish young snob, hurtfully intent on forgetting his origins, especially his most loyal friend, his brother-in-law Joe Gargery. But in the end Pip learns the truth by a series of complex revelations, and by unexpectedly experiencing real love for the returned convict Magwitch, the true source of his 'expectations'. And so the later Pip who relates the story is a sadder and a wiser man, who remembers and relates and at the same time deeply repents the faults of his youth: the modulation of late and early Pip is one of the most impressive aspects of the novel. And although with a fairy godmother figure like Miss Havisham and a self-consciously split personality like Wemmick, whose character is quite different at work and at home, the novel is galaxies away from conventional realism, the success of *Great Expectations* depends on our acceptance of the reality of Pip's psychological and moral progress.

Fergus Lamont's story has a strikingly similar structure. Young Fergus is brought up in the slums of Gantock (Greenock), disturbed by his mother's disappearance when he is three and her reappearance for three climactic days when he is seven, ending with her suicide. His whole-hearted romantic commitment to his mother is combined with the belief that his real father was an earl's son, and Fergus determines that he himself will belong to the aristocracy. He becomes an outrageous snob and social climber, ruthless in self-advancement and in the cruelty with which he spurns all those in his background who love him but who might betray his Gantock origins.

Arguably Fergus never learns as much as Pip. If he does learn, it is from his ten years on the Hebridean island of Oronsay, where he leads a subsistence-level life with the strong and beautiful but not entirely adult Kirstie: this would be his equivalent to Pip discovering that he really loves Magwitch. But Fergus does not experience the same complete reversal that Pip does, and his cure is only partial. The damage he has done himself is not wholly reversible, and he continues to display appalling attitudes even after the Hebridean experience: the exorcism is incomplete. So Jenkins' picture of Fergus's psychological progress is much grimmer than Dickens' picture of Pip's; but perhaps it is psychologically even more realistic, more convincing.

We suggest this is a peculiarly twentieth-century variant on *Great Expectations*, and not simply for the reason just given. Jenkins' attitude toward Fergus, and the older Fergus's attitude toward the younger Fergus, are much less clear cut than the equivalent in Dickens. It is part of the quality of *Fergus Lamont* that we can never rest in a single comfortable attitude toward Fergus, whether of blame or forgiveness: we cannot be sure of Jenkins' attitude, conveyed through pervasive irony which nonetheless has to be conveyed through Fergus himself, the book's only narrator. He *is* the only narrator, but we never know for sure when or whether to trust him, because his improved perception and moral advancement following the ten years with Kirstie are so unclear and uncertain, the lapses so frequent, and because it remains possible throughout that on this subject or that he is simply deluded, and so is incapable of telling us the truth.

We suggest also that this variant on *Great Expectations* is peculiarly Scottish. This is not only because of the accidents of plot and geography, with concentration on the slums of Gantock, the estates of the wealthy and crofting on Oronsay: and it is not only because of the peculiarly Scottish analysis of central subjects, such as class, education, literature and so on. It is a Scottish variant because Fergus's obsession with gentility amounts to a case of making himself one of the Elect at whatever cost and with whatever self-deluding aims thereafter, even apparently religious aims: he sees himself, bizarrely, as future saviour of Gantock and its slums, while never attempting, like his friend and opposite Mary Holmscroft, to change or improve the condition of the people, or to keep any contact with them. Arguably Fergus elects himself to what turns out to be desperate loneliness, lovelessness and delusion: arguably, like Miss Brodie, he thinks he is the God of Calvin. Certainly in his narrative he sees himself as a more than justified sinner, expecting the astonished reader always to accept and acknowledge the necessity that drives him. Fergus is a new statement of the theme of split personality in the Scottish psyche, inheritor of Jekyll and Hyde, but containing the two aspects warring inside him continually (as Mary Holmscroft acknowledges, page 245). And it is Fergus's own determination to become an aristocrat that determines all the splits we see between different and conflicting attitudes, and different roles—officer and gentleman, poet, husband and father, etc. As elsewhere in Jenkins, and in Hogg's *Justified Sinner*, powerful obsession gives the will enormous strength, but is likely to mutilate the psyche and perception of reality: compare Agnes Tolmie in *A Toast to the Lord* (1972). And Fergus's obsession makes him solipsistic, hardly able to care in any real sense for other people.

It seems appropriate to begin with a brief account of the main lines of the story and its main themes, before embarking on a selective approach which will inevitably pay most attention to the first part of the book, or to the pursuance of themes first occurring there and returned to later. The book is being written by Fergus himself, in 1963 when he is seventy-one. It tells the story of his life up to 1941 and his second return to Gantock. The novel is divided into six very unequal parts, some covering many years, some days only. Part One covers fifteen years of Fergus's childhood and early manhood in Gantock, and Part Three fourteen years of his disastrous marriage to Betty, and Part Five the ten years with Kirstie, while Part Two gives a very selective glimpse of his almost four years at war, Part Four covers less than two days, the first return to Gantock, and Part Six, the second return, one day. Always there is great compression: the novel is very full and rich, and because of the ambiguous nature of the narrator and authorial irony, a constant challenge to the reader.

Part One, then, opens with Fergus aged seven, thrilled and appalled at the return of his beautiful young mother who brings out so much savagery in all his acquaintance. The fateful visit of mother and son to the unforgiving Calvinist grandfather begins with a cataclysmic incident for young Fergus, where three women reminiscent of the witches in *Macbeth* gather, one spitting in his mother's face, another wanting to throw dung at the 'whure' with a malice as reminiscent of the Puritan crowds in Hawthorne's *The Scarlet Letter*. Mother and dung-gathering son are rejected by the grandfather, and the mother drowns herself.

Gradually life resumes. Fergus is unconsciously deeply ashamed of his grandfather. He goes to secondary school and is much impressed by the atheist, socialist teacher 'Limpy' Calderwood, and by his bright fellow pupil Mary Holmscroft, who will dedicate her life to the Gantock slums via politics, and remain faithful and close to her family, unlike Fergus. At length Fergus learns that his mother had lived for those four missing years with a rich old man, and that he himself is illegitimate, possibly the son of the earl's son. When his grandfather dies he accepts his inheritance and goes to a fee-paying school, forming ambitions to write, but above all to be accepted as gentry, an ambition that may be furthered by the Great War approaching. He is very much attracted to Limpy's sister, the beautiful but often childish Cathie, and to his early class-mate, the beautiful Meg Jeffries, whom he silently renounces because he will need an aristocratic wife.

Part Two covers Fergus's war experience and his continuing social ambitions. He is intent on copying his fellow officers from aristocratic homes, intent on being accepted as one of them, and ruthless about ignoring any inconvenient ties with the past. We do learn how he won his MC, but his courage is mitigated by his complacent certainty of secular Election: he will not be killed, but has 'a strong assurance of deserved immunity'. He enters into correspondence with a popular authoress of inspirational novels, Betty T. Shields. With many indications of a disastrous, domineering relationship to come, Fergus is sent home to be at Betty's disposal to boost morale.

In Part Three we witness Fergus's craven submission to Betty, the coming of the children, Betty's numerous infidelities. Fergus writes his only two books of poems, based arguably on his only two 'real' experiences before Oronsay (which inspires more poems), the Gantock childhood and the war. Fergus's ambitions here, of returning to Gantock at last as 'absolver and redeemer' (117), are at their most unreal and self-deceiving.

This Part climaxes in Betty's support of one of her lovers, National Government candidate Sir Jock Dunsyre, at the 1931 election, and Fergus, the 'kilted worm', turning and making an arcane speech in favour of Mary Holmscroft—who wins, we suspect, independently of his support. Fergus fights off Betty's subsequent attempt at banishment, and then inexplicably falls victim to pity. After all the occasions when he has failed to revisit relations and old friends, especially Aunt Bella, he responds to the call to visit his foster father, John Lamont, apparently dying. For all its comic sparkle in the treatment of the monster Betty, this Part impresses less than the previous two, as sporadic, rather diffuse and comparatively lacking in direction: arguably in all this it reflects Fergus's life over these long years when he sells out as poet, husband, father, human being, to retain the status he had spent so long and worked so hard to achieve:

> I had to take care lest I throw away with a few plebeian barbarisms what since leaving Gantock I had schemed, lied, deceived, betrayed, and even killed, to achieve: that was, my status as an officer and gentleman (150).

Fergus's first return to Gantock and the consequent break-up of his marriage is rendered in some detail in Part Four, where he necessarily re-encounters many people he has scrupulously avoided: it is seventeen years since he saw his foster father's wife Bessie, for example. Fergus's protestations of affection are hollow and mistaken: other people generally seem unreal to him, except as icons of his imagination and memory. He had learned of Cathie's death two years after the event (158), and now he learns Uncle Tam has been blind for five years, and has the impudence to feel pain (175). His nearest approach to childhood reality here is the imaginary conversation with young Smout at the War Memorial, when Smout tells him some home truths about the comfort and luxury of his circumstances, but Fergus's response, his promise to look after Jessie, is hollow and quickly demolished.

A vengeful Betty comes to confront Fergus and win her freedom by exposing the true conditions of his birth and childhood and his disabling shame about them. Her malice may make us sympathise with Fergus, but we recognise truth in, for instance, her statement that he has been a parasite for years (188). The main accusation is the old one, first articulated by Aunt Bella (24), that, like his mother, Fergus lacks affection. And Fergus makes no attempt to counter it:

> 'Why am I not wanted?'
> 'Because you yourself want no one. I don't think you ever have' (189).

Apart from the long interlude on Oronsay, this seems a factual summing up of Fergus throughout. Part Four ends in the present, with Fergus planning a bizarre and romantic funeral journey back to East Gerinish: the unmoved way in which he and Betty part for the last time is thus juxtaposed to his perpetual loving regret for Kirstie, who is to be the major subject of Part Five.

Clearly Fergus's sojourn on Oronsay, his work with the McLeods at East Gerinish and above all his loving relationship with Kirstie, constituted the happiest ten years of his life. Whether these years purged him of his selfishness and arrogance as much as the seventy-one-year-old narrator believes throughout is much more questionable. Jenkins' work is crowded with saintly innocents with less than full normal adult understanding— Calum in *The Cone-Gatherers* is an outstanding early example. Here Kirstie has had predecessors—'soft-witted' Jessie McFadyen, 'beautiful but glaikit', the only female in his early life to offer Fergus what he calls tenderness, and Cathie Calderwood, the slightly unconvincing mixture of delightful young woman, graduate and teacher, and 'afflicted', ultra-childish little girl. Kirstie outdoes the other two in her 'unimaginable goodness' (259), combining extreme simplicity and sweetness with strength, presented visually as it were as herself a split personality, the broad, mannish figure with cap and pipe, and the stunning Celtic princess. Arguably she is not as fully rendered as these predecessors, or the obnoxious Betty, or Fergus's first sweetheart Meg Jeffries, or his 'sister' Mary Holmscroft: we believe in Kirstie not because of what we see of her but because of the change in Fergus when he lives with her or when he talks about her. Again we are reminded of *Great Expectations* and the change that unawares takes place in Pip when he begins to love the convict Magwitch who has risked so much for love of him. But Fergus's case is again more complex, the change less radical and less permanently convincing. When he sets off for Oronsay, Fergus's humility is minimal; he automatically expects others to carry his case and serve him: after the ten year idyll he still expects his case carried (Kirstie has been there to carry it), and indeed he demonstrates an unpleasant and unjustified confidence in his moral improvement, while continuing to despise all he meets.

The effort of writing about Kirstie is too much for the ageing narrator, and at the end of Part Five he has had a stroke and is content to face imminent death, no longer determined as before (237) to finish the account of the 'second and final return to Gantock', no longer, apparently, seeing this as a precondition of success, or over-concerned about his work.

In the event, Part Six does describe that return, although it is brief and finishes abruptly with the narrator's death before he can tell us what if anything he thinks the return achieved, and what his apparently solitary life has been in the twenty years since. The impact of this last short section is oddly mixed. On the one hand Fergus's conviction of his superiority seems virtually undiminished: it is made perhaps even more unpleasant by his belief in his moral rectitude, his achievement of humility. On the other he is a figure of fun and conscious of it, although he has little sense of fun and is almost never known to laugh. Comic effect is nonetheless integral to the story throughout the novel, nowhere more so than here, when he tries to buy sweets without coupons in 1941, and overhears the reaction:

> 'I think, Mrs Paterson, we're safe in thinking nae German spy would hae the nerve to come in wearing a kilt and ask for purple aniseed balls.'
> 'Without coupons tae' (280).

Like us, Fergus finds it hard to know how much of the laughter is satirical. And so the effect is inconclusive. Before (typically) returning to the comfort of John Calderwood's house, Fergus wants to make an act of expiation to someone—any one—he has treated badly, and finding that Uncle Tam is still alive he ventures to Kirn Street, to find his way barred by Tam's 'pleasantly dotty' wife. Fergus attempts self-justification to us for his long, long neglect: yes, he was a snob, but he also pleads 'fear of Aunt Bella's celebrated breasts' (convincing), and 'aesthetic repugnance' and 'moral anguish' at their sufferings (rather less so). But Fergus does not see Uncle Tam, and when he tests himself and his reactions to his native Lomond Street, to see if the years of Kirstie's love had been wasted, he meets Meg Jeffries and quickly succumbs again to aesthetic repugnance and moral anguish at her twisted mouth and the impossibility of helping her—and he lies to her to get away.

The final encounter with John Calderwood is equivocal. We have the words of their conversation, but only Fergus's authority for his interpretative impressions, Calderwood's 'habitual malevolence', possible insanity, enjoyment of his pessimism—and what sort of authority are we to allow this self-righteous prig?

> My host ate, I thought, with more relish and greed than a cynic should. I felt obliged to eat frugally myself, in some kind of rebuke; but to my chagrin he did not seem to notice (291).

Fergus's quasi-religious ambitions for his return have been eventually reduced, but by no means ended: he no longer expects to be an actual saviour, but still 'a giver of courage and hope' (275). And he is still deluded about his relationship to the people: in Lomond Street he incomprehensibly reflects of the women: 'If they had known me though, how boisterous their mirth, how bawdy their proposals, and how warm their affection' (281–2). By the end, though, he agrees with Calderwood: 'I could be of help to no one'. As the German bombers raid the town, he apparently achieves briefly a pure emotion: 'For the people of Gantock, at that moment suffering terror and pain and death, I felt only pity and love.' After writing this the narrator dies, and in his son's postscript the random, unhappy nature of things is reflected—among the massive casualties in the air-raid Uncle Tam and his wife were killed, and Meg Jeffries was severely injured.

Fergus Lamont is the only one of our novels (and the only one of Jenkins' novels) to undertake the peculiar problems of first person narration, and, as the comparison to *Great Expectations* makes clear, Jenkins makes these problems the more peculiar by the nature of the narrator he chooses. Fergus sees himself as aristocrat, poet and potential saviour and absolver of the slum-dwellers of Gantock: but the literary critic Campbell Aird sees him as 'a selfish, ignorant, conceited, unconvivial, aloof, and unsympathetic bastard' (140). Irony and ambiguity are central features of many Jenkins novels, in a tradition that goes back at least to Hogg: while we try to test and assess Jenkins, he is constantly, strenuously and subtly testing us. Page by page our attitude changes, wavers, fluctuates, and the careful reader is forced into radical self-examination. Fairly typical is the very beginning of the novel, in which the narrator's voice emerges as individual, pompous, absurd, misanthropic and melodramatic:

Half Scotland sniggered, and the other half scowled, when in letters to the *Scotsman* and the *Glasgow Herald*, I put forward my suggestion that prisoners in Scottish jails be allowed to wear kilts, as their national birthright, if such was their wish. Those sniggerers and scowlers may well snigger more moronically and scowl more impatiently when I now confess that I donned my own first kilt, at the age of seven and a half, not with pride and joy, but with reluctance and anguish; and also that for the rest of my life I never buckled one on without feeling something of the grief and shame with which James IV, unhappy parricide, must have put on his penitential shirt of iron.

Puritanic and parochial Scots, you murdered my young and beautiful mother. As one of you, I must share the blame.

The kilted prisoners suggestion is never developed, nor is it important, except as an indication of Fergus's eccentric mentality. It is no accident, surely that in this first sentence Scotland itself is seen as fractured, fundamentally split, in this case into sniggerers and scowlers. The novel goes on to portray a Scotland split into classes, split by religion, split in education between two traditions, 'love of learning and truth, and . . . Calvinist narrow-minded vindictiveness' (58), split in soul and literature between 'mendacious sentimentality' and 'ironic truthfulness' (120). And it is no accident that Fergus's choice of words here, sniggerers and scowlers, implies his contempt for both: we are not attracted to this voice, this vision. The following sentences seem highly coloured, romantic, absolutist, while implying a story to be told which is mysterious and intriguing: that mixture of off-putting teller and enticing tale is fairly typical, but we are rarely exposed for too long to the most unlovable aspects of our hero. And so the novel immediately moves into rendering the anguish, fear, love and anxiety of a seven-year-old bewildered and desperately concerned by the re-entry into his life of his 'young and beautiful mother'. Jenkins is a master at rendering the extremes of misery to which children are susceptible—see both Stirling and Gourlay in *Happy for the Child*—so inevitably the reader, however put off by the first two paragraphs, sympathises with both Fergus and his mother as victims in this clearly serious situation, and the ironies and ambiguities of the novel begin to weave their complex patterns.

The narrative structure, as we have suggested, is not such a complex pattern. The six parts are related in chronological order, and the interruptions of this order are presented naturally enough. The seventy-one-year-old narrator occasionally surfaces in the present, usually at the end of each part, to record some contemporary feeling or experience which may contrast ironically with the events he has been describing, as when he leaves off relating the supposedly healing relationship with Kirstie to tell us of his rejection of his son Torquil, or at the end of Part Two, where the young, handsome, successful soldier sent home to accompany the beautiful authoress on a morale-boosting tour is suddenly juxtaposed with the scruffy—and probably smelly—old man, the solitary who writes his memoirs in the public library in a crumpled and stained jotter, with sandwiches on the side. Occasionally Fergus anticipates events, gives 'flashes forward' as Vonnegut or Spark might do, but the first person narrative makes it seem natural, while effective. So for example in chapter 5 of Part One the first paragraph not only describes the dangers of Puddock Loch but abruptly announces Fergus's mother's drowning, before the chapter reconstructs the child's experience of apprehending and reacting to the news. More elaborately, the futures of Fergus's contemporaries are flatly announced in chapter 2, where Fergus is going through agonies at the public reception of the kilt he wears to please his mother:

> In time to come Jock was to wear a kilt himself and be killed in it. So were Rab and Smout. Their names are on the Gantock War Memorial (10).

Our awareness of this adds poignancy to the later treatment of Smout, his ambition to have a kilt (21), and his precipitate volunteering for service in the Great War: and to Fergus's choice of Smout's real name, William McTavish, as his alias in his solitary later years.

The situation at the beginning of the novel is compelling. We will never know for sure if Aunt Bella is right that Fergus's mother had 'nae affection'

(24): even Fergus later seems to suspect this coldness when he tries to read Betty's mind about his ice-cool, Estella-like little daughter Dorcas:

> She would have died rather than say that Dorcas must take after my mother, but I was sure she often thought it (153).

But the reader inevitably sympathises here with the mysteriously persecuted, beautiful young woman showing courage and disdain in the face of old harridans anxious to spit on her and throw dung, as well as with the boy who will relive that spit in nightmares and experience always 'a sense of unconquerable evil' (6). Fergus's ignorance and limitations are rendered as skilfully as Pip's: we indulgently oversee his strong sense of class within the working class, when he rates people by the street they live in as ably and dogmatically as Dunky Logan's mother, and his acceptance of all the anti-Catholic wisdom of his Calvinist grandfather. (Fergus never totally recovers from the emotional conditioning involved—see his horror when he discovers that Betty's mother not only never married but never 'turned' (152), and his reaction when Meg Jeffries tells him she let her daughters marry Catholics, too (286).)

But it is the Calvinist grandfather who determines the tragedy of Fergus's mother's death. No wonder Fergus is alarmed when she wants to visit her father: he has already told Fergus she is in hell, his mouth 'as hard as railway lines' (3)—one of Fergus's friends has said: 'When he's no' pleased, your grandfather looks like Goad.' Calvinism is a target in this novel, as much as in MacColla, Spark or Mackay Brown, and Fergus's grandfather is its worst manifestation. Fergus has naturally accepted him and all his dogma till now, an important man who runs the Sunday school and the Band of Hope, is an elder and a town councillor, and has eminent friends. Fergus has accepted his detestation of Catholics as only right, and is amazed and confounded at his mother saying: 'Your grandfather has no right to set you against Catholics or anybody else' (11). The rejection of daughter by father is indirect, anticlimactic. After nearly two hours of waiting at his home 'Siloam' (more ironically named than Samuel Whaness's boat in *Greenvoe*), only Fergus sees his grandfather, who simply locks him out of the house. The full impact comes from Fergus, after his mother's death and the continued failure to relent:

> My grandfather did not allow my mother to be buried in her own mother's grave; nor did he go to her funeral. He displayed atrocious callousness; yet, by the sheer effrontery of faith, he compelled most people to think of him as a Christian of formidable and magnificent staunchness (27).

After this, Fergus continued to associate with his grandfather, unconsciously 'profoundly ashamed of him' (27) and beginning to test his reactions to events. Importantly, there is the case of the Frames—wife, reputedly disabled husband and six children evicted, for non-payment of rent, to the rage of neighbours. Fergus was amazed 'that so much misery, and so much hatred, could be caused just by a lack of money' (28), but grandfather says non-payment is the disgrace, that it doesn't help people to give them money, that Frame drank and gambled, all 'with not even the merest tremble of doubt or indeed of pity'. Here for the first time something like the theme of the clearances is raised in the novel, and grandfather is of a mind with MacColla's Maighstirs Tormod and Iain, with no hint of Maighstir Sachairi. His reaction to the overpunishment of a boy in school is just as callous and self-righteous, and contrasts with the humane and angry reaction of Bessie, at this stage a non-believer.

Fergus forces the story of his birth out of Aunt Bella when he is twelve, and is transformed overnight into a terrible snob: 'I began to find it difficult to speak to people without making it too plain that I thought they were beneath me' (50). Indeed, perhaps because of his mother and her attitudes, even before this he has experienced, echoing Wordsworth, 'vague intimations of superiority'. It seems to run in the family! When he goes to his grandfather to consult him about his future, for the second time his grandfather locks the door against him, and that night he dies, the inheritance he leaves Fergus making possible the fee-paying Academy and the start of the road to aristocracy.

He leaves him also, intangibly, an inheritance of inhuman coldness, determination and self confidence: *he* only unbent once, to love his wife, and *she* died in childbirth. The pattern seems to perpetuate itself whether the elements of traditional Calvinism are retained or not. Grandfather sent his daughter into service at Corse Castle 'to humble her'. She in turn is accused of coldness and selfishness; although she does seem, briefly, to have loved the earl's son, there is no suggestion that she loved the rich old man for whom she left John Lamont and Fergus: she loved what his money could provide. When she returns, even her adoring Fergus admits she is 'a bit too beautiful, too perfumed, and too haughty for Lomond Street, and for me' (2). And the strong tradition persists that she is heartless. Fergus in his turn will unbend and love once, with Kirstie, but he will have no idea how to express love for his children: he will remain aloof, wholly committed to his own paltry concerns. And his little Dorcas will be imperious, snobbish and heartless, described in the same kind of imagery as Estella in *Great Expectations*: 'a hert o' ice ... like a tree covered wi' snaw' (152). In her turn she rejects her father for *her* religion of social advancement, and the unfairly rejected Torquil has to seek an obsessional faith also, and finds it in art. A stiff-necked generation! Crucial to our final estimate of Fergus will be his rejection of Torquil's love in his old age, with no such spurious 'justification' as a Calvinist judgement on a scarlet woman.

Education is frequently a major topic for ex-schoolteacher Jenkins, and *Fergus Lamont* is no exception. Although Fergus can be hopelessly deceived about himself and his motives and behaviour, like many of us he has a sharp eye for other people's: so he describes and denounces the primary teachers of his youth in chapter 8:

> In those days not all teachers were physically brutal, but too many of them were spiritually dull. It was no compensation that they were conscientious and diligent: the harder they worked at quelling originality and instilling conformity the less they deserved praise. After forty years they looked back in retirement with benign satisfaction upon careers more heinous than Herod's: he extinguished life only, they had extinguished the spirit (30).

We might say that such teachers, with better motives and blinder vision, are doing on a large scale to their pupils what Fergus does to himself, imposing a foreign character and repressing a native one. The indictment becomes nationwide, although Fergus here denies that the teachers succeeded, and triumphantly asserts the vitality of his boyhood slum companions. This chapter, unobtrusively covering about five years, can interestingly be compared to one or two in *Docherty*, giving the essence of Conn's boyhood experience (for example Book I, chapters 2, 18). And it indicates that Fergus, if a natural leader, was also a happy member of his peer group in these years: the disabling 'expectations' are to come. He implies that his 'seedtime' in the Gantock slums rivalled Wordsworth's in the Lake District (32).

There are more harsh words for education as Fergus goes on to senior school, a prison-like building with tiled walls, spiked fences, militaristic janitor and tawse-bearing teachers. What impresses Fergus is the one teacher who is different, Limpy Calderwood, the 'dominie without a tawse'. The voice and understanding of the older Fergus come in usefully here (33) to fill in Limpy's background, wealth, atheism and socialism. Fergus and Mary both hit the public eye in his first class: Mary intervenes when Limpy mocks Fergus and his kilt, to Limpy's astonished delight and Fergus's ready jealousy. Mary's life hereafter will frequently involve her in Fergus's jealousy, and will constantly and unobtrusively remind us by contrast of his shortcomings, both in relation to reality itself and to his family and background in particular. But one lesson of Limpy's is rehearsed at some length: chapter 10 contains an important theme of the book; it reveals Limpy as a superb teacher; it attacks conventional ideas of education, and is moving, funny and memorable: Jenkins' economy is extraordinary.

Instead of the history of the kings of England, Limpy insists on teaching
Scottish history, and in what at the time would be a most astonishing way:
'His method was to take some ordinary Scotsman or Scotswoman of the
past and imagine what his or her life must have been like' (37). This is the
story of Donald of Sutherland who went off at the behest of his Countess to
be a soldier, and returned many years later to find his native Strathnaver
ruined and deserted, except for sheep. Most of the listening children have
thrilled with patriotic and religious fervour, only Mary scowling scepti-
cally, but all are dumbfounded to learn that the clearances were sanctioned
by police, army and Parliament. The impact on the children is underlined
by the comic protests of the eavesdropping headmaster:

> 'Really, Mr Calderwood,' he cried, 'I must warn you. You are filling these
> children's minds with poison. You are undermining their confidence in legally
> constituted authority. It is a mistake to study the history of one's own country. It
> divides instead of uniting us. . . . Why bother with stuff so out-of-date?'
> 'It isn't out-of-date, Mr Maybole,' said Mary. 'People are still put out of their
> houses' (40).

Fergus remembers the evicted Frames. Like the others, he naturally and
single-mindedly opposes the evictions here: later, his social ambitions will
conflict with his natural sympathies, and overcome them. His outing with
Lady Grizel has an audience of sheep:

> Since that stuffy afternoon in Limpy's classroom ten years ago, the ghost of
> Donald of Sutherland had troubled my imagination. Now, through the sheep, it
> spoke, to rebuke me for associating with the kind of people who had betrayed him
> so cynically, and to warn me that such association would blur my poet's vision
> and numb my poet's conscience (89).

As Fergus is to learn again and again, his social ambitions are incompatible
with everything else he holds dear. Again and again he sacrifices everything
for the ambitions, only to be left with less than a mess of pottage. He is left
without family, without friends, without home.

One final chapter on education will furnish Fergus with yet another
warning. By chapter 15 he has acquired both his expectations and his
grandfather's money, and is at the fee-paying Academy. His main concern
now, he says, is to be a gentleman (56), but he has real ambitions also as a
writer. A crucial incident occurs when he writes an article on 'Quoiting' for
the school magazine. After some thought Fergus the potential poet uses the
word fart, as the only one appropriate to his context, and he is condemned
as a guttersnipe. This causes more thought:

His use of the word guttersnipe was making me wonder. 'Fart' was a truthful word, but was it gentlemanly? Was there a contradiction between truth and gentlemanliness? (57).

(Years later on Oronsay Fergus the gentleman has to describe Kirstie's breaking wind, but significantly avoids the word fart.) Here he refuses the belt, and there ensues the confrontation between Classicist headmaster and 'gaunt Presbyterian' teacher which Fergus describes as 'a clash between two traditions in Scotland, that of love of learning and truth, and that of Calvinist narrow-minded vindictiveness' (58). Again, we have Calvinism and an educational system influenced by it condemned.

Warnings or no warnings, Fergus sacrifices everything to his ambitions. Some are satisfied, but the results after all are entirely unsatisfactory: others, the quasi-religious dreams of salvation for Gantock, frighten us by the distance from reality they indicate. Let us sketch briefly his progress, after his instantaneous conversion to aristocratic pretension in chapter 13. His first problem is his foster father John Lamont, whom he avoids as Pip avoids Joe Gargery. He has no problem about his good friends, his schoolmates:

> Theirs was by birth the Scotland of tenements and low-paid jobs. Mine was the Scotland of castles, famous families, and heroic deeds (52).

When his grandfather dies, Fergus evinces no emotion, but he takes great care to look distinguished at the funeral, and is overwhelmed by Lord Baidland's voice:

> From his lips I heard, for the first time, the authentic confident bray of the upper-class, and noted the instant obsequious effect it had on those bourgeois Scots. I knew then that I must acquire it too (53–4).

Major Holmes at Gantock Academy will give him further advice (60–1). Meanwhile John Lamont tries to articulate his decent feelings for Fergus, and Fergus aims to devise 'a new mode of behaviour that would impress but not infuriate' (55): his outrageous openness in his snobbery is almost disarming. (Could Jenkins be tilting gently at literary figures as diverse as James Boswell and John Buchan?)

From now on his tendency to self-deception increases. He tells us that he did his best to keep in touch with Lomond Street and friends like Smout, but this amounts to occasionally cycling through Lomond Street with cheery waves on his way home to Siloam. When he returns to Lomond Street at the declaration of war, he finds 'forgiveness and conciliation' in the rough greeting of the women, but when he is reproved for never visiting Aunt Bella, now dying, he has no defence and no explanation. We are being prepared for the ruthless and wholesale determination with which he excises his background once he has become an army officer. He insists that this is 'imperative' and 'strategically necessary', and first announces the 'Return to Gantock' ambition: 'One day, years later perhaps, I would be able to return to it, bringing my honour and fame as tributes' (83). Despite his appalling behaviour, and his dismissal of the efforts of the aristocratic but sincerely Christian Archie Dungavel to understand the poor, Fergus has the impudence to assert: 'My profounder loyalties . . . though of necessity kept secret, were alive and developing' (87). By this time the fundamental and self-induced 'splits' in Fergus's personality are evident to his complacent consciousness, as he catalogues his different attitudes to Mary Holmscroft, whether as officer, as aristocrat or as 'poet and seer' (84).

Fergus wants to be poet and seer speaking for the Gantock tenements— but from the safe distance of an aristocratic home. He admits this when he explains his admiration for Sir Walter Scott:

> He was a Scotsman who had done with success what it was my ambition to do: that was, write about common people and assort with nobility (90).

He probably feels he is being unnecessarily humble when he adds: 'I had the advantage over him of having aristocratic blood in my veins; he, perhaps, had the advantage over me of superior talent.' If that is not in itself the sign of a man whose obsession has driven him to lose touch with reality, his attitude to the war certainly is such a sign. Although he claims to have written great anti-war poetry, and afterwards professed to admire anyone who took part in the war far above anyone who profited by it (120), he self-evidently and deliberately did both at once: 'The war would be pointless if I could not make use of it to distinguish myself' (95). It becomes clear that he has achieved confidence in a kind of (non-Christian) Election: 'I felt I had a greatness in me, too valuable to be lost.' It seems almost a Christ-complex: 'The men in my company called me anointed. They intended sarcasm and achieved truth.'

After the war, in his unhappy marriage to Betty, Fergus's social ambitions are more or less fulfilled: he has come 'almost as far as his mother would have wished' (166)—and he is miserable. What it has cost is spelt out on his first return to Gantock, which seems prompted by *some* real and generous impulse. He had refused to return in the glory of his MC, declaring 'I wanted to be brought as close to them again as I had been long ago as a child of eight' (116), but now he is nervous on a rather different score: 'I felt I could manage the condescension confidently enough, but not the implicit kinship' (171). His initial telephone call to Bessie is momentous: he compares its potential impact to his grandfather's rejection of his mother. He acknowledges to us how important her love and encouragement were when he was a boy, and how he has ignored her: not surprisingly, he has difficulty in finding the right tone: 'God knew I tried as hard as I could to sound affectionate, letting hauteur speak for itself' (172). He cannot understand the weeping Bessie's responding, 'shame between the living grows too great, if you see what I mean'.

The extremity of Fergus's self-deception is displayed as he plans the return:

> I reviewed that preliminary skirmish with Bessie and decided on future tactics. No matter whose feelings were hurt, including my own, and no matter what last ties of loyalty were strained or broken, I must use my landed-gentry manners and accent, even in Lomond Street itself. Surely the last thing anyone in Gantock wanted was for me to return humdrum and humble. Any distinction I brought would be shared by all. It was therefore for everybody's sake that I should speak as lord to serfs, hero to cravens, and poet to groundlings, though always with undercurrents of affection (173).

The more he postures like this, the more we feel that Betty's cruel and malevolent uncovering of some basic truths is good and necessary for him in the long run. Once again Fergus proceeds to hurt Bessie, refusing her invitation to lunch, denying her any hope of meeting her idol Betty, and this time even Sammy Lamont, son of Bessie and John, objects. Samuel Lamont is on the whole a slight character, but a 'sleekit' one: he is a careerist and a smooth one, who keeps in with everyone, including even Fergus, evidently with an eye to the main chance. But now:

> Sammy said little, but as he drove me to the hotel he became quite loquacious.
> 'Pretty convincing,' he murmured.
> 'What do you mean?'
> 'You hurt my mother's feelings, you've hurt them for years, and yet I'm ready to wager that at this moment she's thinking of you with more pride than anger. I would say that was as good a test as any.'
> 'Of what?'
> 'Of hubris. To make people whom you've insulted feel they have been honoured.'
> 'I did not insult Bessie.'
> 'Ah, so part of the secret lies in not being aware that you've been obnoxious' (178).

Sammy goes on to report that many regret Fergus's giving up writing poetry, and to suggest shrewdly that his parasitic country gentleman's life is probably less than inspiring.

Early in Fergus's relationship with Betty he dreamt, wildly, of returning to Gantock 'not just as hero, aristocrat, and poet, but as absolver and redeemer' (117). At times he talks as if his first return to Gantock was a crucifixion, and his second a Second Coming. His God complex is still apparent after he arrives on Oronsay and is inspired by the radiant light. Yet again, after claiming to be on the verge of a nervous breakdown (206), he aspires beyond the mere human condition:

> If I stayed here I would be seer as well as poet. There were few places in the world where a man of compassion and intelligence might prepare to take up, for a moment or two, without sentimentality or vainglory, the burden of all the multitudinous evils and miseries of humanity, and by showing that they could be borne, even for so short a time, make them less incomprehensible and less terrible; but if it could be done anywhere it could surely be done here (234).

His over-reaching is conveyed out of his own mouth, and so when Mary Holmscroft analyses him by letter she is able to be relatively gentle and non-judgemental, as she was long ago when she refused to blame him for his hard-hearted abandoning of friends and relatives (78). Now, Mary writes from Barcelona during the Spanish Civil War, and the war seems to her to enact the confusion in Fergus's mind:

> On one side are the Republicans dedicated to do away with stairhead lavatories or their Spanish equivalents, and on the other the Royalists determined to preserve those refinements of body and mind which generations of ease and privilege have brought about, and which of course the materialistic multitudes wish to destroy out of envy and spite. Am I being fair to you, Fergus? If I am, and these two loyalties really have been in opposition in your mind, and you haven't just been striking attitudes, which side would you fight for, if you were here in Spain? (245).

In response, Fergus dreams of a Scotland in which poverty is abolished without sacrifice of refinement and spirit, although he does nothing about it: nor does he answer Mary's letter.

So when we compare Fergus to Pip, it is not surprising that their awareness of guilt is so different. Even when Fergus does accuse himself, we would suggest it is with the wrong stress, often again caused by his arrogance and distance from reality. In Part One, talking of love, he sees himself as central, and destructively central, to the fates of Cathie Calderwood and Meg Jeffries: 'My deficiencies as a lover were partly to blame for Cathie Calderwood's going mad, and Meg Jeffries's making an ill-fated marriage' (62). Is this truth or hubris? Hubris, probably. So far as we understand it, Cathie's madness is something which has been threatening for years, before fifteen-year-old Fergus tries to spy on her through the bathroom key-hole, or eighteen-year-old Fergus tries to seduce her, to be stopped, comically, by the agitated self-sacrifice of her goldfish. Fergus's regret for this attempt (66) will do him no harm, but he has no reason to claim responsibility for her progressive condition. Perhaps he should have intuited something of it sooner: the prevailing image of butterflies is often associated with Cathie, and young Fergus understands early on that 'once the powder was off the wings they lost their power of flight' (31). Cathie, Jessie and Kirstie, all beautiful, gentle and somewhat soft-witted, are butterflies—Betty is a bumble-bee, and 'bumble-bees had stings'.

He seems wrong, too, about Meg Jeffries. Never as clever as Mary, Meg is always beautiful, gay and good, and he is certainly wrong about her when they are courting:

> Because she chose me I was considered in the East End more forunate than Mark Antony or Priam of Troy. It should really have been the other way round, she being thought fortunate because I showed her my favour, but it was not, I was the one congratulated, envied, and above all warned (67).

But Fergus's selfish ambitions mean that Meg is safe from him. He determines to marry a woman aristocratic and wealthy, and one who will not laugh at his posh accent. There is no suggestion of truly deep feeling between Meg and Fergus. We see from her account of her lover McHaffie (68–9) how true her feelings are: for her Catholic schoolteacher Meg will brave her Orange family and after his death in 1917 she will uncomplainingly raise her family quite alone.

No: Fergus fools himself when he claims responsibility for Cathie and Meg, at the same time as he evades full responsibility for his greatest fault, ingratitude to his family, his friends and his class. This is his most coldblooded, least excusable fault, the kind of cruel ingratitude that drives the ageing Lear mad: his punishment, appropriately enough, is to marry Goneril. Betty is a monster regularly described in comic terms, but a monster nonetheless, and Fergus is helpless in her hands. When he first sees her picture he reflects that it is like 'a Viking princess capable of strangling, with one of her thick plaits of hair, any lover who failed her' (106). He is tempted by her wealth and situation, and persuades himself he can surely manage one woman, 'no matter how many sharks were in her blue eyes' (112). Betty gradually devastates Fergus, and makes him pay very highly in humiliation for his position at Pennvalla as the relatively unsuccessful writer husband of the superlatively successful writer Betty T Shields. She dominates and manipulates him from the first.

Betty has so little going for her, so few good points, that we are not generally troubled by the suspicion that Fergus's account is too biassed. Like him, she has two personalities, one for her adoring public—and the other. Her treatment of him is consistent, and her sexual appetite voracious. We are drawn to sympathise with Fergus again as we did at the very beginning, when she behaves so outrageously during her pregnancy with Torquil, and his birth, when the openness with which she and Mutt-Simpson carry on their liaison is extraordinary, and we share with Fergus the strong suspicion that Torquil is, like his parents, another little bastard. Fergus does admit (144) that Torquil gradually began to look less like Mutt-Simpson and more like his own grandfather, worshipping instead of 'a retributive God', 'the beauty of artistic creation'. He also admits that Torquil never looked down on him the way Dorcas did, which makes even more unfair Fergus's posture of eternal devotion to the ice maiden, and his rejection of his son's affections.

Betty and Fergus are hopelessly mismatched. Fergus has confided in the reader long since (127) that she is incapable of tenderness, when Betty justifies her relationship with Mutt-Simpson with the opposite accusation. This is only a comic extract of a conversation in which the two reveal themselves as equally unlovable:

'You lack tenderness. Why look shocked? You handle my most sensitive and fastidious parts as if they were nuts and bolts.'

What shocked me was not so much her accusation that I lacked tenderness as her assumption that she possessed it. After all, her simile of nuts and bolts applied far more accurately to my sensitive and fastidious parts (147).

So the marriage is hopeless. Fergus attempts to have it out with Mutt-Simpson, only to find himself breaking the news to Betty that her lover is to marry, knowing himself from that lover who is next in line for Betty. But none of this, surely, excuses his lack of interest in his children.

Really the only positive for Fergus in these fourteen years of his marriage is the composition of his two books of poetry, on the Gantock slums and the Great War. It seems we are to believe that Fergus is a real poet: evidence to that effect from Campbell Aird, Mary Holmscroft and John Calderwood cannot be gainsaid. But the suspicion is that without his self-destructive and deracinating ambitions he would have been if not a better, certainly a more prolific poet. Two chapters are devoted to literary topics (Part Three, chapters 5 and 6), and their main thrust, besides establishing Campbell Aird as a reliable judge, is to advance the thesis that Peter

Schaeffer made central to his play about Mozart, *Amadeus*, that the greatest musician may be a failure as a human being, while no amount of virtue will turn a second class musician into a great one. Campbell Aird is a trenchant critic and a man of few words. Most new books are 'kach': a few in any generation are 'manna', and he sees Fergus's two slim volumes as manna. But in a later article on Scottish poetry he restates the *Amadeus* paradox, comparing Fergus's poetry to that of a much pleasanter, less talented contemporary:

> It is a melancholy fact of literary life that the nicest of men do not write the best poetry. In order to be able to write good poetry it is necessary to have what the poet himself will call god-like confidence, but what seems to the rest of us to be infernal conceit. . . . With Mr Fergus Lamont . . . we feel we must heed his poetry because it has on it all the authentic signs of the divine scorching; but we have no urgent desire to seek his company. In mundane circumstances that god-like confidence without which admittedly great or even good poetry cannot be written becomes insufferable. . . . Mr Lamont, it seems, cannot set it down (130–1).

Fergus pityingly and unconvincingly comments on Aird's blindness: he cannot see that Fergus's aloofness is merely a husk round a growing humility. Well, no. In chapter 5 Fergus deliberately juxtaposes the poet and champion of the slums to the aristocrat who has to protect his privileges and please his snobbish toddler daughter by harshness to petty poachers. At the end he is prepared to defend himself, a defence which rings hollow, but which in less extreme form has often been offered by writers before:

> Only arid perfectionists would have expected me to be as understanding of and compassionate towards the poor in my capacity as an ambitious social being, as I was in my capacity as inspired poet. . . .
>   Poets have a hard enough task showing mankind what truth and love are, without their having to be truthful and loving themselves, at any rate all the time (136).

Chapter 6 combines an account of the reception of Fergus's *First Poems* and a short critique of the literary establishment. Campbell Aird assures him the reviewers are ignorant of—and envious of—'the red-blooded vigour of your East End streets' (137). Mary misreads the poems, the Lamonts will not read them, and Fergus's fellow poets refuse to admit his superiority. Aird 'jestingly' assures Fergus:

> I should not wonder therefore that my fellow writers, who considered themselves large-hearted, idealistic, and knowledgeable, should find it quite intolerable that their own poetry was so much inferior to that of a selfish, ignorant, conceited, unconvivial, aloof, and unsympathetic bastard like me (139–40).

His poetry remains most important to Fergus: he is immensely pleased when on his second return to Gantock John Calderwood answers the telephone: 'Fergus Lamont? Fergus Lamont the poet?' (276). But Fergus deceives himself as usual: here he says, 'Whatever he had become, I would love him': that same day and a few pages later, he disparages, disapproves and dislikes his early mentor.

The final question to be considered is whether Fergus does manage to love Kirstie, and to what extent, if any, this relationship redeems his monstrous selfishness. The Hebridean idyll is otherwise so marginal. Mary sees Fergus 'skulking', in retreat, and John Calderwood sees the desperate effort to subsist in East Gerinish as 'stupid and misguided' (292): after all the emotion that the clearances evoked in Fergus, why did he break his back struggling with the wilderness instead of reclaiming the fertile acres from which his ancestors were driven?

We suggest that the love of Fergus and Kirstie is very real, and very flawed, and yet presented as very valuable. Kirstie comforts Fergus for all his vexations, all the wrongs he had endured and inflicted, and all his 'crippled and blinded expectations' (224). Perhaps Fergus could only relax with a woman clearly much less intelligent than himself: like the rest, he calls her feeble-minded. Also, to his great satisfaction after Betty, he finds her 'that most reassuring of creatures, a woman who knew her place' (222). Her place is inferior, attendant. He naturally sees her as bondswoman to a biblical patriarch (221), and falls easily into the latter role himself. Waking after their first night together he lies in bed, while she of course makes the breakfast, and he wonders whether to 'command' her to wear women's clothes and stop smoking her pipe, or to 'let her go on as before': on the whole that seems best, and he looks forward to her nightly transformation:

I myself would have it revealed to me every night in a ceremony of surprise, as if I was not only her lover but her high priest too (227).

Nonetheless, the relationship seems to suit both of them, and they live in happy harmony. Fergus smiles, lying in bed with Kirstie, at Betty's angry taunts, her accusation that he wanted 'not the tempestuous sea of love but the haven of maternal affection', that he was a timid lover because he was 'Oedipus in a kilt' (226). He can afford to smile, because he has found fulfilment, but Betty is not necessarily wrong: strong, gentle, tender Kirstie, herself frustrated by having no children, has wells of mother-love to offer Fergus, who suffered so radically for lack of it in his early years. Jenkins' novels regularly lament the rareness of love and celebrate it when it is found, in however imperfect a form, and he celebrates it here. But it is imperfect.

Fergus 'forgives' Kirstie for being a freak when he first meets her, reckoning, 'If I had lived here all my life I would be a freak too' (215). But he never fully realises, even made happy in her love, that she is *not* a freak, but a widely loved and respected member of the island community (see the turnout for her funeral): even after five years he likes to accompany her to 'cudgel' with his eyes 'anyone who dared to snigger at her' (242). They don't, of course, although they probably do at Fergus, and after her death there is a unanimous recommendation from the islanders that he should leave (269). But his arrogance in this is trivial, compared to the one great instance of his cruelty to Kirstie, his refusal even to consider giving her a child. Fergus has seen close up, in Aunt Bella, the anguish and frustration of thwarted motherhood, but when the practical possibility of conception arises his response is instant, selfish and final: impetuous sex 'could have bitter lifelong consequences' (226), too evident to one who, 'already martyred by fatherhood, . . . had no wish to be nailed to that cross again' (227). So his much professed love for Kirstie, while real, is very much on his own terms. He never weakens over her 'maternal longings': he never seems even to consider the question. He just patiently refuses, even in the comic-pathetic little scene (243–4) when she pleads that if she had a child she would not wear trousers, she would throw away her pipe, and she would feel like a woman.

After her death he believes that her love has transformed him: 'It could well be that . . . my love for Kirstie and hers for me, had made me, unknown to myself, a good man' (275). He expects too much. A most imperfect man, he has been in many ways healed and helped by Kirstie and his imperfect love for her, but he can hardly be called a good man. The narrator interrupts his account of Oronsay and Kirstie to report his most dramatic act of selfishness and cruelty, his rejection of his son. Flamboyantly dressed, an 'effeminate aesthete', Torquil has come from Paris and flown to America and back in his search for his father, whose 'immediate impulse was to shut the door on him' (238), and who, after more than thirty years, can find 'nothing to say to him'. When Torquil calls him 'Fergus Lamont, the poet', he registers none of the thrill John Calderwood gave him with the same words. In desperation—and thinking longingly of Dorcas—Fergus begins pushing Torquil toward the door:

> *After I had shut the door on him I stood behind it knowing that I had been wrong to reject him, as my grandfather had been wrong to reject my mother; but like my grandfather I did not open the door and shout the forgiving words* (241).

The major differences between Fergus's situation and his grandfather's are that his grandfather's harshness was abetted by a genuine belief in a harsh and unforgiving creed, against which his daughter had openly sinned: Fergus has no such faith, only his endless interest in himself and an unwillingness to be otherwise interested, and he certainly has nothing to forgive. At most as a small boy Torquil had 'offended' him by lack of interest in playing with a girr. And Fergus had long ago turned his back on Torquil as resolutely as his own mother turned her back on him, more than justifying Torquil's sad remark here: '*I never knew you.*' (Seven-year-old Fergus says of his returned mother: 'I didn't know her well.')

So Fergus remains an enigma to the end. The last time we wonder whether to accept his account is in the book's last sentence, when he claims to feel for the people of Gantock 'only pity and love'. Jenkins has brilliantly exploited all the tensions inherent in making the narrator of such a diverse and wide-ranging book a character allied in many ways to Hogg's Justified Sinner, or Horatio Pagan, the hero of John Herdman's *Pagan's Pilgrimage* (1978). Comedy becomes a major characteristic and the ironies and ambiguities are legion. In 1955 Jenkins wrote an essay called 'Novelist in Scotland', in which he famously asserted:

> We have been a long time in acquiring our peculiarities: in spite of ourselves, they are profound, vigorous, and important; and it is the duty of the Scottish novelist to portray them.

He has done this in *Fergus Lamont* and many other books. In the essay he also talks about the neglect of native themes and the 'superficial dreichness of the Scottish scene': in our opinion, he gives a fine prospective account of one of his finest achievements, *Fergus Lamont*:

> Admit the superficial greyness, therefore, and put it boldly in the picture: it can itself be a source of strength, as George Douglas Brown showed. To alleviate it there will be a virility that could blow like a West Wind through the becalmed pages of English fiction; a comic bravado; bursts of devastating self-criticism; humour sardonic, hard-hitting, irreverent, and courageous; and a resolute sadness that harks back to our old incomparable ballads.

FURTHER READING

Our references are to the Canongate edition of 1979.

Robin Jenkins was born in Cambuslang, Lanarkshire in 1912, and was educated at Hamilton Academy and Glasgow University. He taught English in Glasgow and Dunoon, where he still lives. In the 1950s and 1960s he held teaching appointments abroad; in Kabul, Afghanistan, in Barcelona, Spain and in Sabah, Malaysia: all this experience enriched his fiction.

He has published twenty novels and a book of stories. The novels are hard to obtain, but even their titles indicate Jenkins' range of interests. They are: *So Gaily Sings the Lark* (1950); *Happy for the Child* (1953); *The Thistle and the Grail* (1954); *The Cone-Gatherers* (1955); *Guests of War* (1956); *The Missionaries* (1957); *The Changeling* (1958); *Love is a Fervent Fire* (1959); *Some Kind of Grace* (1960); *Dust on the Paw* (1961); *The Tiger of Gold* (1962); *A Love of Innocence* (1963); *The Sardana Dancers* (1964); *A Very Scotch Affair* (1968); *The Holy Tree* (1969); *The Expatriates* (1971); *A Toast to the Lord* (1972); *A Far Cry from Bowmore and Other Stories* (1973); *A Figure of Fun* (1974); *A Would-be Saint* (1978); *Fergus Lamont* (1979). The *Thistle and the Grail* has now (1984) been re-published by Paul Harris (hardback and paperback).

In 1955 he published a most interesting essay, 'Novelist in Scotland', in the *Saltire Review* (Number 5, pp. 7–10), and in 1982 he published another in the *Glasgow Herald* (12th October), under the heading 'Why I decided Scotland must be seen through fresh and truthful eyes'.

The following are some of those who have written interestingly about Jenkins' work.

Moira Burgess, 'Robin Jenkins: a novelist of Scotland' in *Library Review* 22(8) (1970), 409–12
Francis Russell Hart, *The Scottish Novel: A Critical Survey* (1978)
Edwin Morgan, 'The Novels of Robin Jenkins' in *Essays* (1974)
Alexander Reid, 'The Novels of Robert Jenkins' in *Scotland's Magazine* (October 1958), 43–4
Alastair R Thompson, 'Faith and Love: An examination of some themes in the novels of Robin Jenkins', *New Saltire* 3 (Spring 1962), 57–62

CHAPTER ELEVEN

Alasdair Gray:
Lanark

In our Introduction we note, among other things, two contrasting features of modern Scottish fiction. On the one hand, there is its variety which sometimes shows itself in a marked individuality and even singularity of approach. On the other hand, similar preoccupations tend to crop up in different ways in works by writers with very different standpoints and methods. We noted that the variety and inventiveness displayed by Scottish writers has often meant ingenious adaptation of already established fictional modes and techniques to suit their particular purposes. It has less often meant self-consciously innovative experiment with the novel as a form or genre.

As it happens, it is highly appropriate to recall those features now that we come to the last novel in this particular set of ten: For, arguably, Alasdair Gray's *Lanark* is, both in form and content, the most exuberantly unusual and inventive work of fiction to have appeared in Scotland during the entire period represented by our selection. It even looks different. It proclaims its distinctiveness challengingly and perhaps provocatively—the author secure in the logic of his exploitation of the very conventions he appears to flaunt. It certainly plays ironically around a usually sensitive nerve. It is odd but true that in a country where art or writing is so often considered a marginal and spare time activity (almost a pastime), people are apt to wax indignant if they think some chap isn't taking the job seriously enough and is being jokey about it.

Happily, what the appearance of *Lanark* provoked when it appeared in 1981 was a warm welcome amounting to acclaim from reviewers both inside and outside Scotland. If anything its more outstandingly unusual features seem to have encouraged that response.

There is, for a start, the odd business of its four main sections, called Books. They appear to be printed in the wrong order. Book Three is followed by Books One and Two and then we have Book Four at the end. The Prologue as a result of this appears after Book Three although admittedly before Book One. There is also an Epilogue which seems even more peculiarly out of order since it turns up four whole chapters before the end of Book Four; and in a footnote it is alleged that it acts as an introduction to the work as a whole. There are, indeed, thirteen of these footnotes and in addition numerous marginal notes too in the Epilogue, an incongruously academic-looking piece of apparatus to appear in a novel, especially since the marginal notes provide an index of the author's plagiarisms. At least two of these notes refer to chapters which do not exist or, at any rate, have not been printed. And, just to complete this catalogue of visually conspicuous items, each of the four Books is introduced by an elaborate and rather archaically mannered frontispiece, the work of the author. For Alasdair Gray is an artist as well as a writer. As an artist he has an impressive range of styles and techniques at his command, along with a penchant for visual as well as literary parody. These frontispieces distinctly recall a bygone era of book production.

All very intriguing this might be, but there was also a danger that it might be considered a touch gimmicky, quirky or downright eccentric. Leaving the matter of the author's underlying seriousness of purpose until later we may note that the literary climate in Britain and at least in patches of Scotland had altered in favour of a decent reception. Salman Rushdie's 'fabulous' tale, *Midnight's Children*, won the Booker-McConnell prize in 1981. D M Thomas's almost equally unconventionally narrated *The White Hotel* was short-listed for the same prize in the same year. Having, it seems, assimilated the tricks John Fowles could play with narrative, there was a readership prepared to venture out to new frontiers. It should be said, to allay any suspicion that Alasdair Gray is an agile boarder of bandwagons, that *Lanark* was well over ten years in the making. It arrived, luckily, at a good time to generate the attention it has deservedly received.

Gray's unorthodox approach takes him much further than the kind of play on conventions we have already indicated. Much more importantly there is the nature of his material and the way he handles it. *Lanark* is sub-titled 'A Life In Four Books'. However, the reader quickly discovers that, contrary to what the sub-title might lead him to expect, there are two quite different kinds of stories told about at least two main protagonists, Thaw and Lanark. In Books One and Two, the central portion of the whole work, the story of Duncan Thaw is presented in a familiarly realistic and almost documentary manner. This story is bound in, so to speak, by Lanark's tale (Books Three and Four). It takes us into a strange world of grotesque characters and monstrous creatures that bespeaks a highly inventive imagination at work. Nonetheless the plain implication of the sub-title remains. This is indeed a life in four books as well as anything else it may be. It follows that Gray is *combining*, in some as yet undefined but strong sense of the word, a kind of conventionally realistic narrative and a kind of 'fantasy' narrative in order to create this singular life story.

It is this combination of 'realistic' with 'non-realistic' narrative, and particularly the way in which Alasdair Gray operates that combination, which gives *Lanark* a high degree of originality. There are plenty of precedents for serious writers opting for one or the other. There are precedents for some combinations of both. It is, however, highly unusual for an author to imply that both kinds of story he tells come together to constitute a single life story while at the same time insisting that 'the fact remains that the plots of the Thaw and Lanark sections are independent of each other and cemented by typographical contrivances rather than formal necessity. A possible explanation is that the author thinks a heavy book will make a bigger splash than two light ones' (footnote, 493). Gray makes a joke of it. At the same time he means what he says perfectly seriously. We find ourselves in a Gray area: precisely so. It is both a joke and not a joke that the Thaw and Lanark sections of this novel do and do not interrelate.

Simply in order to provide later discussion with a point of reference we may ignore such complications for now and summarise what, from one point of view, appears to happen in the novel: beginning with Book One and following events through in chronological order. This life story, then, begins with a description of the experiences of someone called Duncan Thaw from childhood to early manhood. This preoccupation with themes of childhood and youth, with the formative phases of growing up, instantly strikes a chord—cf Gunn, Jenkins, Williams and McIlvanney, for example. Duncan Thaw's story is set in the 1940s and 1950s in Glasgow and—mainly while Duncan is a wartime evacuee—among the hills and glens of the west of Scotland. It is a working-class boyhood. Duncan Thaw is introverted, something of a dreamer prone to asthma. As he grows up he struggles against a sense of personal insecurity which, in turn, collides with a conviction that he is specially gifted. He contends with isolation, sexual anxieties and the indifference or contempt of most other people (with the notable exception of his patient father) in his attempts to find fulfilment in love and in art. This we may call Duncan Thaw's quest, because themes of lifelong personal quests are central to the novel (again we would suggest a point of comparison with Gunn). In despair at his sense of his utter failure to fulfil either ambition he ends up, ill and desperate, possibly murdering a girl and by all appearances committing suicide by drowning.

In its own bleak way, this part of the book has ingredients and a narrative style typical of a complete *bildungsroman*, an account of the experiences and education of a young man described mostly from his own point of view. Specifically what we have is one Glasgow variant on the theme of *A Portrait of the Artist as A Young Man*. Books Three and Four, between which the story of Thaw is sandwiched, are very different. Here we find Lanark (or Duncan Thaw in quite another form) plunged first into a hellish, dark city called Unthank and then deeper still into the nether regions, finding himself in a very curious quarter called the institute. These other-worldly parts of the world with their bizarre inhabitants and sinister rulers are very much products of Alasdair Gray's invention and imagination. However, Unthank is plainly enough intended to represent an infernal version of Glasgow (and more generally, modern industrial cities). The institute in conjunction with a governing body called the council and industrial interests called 'the creature' all add up to a ruling nexus. Together they represent scientific and technocratic plus political plus economic forces dominating life on the planet. By implication they have been the hidden powers circumscribing the life and times of Duncan Thaw.

Lanark's quest is first of all for a means of escape back to a world where there is light. He seeks freedom for himself and, if possible, for a woman called Rima whom he would claim to love. His quest widens for a time to take in a greater and more generous ambition when he is conned into making a bid to save Unthank and its people. When this attempt ends in fiasco and disillusionment he finds himself left with very little he can care about at all, facing death alone (again?) amid scenes of apocalyptic disaster viewed from Glasgow/Unthank's Necropolis, its city of the dead. Lanark has become an old man in what would be a very short space of earthly time were it earthly time we had to deal with. Instead, the space-time continuum undergoes very peculiar contortions and distortions indeed in the world explored by Books Three and Four. Of course, Lanark's encounters and what he learns from them and his point of view at the end are substantially what this story is about.

But we can come back to the story in due course. When we do, much of our discussion will concentrate on Books Three and Four. This is partly because of the intricacies packed into those Books. By contrast the content and concerns of Books One and Two are in themselves more straightforward. Thaw's story provides an indispensable dimension to add to the world, the experiences and the perceptions of both Lanark and Rima. It contains important characters and viewpoints, notably Thaw's father, Mr McPhedron the minister, Robert Coulter and Marjory Laidlaw. But what excited the imagination of many readers and reviewers, and rightly so, when the book came out was the verve and ingenuity with which the whole thing was put together. We would suggest that a key to the fascination and attraction exercised by *Lanark* lies in the contrast—the ironical and paradoxical contrast—between the starkness of much of its content and the vitality of the creative performance. When, as we shall see, the author appears on this stage as a character he describes himself as a conjuror. His great trick, arguably, is to conjure up defiant pyrotechnics as evidence of an undefeated capacity for delight and illumination on the very edge of the abyss.

The content of the book is, after all, often sombre. The ending might be described as grim and hopeless if not (less approvingly) as melodramatic. The overall abiding impression could be that of a world viewed with the deepest foreboding and gloom. Yet the overall effect seems to us not to be one of such dire despair. How exactly one 'reads' this will depend in part on how the ending is interpreted and in particular on the view one takes of Lanark's feelings and outlook at that point. Still, irrespective of the ending, we opt for a somewhat sunnier reading of *Lanark* largely because of its creative power as a *tour de force*.

Confronting the bleakness of its own subject matter, so to speak, *Lanark* at times displays a dour determination to concede nothing to sentimentality or the very suspicion of softness. Thaw's story is in no sense mirthful. The drearier aspects of his circumstances and his preoccupations are presented so much from the standpoint of a young man's brooding and obsessive 'gravitas' that the patience of a willing reader may be tested, especially since Gray tends to grind his prose down to an evenness of tone which verges on flatness. This tendency is still apparent in Book Three, in the early stages of Lanark's tale, in striking counterpoint to the almost extravagant oddity of the goings on there. Lanark's world (in Books Three and Four) may be in some respects deadening and deadly, more than one kind of hell, but it is also illuminating. Lanark may be dim, unreliable both in love and perceptiveness; yet he does also learn; and in the end, left with virtually nothing, he is wiser and warmer than at any earlier stage. All this involves a rich appreciation of bleak and uncompromising ironies about human endeavour and prospects for the species. But by way of the very energy with which these perceptions are realised and their implications pursued, Gray and the highly ironic 'author' who comments on it all in the Epilogue affirm something rather less than hope but much more interesting, indeed more *entertaining*, than gloom. There is in this pervasive spirit of humorous affirmation a quality of sheer liveliness that cannot be reduced to anything as simple as despair.

We recognise freely that there are a number of possible ways of reading *Lanark* and hence evaluating it as a literary achievement. Almost for the sake of argument we proceed to take the view that it is best read in the light of the final Book, Book Four. In part this is because Gray's writing in Book Four is at its liveliest, most varied, most paradoxical, parodic and ironic. This is in turn a reflection of the way in which he brings about a satisfying culmination of the main themes and preoccupations of the novel which have gradually, and in some cases only implicitly, been developed hitherto. Only in Book Four do we fully discover the nature of the power matrix governing the planet and the interconnection between 'hell' and a higher order of things in the universe. Thus we begin to appreciate in retrospect much of what has gone before. When Gray introduces 'the author' as a character into this life-story-in-four-books we see that this one life is acted out by three protagonists or personalities, none of them altogether rounded or complete. That is, as well as Thaw and Lanark we must also take into account 'the author', part of whose autobiography is contained in Thaw's story and who exists in this world only by extension: through his creations, who have different and sometimes conflicting perceptions of what 'really' happens.

We can make more complete sense of the apparent impossibility of satisfactory *human* relationships and of the bizarre happenings both in Unthank and in the institute as described in Book Three. It becomes clearer in the end why the personal quests of Thaw and Lanark are doomed to total or partial failure while, on the other hand, together their lives combine in a process of illumination and enrichment: a process which, most paradoxically of all, involves forms of death—loss of certain aspects of self at least—and rebirth. (Thaw dies, literally or metaphorically, at the end of Book Two. Lanark hesitantly undergoes a form of death in Book Three, at the end of Chapter Six. He faces death again, but more squarely, at the end of Book Four.)

Much of *Lanark*, then, can only fully be appreciated by hindsight and as a result of a cumulative and gradual series of revelations about the nature of the world through which Thaw and Lanark try to find their way. The reader must take a lot on trust. Confronted for a start with Lanark's first encounters in the odd world of Unthank, the reader's interest is no doubt nourished by the steady supply of intriguing, surprising and mysterious events. Even so, much of Book Three is presented in a spare and unemphatic prose which provides little by way of explanation and few pointers as to moments of special significance for the later stages. This can do wonders in terms of creating the sense of being in a milieu where we must expect the unexpected. The corresponding danger here, and in general, is obvious enough too. We may miss something rather important. We may lose any confidence in our sense of direction in a landscape so short of signposts. There is a further potential problem stemming from the nature of the characterisation in Book Three. When we first meet Lanark he does not know who he is. Indeed, he is so lacking in identity that there is very little for us to latch onto. And those he consorts with throughout the first six chapters can hardly be said to be rounded characters in any of the usual senses of the term. All of this is entirely deliberate; but Alasdair Gray is certainly making no concessions to readers whose responses are conditioned by expectations of a more recognisably human world and a (perhaps reasonable enough) reliance on the author pointing up clues as to future developments.

But with patience we see the point of this. We come to realise that we are being presented with a remarkable ironic parody of the venerable epic technique of plunging the reader into the middle of the action, *in medias res*. The most obvious aspect of this is that at the end of Book Two young Duncan Thaw is swallowed up by the sea and at the beginning of Book Three we have a young man of about twenty-four who has no idea who he is or what's what.

Gray solemnly refers us to Homer, Vergil, Milton and Scott Fitzgerald as respectable antecedents in the use of the technique of throwing the reader into the thick of the action. His own version of the practice has some originality. None of those others chose to open a *magnum opus* with one of their key characters in quite such a state of vacuous inertia bordering on paralysis.

Sometimes he gazed in a puzzled way at the black sky, sometimes he bit thoughtfully on the knuckle of his thumb. Nobody else used the balcony (3).

No wonder, for the balcony upon which we find Lanark is rain-drenched as well as dark. It is almost perpetually dark in Unthank. The balcony, complete with its drooping parasols, is the most redundant part of a drab and dimly lit café which is incongruously called the Elite. It is tended by a smiling but utterly uncommunicative fat man whose countertop encircles him like one of the rings around Saturn. The clientele consists of mutually exclusive circles or cliques. These people occupy their time chattering about politics, crime, religion, art and other pastimes.

Typical of these, for it is perhaps not even exceptionally unattractive, is a clique whose only focal point is another young man with a name like a mouthful of something nasty: Sludden. His adherents seem to have little better to do than adhere to him: especially the girls, recognising as they do the erotic appeal of a man who does supremely well what others only fumblingly and uneasily practise. Sludden does nothing, with fantastic ability. This character really has the makings of a very smart political operator. In the context of Unthank, this means that he understands better than most the art of doing nothing, effectively.

For although we may well not suspect as much at first, Sludden is more than merely smart. He is a genius. The extraordinary power of his malign genius is, again, only fully revealed in the light of events described in Book Four. There we find his ultimate achievement, harmonising an aesthete's exquisite appreciation of his materials and techniques with a deadly callousness in his use of them.

The materials Sludden works on are other people. His techniques are those of the masterly manipulator and *poseur*. His greatest achievement

will be to take the entire population of Unthank for all they have. He will
con them out of the last of their (mineral) resources. In doing this he will
also outwit all or most of the world's 'ruling' council (with the possible
exception of its president, Lord Monboddo) by refining its intention to
consume the population of Unthank without further ado, using them as a
cheap supply of energy. Sludden's master-stroke is to extract more from the
people while appearing to save them. It is no more than a temporary
reprieve for some. The end will be the same. Sludden is an artist in the grand
tradition of confidence tricksters. His final flourish is an ultimate kind of
'sting': taking even more suckers than expected for even more than they
were perceived to have, at the same time doing down his own confederates.
There is a terrible beauty about this. Lanark, persuaded by Sludden
to make a dangerous, time-consuming and life-consuming journey to the
great assembly of council delegates in Provan (a place reminiscent of
Edinburgh) in order to plead for Unthank's future, is only one of the many
whom Sludden dupes. Lanark's role, as stage-managed by Sludden, is to
create a diversion while the real business is done. Lanark's fate is to suffer
the indignity of making a comical mess of everything, including himself:
which is diverting enough (Chapters Forty to Forty-Two).

When Lanark and Sludden first meet at the Elite café, of course, we are
back in the early days of Sludden's career. He has so far given no overt sign
of political aspirations. On the contrary, he appears to regard politics as
disdainfully as he regards most human activities, especially those directed
towards making a living. He is not only fastidiously selective about
the kinds of work a person might be prepared to contemplate; it is clear
that he prefers to contemplate work rather than do it. With no visible
means of support himself, he appears to hover languidly in his own air of
superiority.

There is more to this pose than a trick by which he can impress members
of his pathetic little clique, male and female alike. It does evidently beguile
them. We can see that they are mostly feckless, apparently unemployed or
in various ways insecure, anxious and in need of reassurance. Someone who
does little or nothing with such great aplomb, who has all the time in the
world and is not afraid of it, might well in those circumstances prove to be
a baffling but compellingly attractive figure with a secret which others
might hope to learn by contagion. That much is the trick in Sludden's
performance.

Beyond that, however, Sludden's pose illustrates crucial qualities of his
genius and his art. By his pose he has, in the first place, created an image of
himself: the very picture of the unconcerned man of leisure, the satisfaction
of whose needs is assured. It works. They are queuing up to satisfy his
needs.

Sludden's genius essentially lies in his appreciation of how to achieve maximum benefit and gratification from an absolute minimum of personal effort. We stress the element of gratification. He is not the kind of man to demean himself by some grubby pursuit of benefits—goods and services in quantity—merely in order to possess or consume them. He requires, over and above all that, the ego-massaging intellectual and sexual satisfactions which come from playing with power. That pose which he strikes in the early days at the Elite exemplifies how little exercise power sometimes requires in order to ensure its rewards.

Art, Sludden explains to Lanark (6), is like certain 'superior' forms of work and love: they are all of them means of dominating other people, characteristically by imposing one's personality on them. Sludden cultivates this style to greater and greater effect throughout the book. The nature of Sludden's hold over his entourage at the Elite may seem shabby and marginal. Nonetheless it does show his insight into something close to the heart of human affairs and provides a kind of metaphorical model for later operations more ambitious in scale, when he requires the support of the population of Unthank. (By the time he loses it, it clearly no longer matters to him; for they are doomed and he is not.) Art and 'love' are factors he twists to his purposes. Using sexual stratagems, he plays on the insight that desperate people with a profound sense of their inadequacy are liable to spend energy uselessly from their point of view (profitably from someone else's) in feverish pursuit of any comfort, consolation or distraction they can find. Erotic pursuits fit the bill perfectly.

Thus it is no accident that the Elite café adjoins a cinema which shows a continuous programme of pornographic films. Having first drawn his victims into his ring of confidence, the ringmaster Sludden carefully controls the supply of reassurances and caresses, feeding but never satisfying the demand, so as to make them serve him in more senses than one. Not only Gay his 'fiancée' but the other females too are more or less under his spell. It is a relief to report that his hold is not total although it is usually destructive and always damaging. Gay herself rebels, at evidently great and painful cost. She it is who eventually, as a battered but undefeated middle-aged journalist, educates the still somewhat dim Lanark and spurs him on to blow the gaff on Sludden's rotten deals (530–1). A much more important character is Rima, who weaves in and out of Sludden's orbit as well as in and out of a relationship with Lanark.

The Lanark–Rima connection constitutes the most important and most nearly human relationship explored in Books Three and Four. Indeed, when Rima evidently expresses both fear and contempt for Lanark and a desire to kill him, along with sympathy, need and some attraction (and Lanark does not reject this peculiar way of getting along), we may feel assured that a genuine human relationship of a kind has been established between them and will not end there (Chapter Five).

The lifelong on-and-off affair between Lanark and Rima is crucial to our understanding of *Lanark* as a whole and complete work. This is so for a considerable number of reasons. Perhaps one way to sum them all up before looking at some of them in more detail is to say this: in so far as there is a central hope which is explored, illuminated and then dashed in *Lanark*, it is the hope of all the male protagonists (Thaw, Lanark, 'the author'/the author) that they might find a basis for the sharing of human bonds of trust and care. Lanark and Rima never do. Again referring to Book Four we can see that what they salvage out of their bruising and battering encounters is a sense of having been of some help to each other along the way, a sense of having gained some wisdom from the experience, and a sense of reconcili-ation to each other—in spite of their final separation. It is perhaps not such a bad total of gains at that: considering that they start off in a world, Unthank, in which trust is inadvisable and virtually impossible because (as we fully appreciate from reading Book Four) the strong can usually only hope to survive by devouring the weak or by turning them into their creatures, mouthpieces for their own egos. Consider, again, the example of Sludden and what he does to Gay. It comes as an appalling shock to Lanark.

Estranged from Rima and searching for her (a situation he will repeatedly find himself in), Lanark happens to run into Gay. Lanark himself has been falling victim to a disease called dragonhide, which comes of having to develop a thick skin in Unthank and which is a common defensive but debilitating condition. Gay coyly offers to show Lanark her disease if he will show her his.

> He began to say he was not interested in her disease but she pulled off her fur gauntlet. Surprise gagged him. He had expected dragon claws like his own, but all he could see was a perfectly shaped white little hand, the fingers lightly clenched, until she unclenched them to show the palm. He took a moment to recognize what lay on it. A mouth lay on it, grinning sarcastically. It opened and said in a tiny voice, 'You're trying to understand things, and that interests me.'
>
> It was Sludden's voice. Lanark whispered, 'Oh, this is hell!'
>
> Gay's hand sank to her side. He saw that the soles of her feet were an inch above the pavement. Her body dangled before him as if from a hook in her brain, her smile was vacant and silly, her jaw fell and the voice which came from the mouth was not formed by movement of tongue or lip (45–6).

Gay dwindles then almost to vanishing point, moving in the direction of the café. She has been no more than an apparition, a projection, sent by Sludden to recruit Lanark as a promising prospect if he will only use his intelligence to his own advantage instead of worrying about 'the wrong things'—e.g. creating a loving relationship.

Interestingly, Lanark is so terrified by this incident that he does forget his quest for Rima and frenziedly seeks some means of escape, any means, so long as he can get away from Sludden, Unthank and all it entails. It is then that Lanark makes one of the darkest leaps of faith to be found anywhere in fiction. For, in spite of understandable fears and hesitations, he accepts a bizarre invitation in a Necropolis, a city of the dead. Another mouth miraculously appears, this time on a marble block offering itself as 'the way out'. It is and it is not. For Lanark duly discovers himself in the institute, a deeper and more central circle of this comprehensive hell where he will find Rima again, this time almost completely transformed into a dragon, in a part of the world where human relationships are possibly even less attainable, since 'people' there are mostly defined and delimited by disease or function.

The conditions, then, in which Lanark and Rima have to try to construct their relationship are unpromising to begin with and then go from bad to worse. Perhaps 'reconstruct' would be a more accurate word to describe their task: the task of characters who have to re-make themselves anew. For we have suggested that the affair between Lanark and Rima is crucial to our understanding of *Lanark* as a whole and not only a key element in Books Three and Four. This inevitably raises the whole question of links between the two stories of Lanark and Thaw about which we have already noted that it is both a joke and not a joke that they do and do not interrelate: a characteristically Gray area. In *Lanark* a thing is what it is; but it may also be other things. This variation on a famous old philosophical rule applies to characters and apparently complete stories too.

We recall now that when Lanark first appears in Unthank he has scarcely a shred of human identity he can call his own. At first, by his own account (Chapter Three), he feels pleased and relieved to find himself alone, unburdened by a sense of identity. This adds another twist to Gray's paradoxical version of plunging us into the middle of the action. Not only do we find ourselves in the middle of inaction on Lanark's part: he is apparently as near as one can conceivably get in human terms to a clean slate, the *tabula rasa* of empirical philosophers. Character has still to be formed by experience. Yet we also see that in some sense or another he must also have been Duncan Thaw. We may recognise one or two incompletely erased traces of Thaw's character. There is an endearing but somewhat idiotic stubbornness which he appears to have in common with Thaw: perhaps that much of the latter has survived his suicide, his death by drowning, his self-immersion—however we choose to describe his end. Other points in common include a need for a satisfying sexual relationship with a woman (which soon displaces Lanark's initial cheerfulness at being on his own) and an acute lack of self-confidence in pursuing that end, so to speak.

The most important evidence that Lanark and Thaw are 'really' one and the same comes in a Prologue at the very end of Book Three (117) from the unseen 'oracle', who has been summoned precisely in order to supply Lanark with information about his past before he and Rima set out from the institute on their return journey to Unthank. The 'oracle', having just told his or its own story, proceeds to the story of Duncan Thaw, with the clear implication that this is the story of Lanark's early life.

However, it is always necessary in *Lanark* to be wary of the narrators, to question who or what they actually are. The oracle has, ironically, explained that owing to his passion for finance and numbers he became a non-person, a non-entity. He can only tell a story from someone else's point of view because he can only exist at all that way: by extension, through a character. The oracle of the Prologue, in effect, is a 'financial wizard' version of the 'conjuror' author to whom we—and Lanark!—are introduced in the Epilogue.

At the beginning of Book Four Lanark confidently refers to what he has just been listening to (Books One and Two) as the 'oracle's account of my life before Unthank. He's just finished it.'

Rima has a very different story:

> Rima said firmly, 'In the first place that oracle was a woman, not a man. In the second place her story was about me. You were so bored that you fell asleep and obviously dreamed something else.'
>
> He opened his mouth to argue but she popped a fig in, saying, 'It's a pity you didn't stay awake because she told me a lot about you. You were a funny, embarrassing, not very sexy boy who kept chasing me when I was nineteen. I had the sense to marry someone else.'

(This now implies that Rima has heard, or has dreamed, that she was once Marjory Laidlaw. Lanark has a different 'memory' or 'image' of Rima/ Marjory. He certainly cannot believe that it was Marjory whom he may have killed.)

> 'And you!' cried Lanark, angrily swallowing, 'were a frigid cock-teasing virgin who kept shoving me off with one hand and dragging me back with the other. I killed someone because I couldn't get you.'
>
> 'We must have been listening to different oracles. I'm sure you imagined all that' (357).

We now even have the extreme possibility that Duncan Thaw did not really exist at all, except that in that case what Lanark imagines in some respects corresponds with what Rima has imagined. At very best, Rima here brings out the point that in their experiences and in their perceptions of their lives *past and present* she and Lanark only sometimes intersect and in important respects they cannot share experiences. This, naturally, undermines to a considerable extent the possibility of their having a satisfactory relationship. The further implication is that in *Lanark* the characters, including 'the author', are doomed to live in somewhat lonely, solipsistic worlds substantially different from each other. That is no joke. It is also no joke that a person's own past may be irretrievable, in the sense that in the attempt to describe it mistakes will be made and illusions formed—and even records of the time will not be quite as once they seemed. The very last words in the book, set out in bold type and capital letters, seem sadly to highlight that point.

I STARTED MAKING MAPS WHEN I WAS SMALL
SHOWING PLACE, RESOURCES, WHERE THE ENEMY
AND WHERE LOVE LAY. I DID NOT KNOW
TIME ADDS TO LAND. EVENTS DRIFT CONTINUALLY DOWN,
EFFACING LANDMARKS, RAISING THE LEVEL, LIKE SNOW.

I HAVE GROWN UP. MY MAPS ARE OUT OF DATE.
THE LAND LIES OVER ME NOW.
I CANNOT MOVE. IT IS TIME TO GO (560).

What is a pleasant enough joke is that we are free to read, to experience, the Thaw and Lanark stories and their interrelationship in a number of possible ways. We may accept them as substantially the one tale, however come by, simply following on from each other sequentially. If we don't like that, then we can take the Thaw story as a version of actual facts (autobiography) or possible facts (fictional biography) and the Lanark story as a fable projecting fears about an after-life or a co-existing and contemporaneous underworld. We may take it that Thaw actually drowned and that was the end of him; or we may interpret his end metaphorically, with 'immersion' as a plunge into worlds of the subconscious and unconscious: the possibilities are as various as in Golding's *Pincher Martin*. Or, most interestingly of all, perhaps, we may regard them as representing a person at two different *stages* in life, stages defined by quite different levels or kinds of consciousness. In this last case the joke is that, although Thaw and Lanark may be the same person in a limited sense, because of the passage of time or a definitive shift in viewpoint they are also substantially different selves.

In some respects Lanark's experiences are more illuminating than any Thaw seems capable of having. In the end, Lanark achieves a kind of understanding which Thaw seems incapable of attaining. However, *Lanark* is not a straightforward story of accumulated gains in experience and knowledge. While on the one hand, of course, Lanark's world is beyond Thaw in more senses than one, Lanark cannot fully understand what Thaw was all about either: which is to say that Lanark cannot fully see himself in that previous personification. In particular he is puzzled about what really happened when a stony-mouthed Thaw appears to kill Marjory (348–50), and he is even more puzzled about whether Thaw drowned himself 'for a fantasy' instead of out of proper remorse at having committed murder. Furthermore, while to Lanark's mind Marjory remains some person quite different from Rima, to Rima it seems that Marjory was herself at the age of nineteen. Indeed, it is Rima who tends to recognise continuities which Lanark cannot see.

Her *alter ego* Marjory finds Thaw too unsure of himself, not very sexy, an introverted oddball; and Rima maintains to the end that Lanark (who takes a fairly generous view of his own motives and action) is essentially self-centred and self-willed. This makes him unreliable, as she sees him. She accuses him of several times (nastily) driving her away (558). To Lanark it is Rima who is the unreliable and unfaithful one. Thus they certainly appear to misunderstand each other in a fundamental way; and it is at least possible that the relationship between Thaw and Marjory was blighted by a similar misunderstanding. Neither relationship is helped, in any case, by the woman's (or women's) reservations. Marjory seems more than a little doubtful about Thaw's appeal, although evidently she is somewhat attracted to him and in some sense, probably obscure to herself, she needs him. Rima is clearer and more categorical about the reasons for Marjory's hesitations about Thaw and her own very important reservations about Lanark. According to Rima, Marjory found Thaw 'funny, embarrassing, not very sexy' and in saying this she is identifying herself with Marjory and Thaw with Lanark. More significantly still, Rima considers Lanark decidedly ordinary and something of a disappointment, despite his having saved her from burning up in the institute.

'Were you the only one who could help me, Lanark? Nobody special? Nobody splendid?' (96).

The hapless Lanark has at this point just performed the quasi-chivalric feat of saving his lady from her own dragon-self. He might have expected to be considered something of a hero figure by a duly grateful damsel. What comes out instead is that he does not fit Rima's conception of glamour, and that glamour and excitement are at the heart of Rima's quest in life. Unfortunately for Lanark, the confidence trickster Sludden projects the requisite qualities sufficiently well to be able to take Rima from Lanark when he likes. Worst of all, Sludden lures her away just after she has presented Lanark with a son (424).

Robbing Lanark of this son, Alexander or Sandy (for Rima and Lanark are at odds even about his name), is the cruellest thing that Sludden and Rima do to him. Just as Thaw had his compulsive need to create his own vision of the world, so Lanark has a desperate need for a child in order to make the world something worth caring about: he needs something of himself in the world in order to make life worth going on with.

Unlike Thaw, Lanark is no artist and so cannot direct his energies into producing a version of creation in which he can dream that he appears as God (338). Lanark's energies are spasmodic; but once he gets going he becomes endearingly earnest and determined about the job in hand. To that extent he is a kind of Don Quixote. In other respects he is a version of Everyman, the Common Man, trying to set things to rights: between himself, Rima and Sandy, and between Unthank and the rulers of the world. It is perhaps more for Sandy's sake than for any other reason that Lanark allows himself to be persuaded by Sludden to undertake the heroic but farcical mission to the general assembly in Provan. At the very moment he is about to set off (characteristically it is a moment too late) Lanark recognises the absurdity of this self-sacrificial gesture, knowing that it will take a great chunk of time out of his own life and with that time all his chances of forming a relationship with the boy (467). But Lanark's decision to fly to Provan is inevitable in any case, since to Lanark (as to Thaw's father before him) a son makes intolerable circumstances and many crazy sacrifices at least relatively meaningful.

If Lanark is no artist, and yet he is in other respects a later version of Thaw, it is because the role of the artist-creator has been taken over by 'the author', whom we may regard as the third person in the trinity of protagonists struggling for understanding throughout this one 'Life in Four Books': three personalities in the one key figure whose story this is. We believe that 'the author' has to be taken into account in this way, as a character in his own work of fiction, because *Lanark* as a whole may be regarded as the record of a quest for comprehension on the part of the writer. The trinity of Thaw, Lanark and 'the author' is, to be sure, a peculiar one: a personality so split, that its different bits go adrift and at times cannot even recognise each other. However, such incongruities make this an even more interesting variant on the familiar enough Scottish motif of the split personality. We must also note that, as if to complicate matters further, Gray offers us another to consider (495): the 'author' as God the Father, Lanark as the sacrificial Son, and the reader as a Holy Ghost whose attentive spirit is required in order to keep the whole show together. But since we are discussing a work which belongs to a culture famous for its theological schismaticism, two trinities can only be better than one.

Our 'first person', then, is Thaw the artist who lives and 'dies' within the confines of subjective obsessions: self-disgust and repugnance at the spectacle of human life in general. He considers it 'a disease of matter' (179). These obsessions cannot be relieved either by his fantasies of being the benevolent and beloved leader of a liberated Scotland or by his rather more insightful depiction of creation, his mural on the subject of Genesis. In order to break out from own fevered imagination and thus be in a position to proceed, our hero has to be re-thought by 'the author'. Ironically, Lanark, the transformed 'second person', has less imagination of his own to go by than the first. So as Lanark we see him stumbling onwards through labyrinthine interiors and time zones, through the critical consciousness of his own author. This 'author' confesses that he is no god himself. This trinity is not, we see, a godhead. He is merely a part of that long ago fragmented whole. Moreover he is a part which once went bad and was duly excreted (481). He is condemned to a process of recycling a festering creation of which he can only see a part at any given time. Since he has only partial vision, the 'author' is liable to be surprised by events in his own world, such as the unplanned birth of Lanark's son. Also, he can only see bits of himself strewn along the trail behind him. For example he knows that he was, once upon a time, but in part only, the person he describes as Duncan Thaw.

The 'author' exists by conjuring up versions of himself and others who might once have been or who might be. There is, as we have suggested, considerable uncertainty about what's what and who's who in this world of his. Instead of comforting certainties of that kind there is, however, a constant and pervasive fear. Our 'author', so painfully lacking as he is in godlike powers to ensure a benign continuing creation, is evidently convinced that everything he sees is heading towards self-destruction, propelled in that direction by anxiety and greed. Thus what we in turn see are reflections, conjured up by him, on themes of an individual and epic tragi-comic character. What these themes all have in common are endings involving failure (a very popular notion, we are assured), disaster and impotence. (In our selection the only quest novel that ends positively is *The Silver Darlings*.)

The character who comes closest to representing and enjoying real power in Gray's fictional universe is Ozenfant. At the end of the whole story he is the lord president of the council, the political supremo, a personage always known by the title Lord Monboddo. If Sludden is the joker in this pack, Ozenfant-Monboddo is the philosopher king. But long before he acquires that elevated status we meet Ozenfant in the institute (in Book Three), where he is a youngish but already fairly senior and influential 'doctor'. Under the influence of Ozenfant's musical therapy, patients are less likely to be cured and re-humanised than they are to burn themselves up in spectacular conflagrations. But for Lanark's impetuous intervention, Rima would have gone that way too: all part of a scheme whereby warmth repressed by human beings can be released as an explosive energy source for the system. Other human beings who are not so hot are commonly reduced to processed food, bland concoctions from which every hint of life and taste has been extracted. Ozenfant displays a voracious appetite for this stuff.

Ozenfant's chilling professionalism with its touches of dandyism is contrasted with the philosophy of the mournfully wise yet tenaciously caring Monsignor Noakes. There is surely a pun in that name Noakes; for his attitudes also markedly contrast with those of John Knox whose columnar statue so balefully dominates the Necropolis (348), symbol of a male rigidity that can yield to death but not to tenderness. At some time in the past, Ozenfant himself has been cured or 'saved' by Monsignor Noakes. But the former *protégé* has become not only a rising star: he has also become a tormentor to the man who was once his salvation. As Ozenfant goes up in the world, so Noakes declines and becomes more and more worn out and impotent. Noakes's sadness stems from a bitter realisation that the institute gets away with murder, literally consuming people for food and fuel, because so many have a stake in it: 'It is like all machines, it profits those who own it, and nowadays many sections are owned by gentle, powerless people who don't know they are cannibals and wouldn't believe if you told them' (102). There are shades here, indeed, of property-owning democracies with their pension funds distantly invested in wars and pollution: Gray's idea of a Scottish petit-bourgeois model of the universe. Ruefully reflecting on history, Noakes at one point remarks:

> Cannibalism has always been the main human problem. When the Church was a power we tried to discourage the voracious classes by feeding everyone regularly on the blood and body of God (101).

Noakes makes that more or less explicit allusion to Catholicism without irony, but there is irony in it. For what he describes presents no solution to 'the main human problem' whichever way he defines it; and he provides in effect two definitions. The problem is 'cannibalism'. But that is merely the logical terminus of a process of human division due to which the only provisional bonds now possible are 'mutual assistance pacts based upon greed', in a world where there is no faith, hope or charity to keep people together (80–1). Ozenfant knows that Noakes is, to say the least of it, out of touch with the spirit of the times; for Noakes remains opposed, however ineffectually, to that spirit of greed.

The character of Ozenfant-Monboddo is especially interesting because of his sense of the peculiar limitations of the power which he (and his allies in the industrial corporations) can exercise. They have surprisingly little room for manouevre. When Ozenfant-Monboddo grants Lanark an interview his first remarks are preceded by a sigh:

> He said, 'At last the Common Man confronts the Powerful Lord of this World. Except that you are not very common and I am not very powerful. We can change nothing, you and I' (549–50).

As political supremo Monboddo unquestionably conducts and helps to orchestrate events. So in that sense he is more in charge than anyone else: more in command of the situation and himself than are any of the querulous or self-important delegates to the general assembly in Provan. However, this is mainly due to the single advantage that he is able to see behind the scenes. He understands and foresees the working out of the latent forces of greed. He knows the score and has always played in tune with those forces. But even as master of the music he remains their instrument. His superior power rests on his ability to stand apart and anticipate the future.

A minor character called Grant (nicknamed Polyphemus) has already defined the wealthy and the powerful for us in this way: 'They pay themselves with time: time to think and plan, time to examine necessity from a distance' (410). Considering the way in which time itself is manipulated, and how Lanark suffers from it, this is a telling observation. What it also means is that Monboddo's freedom boils down to Hegel's terrible paradox: the only freedom is the consciousness of necessity.

Monboddo considers that the economic laws which he, and the corporations, must serve are as inexorable as laws of nature: 'We can only help people by giving less than we take away from them. We enlarge the oasis by increasing the desert. That is the science of time and housekeeping. Some call it economics' (550). It is a kind of economic entropy. If production on our crowded planet does entail *concentration* of scarce resources, then the poor will lose the little that they have; and the number of those thereby impoverished will increase relative to the number of those who temporarily gain. Ozenfant-Monboddo refers to this problem of a surplus population in his speech to the assembly and he has argued that surplus populations may be considered as 'wealth': but only so long as clever people can organise surplus people into great enterprises. The ultimate great enterprise he proposes for mankind is to establish a city floating in space, an oasis, which will divert the heat of the sun directly into the production of food from 'dead matter' (544–6). More than one problem can be solved by this refinement on the usual clumsy expedient of having to employ those marked down as disposable before actually disposing of them. The survivors in space will not only be sustained. They will also be freed from the clamorous objections of the redundant population whom they will have deserted and who will no doubt in due course constitute part of that 'dead matter', excreta.

Monboddo is able to contemplate such a future with remarkable equanimity, considering that it may well entail his own redundancy as well as his impotence. He chides Lanark for his babyish, instinctive and selfish demands for change: 'You suffer from the oldest delusion in politics. You think you can change the world by talking to a leader. Leaders are the effects, not the causes of changes' (551). He has also announced to the council 'that in three years all the limited skills of a council supremo will be embodied in the circuits of a Quantum-Cortexin humanoid' (537): even political leaders will in future be robots. Lanark protests that since Monboddo's rational civilisation can only continue by damaging the brains and hearts of children (and, we would add, everything else), it must surely destroy itself. Monboddo merely yawns and remarks that it can probably be made to last his time. Perhaps he has momentarily forgotten his own prediction that he has only three years of active life to go. Perhaps he has not.

Monboddo's position, then, entails coldly accepting his own demise as well as the probability of the end of the human race. His account of history and of the nature of the modern Leviathan, the nexus of States and corporations, is not only comprehensive. In its threatening way it is the most grimly persuasive picture painted in the book, reflecting as it does the workings of that entire hellish universe. However, Monboddo is neither the 'author' nor the writer; both of these leave us with Lanark to consider at the end.

This Lanark has come to understand many things about his world, not least from Monboddo's final revelations. Back on the slopes of Glasgow's Necropolis he awaits death, prepared to take it as it comes, having gone through several 'rehearsals'. So we have to consider whether Lanark is after all so very different from Monboddo.

We have already argued that Lanark's attitude at the end, in the overall context of the book, cannot be reduced to anything as simple and empty as despair. No more than Chris Guthrie's end on the Barmekin does it offer much by way of hope for the future or consolation for the past. But while Monboddo can unfeelingly submit himself to whatever happens, Lanark evidently cannot do so. In this he is human: Monboddo is not. Lanark still complains. He would have liked a fancier ending, something a bit special. He is more than a little like Rima after all, with a yearning for glamour and excitement. He also complains that he ought to have had more love. Further as regards love, he has feelings of regret and guilt about his own shortcomings. He cannot even resist a final little display of self-pity and petulance, a sulky little show of dissatisfaction performed for the chamberlain, the angel or messenger of death who has come to tell him his time is up. This person is a composite figure made up from a certain Dr Munro from the institute and one Gloopy, whom Lanark first encountered as a pathetic wheedling creature, and who has duly wound up as a very well connected pimp. Such a creature can hardly be expected to be of genuine help to anyone in their last hour, least of all when their task on that melancholy occasion is, at most, to sugar the pill. There is one thing such functionaries can be forced to do, at least for a little while: and that is, they can be made to stand there and listen while a man indulges in a final moan and groan about everything. However, Lanark does not merely act here out of childish perversity. He is deeply indignant and serious about at least one thing. He demands to know who will look after Sandy and *the world* when he is gone. The chamberlain shrugs. There is really no answer to that and, realising perhaps that this is so, Lanark relents and in a kindly way dismisses this mere emissary and plaything. Lanark's mind has cleared to the point that he can cast such insubstantial, dark concerns out of it and be receptive instead to whatever brightness remains. Even as the moment of death approaches, the messenger of death is sent packing.

> Lanark forgot him, propped his chin on his hands and sat a long time watching the moving clouds. He was a slightly worried, ordinary old man but glad to see the light in the sky (560).

This mixture of equivocation and affirmation irresistibly reminds us of Chris Guthrie at the end of *Grey Granite*: in our end is our beginning.

FURTHER READING

Our page references are to the Canongate edition of 1981.

Alasdair Gray was born in Glasgow in 1934. His writings include television, radio and stage plays. He is also a painter. Murals and portraits are two of his pre-occupations as well as means whereby he has made a living. His own illus-trations are features of *Lanark* and *Unlikely Stories, Mostly*.

   Lanark was first published by Canongate in 1981 and subsequently, in paper-back, by Granada. *Unlikely Stories, Mostly* is a collection of short stories, also published by Canongate (1983) and by Penguin (1984). His second novel, *1982, Janine*, is published by Jonathon Cape (1984).

Lanark attracted considerable favourable publicity and numerous reviews and has ensured that Alasdair Gray's work will now be looked at with great interest. However, in the short time since *Lanark* was first published there has been little by way of extended analysis and commentary. The most interesting article so far is by Cairns Craig: ' "Going Down To Hell Is Easy": Alasdair Gray's *Lanark*' in *Cencrastus* (No 6, Autumn 1981 pp 19–21). There is a valuable interview with Alasdair Gray in a later edition of the same magazine (No 13, Summer 1983 pp 6–10).

Index